BIKE&BREW AMERICA

Midwest Region

**Todd
Bryant
Mercer**

VELO *press*®

VeloPress

and

Brewers Publications

Boulder, Colorado USA

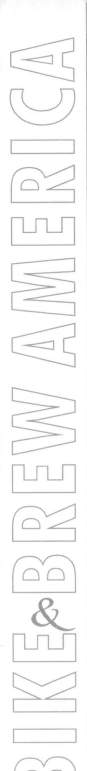

For our parents, Glenn and Judy Mercer, George and Mary Jane Schuster

Bike & Brew America: Midwest Region
© 2001 Todd Bryant Mercer

Printed in the United States of America

Distributed in the United States and Canada by Publishers Group West

International Standard Book Number: 1-931382-00-X

Library of Congress Cataloging-in-Publication Data
Mercer, Todd Bryant.
   Bike & brew America, Midwest Region / Todd Bryant Mercer.
      p. cm.
   Includes index.
   ISBN 1-931382-00-X (pbk.)
      1. All terrain cycling—Middle West—Guidebooks. 2. Bars (Drinking establishments)—Middle West—Guidebooks. 3. Microbreweries—Middle West—Guidebooks. 4. Middle West—Guidebooks. I. Title: Bike and brew America, Midwest Region. II. Title.

GV1045.5.M54 M47 2001
917.704'34—dc21   2001026789

COVER PHOTOS: The Sugarloaf Trail (top), Marquette, Michigan; © 2001 Kevin Bauman. Fitger's Brewhouse Brewery & Grille (bottom), Duluth, Minnesota; © 2001 Amanda Mercer.
Interior photos (unless otherwise noted) by Amanda and Todd Mercer
Maps by Amanda Mercer
Cover and interior design by Ann W. Douden
Production assistance by Pauline Brown

DISCLAIMER: Neither the publishers, editors, nor author shall be held liable for the use or misuse of information contained in this book. Readers assume the risk by participating in the activities described herein. The act of operating a bicycle or any vehicle after consuming alcohol is not advocated by this book and is strongly discouraged.

VeloPress
1830 North 55th Street
Boulder, Colorado 80301-2700 USA
303/440-0601; Fax 303/444-6788; E-mail velopress@7dogs.com

Brewers Publications
A Division of the Association of Brewers
736 Pearl Street
Boulder, Colorado 80302
303/447-0816; Fax 303/447-2825; E-mail bp@aob.org

CONTENTS

CONTENTS

BIKE BREW AMERICA

ACKNOWLEDGMENTS

I am deeply indebted to many people for the successful completion of this book. And once again, the one I'm most grateful to, and the one tortured the most, is my wife, Amanda. To her, I will always be grateful. However, it's because of four other people that this book is in front of you at all. Special thanks to our parents, Glenn and Judy Mercer and George and Mary Jane Schuster—not only for having reared us, but also for putting a roof over our heads, both in Michigan and Florida, so I could write this thing.

A huge thanks to all of the following for their invaluable insights into the local trails and ales: Dean "The Night Train" Mayne for taking care of the "Club House" until I return, Fred Caruso for the Tour de Palos Hills, Nick Ranson for an unforgettable trip through Missouri, Michael Green—I got it, I got it already . . . spokejunkies.com, and Ryan and Adam from Brick Wheels in Traverse City for putting the hurt on me and Katie and Adam (again) for getting some beers afterward. And Adam? You are the wheel MASTER! Thanks, man, I owe you a pint. Also thanks to Randy Furman—the coolest mayor in Minnesota—and the rest of the guys from Bike Blast. Keith Klemp gave me early encouragement and insight into Bike & Brew America destinations and "kept the hammer down." One day, pal, we'll ride, you just wait. I also thank Benjamin Swisher for doing all the work I should have done while I lived in Indianapolis, but didn't. And, of course, Leroy and Jacob for the Maah Daah Hey lesson in North Dakotan riding.

As I realize that my talents lie in words rather than photography, many thanks to the picture people out there who gladly donated their work for the greater good of mountain bikers everywhere. Quinn Kirkpatrick, you saved my butt and made the Quad Cities sparkle as they should at the same time. Lori Hauswirth, Bill Thompson, and, of course, Matt Koss for riding that insane Houghton Tech Trail ramp! Dave Pryor and friends from *Bicycling Magazine*—you guys are the Rock Stars everyone wants to be! Rob Stitt from one of the greatest mountain-bike clubs in existence, Earth Riders of Kansas City, Missouri. Lyle Riedy from the Kansas Trails Council for coming up with some great photos during one of the rainiest seasons on record. And, to all the brewpubs and trail managers whose photos appear throughout the book—thank you very much! Did I thank all the folks from Duluth who came down to drink free beer and hopefully get their pictures on the cover? Well thank you very much, compliments of The Brewhouse. Last but with no slight intended, Kevin Bauman for coming through just under the wire and supplying most of the photos for my home state of Michigan. Thanks to you I can some day return, head held high.

And finally, keeping the rain off our heads throughout the journey were Nikki's adopted parents Beth and Ray Langer, John and Kathy Sheard, Sean Hickman, Mark Stucky, John and Mary Carole Masson, and, last on paper only, Rod "Ironman" Raymond. And let's not forget to mention the pop-up camper Amanda's parents lent us throughout the dark and blustery Midwest fall. We'd still be under 6 inches of snow if it wasn't for that thing— thanks again, Mary Jane and George!

Of course, the reason this book looks so good is because of the awesome publishing and editorial crews over at Brewers Publications and VeloPress: Toni Knapp, Amy Sorrells, Theresa van Zante, Ann Douden, and Mary Eberle.

I'd also like to raise a pint to all the people I met along the way in the bike shops, brewpubs, and everywhere else, for all the information, directions, advice, stories, rides, places to sleep, laughs, and friendly faces. And last, but certainly not least, I once again thank Mark Stucky for designing the now famous Bike & Brew America™ logos.

PREFACE

I don't feel I stand alone when I proclaim, "I love bikes!" And, of those who stand in agreement, many also hail this next statement with equal passion, "I love beer!" For whatever reason, the two seem to go together like peanut butter and jelly; alone, each a fine delicacy, but together . . . ahhh. Words cannot describe the feeling of completeness, happiness, and nirvana—the total rapture attainable— when both are experienced in proper quantity and quality.

This bond, kinship if you will, is for me somehow fitting. My indoctrination to all things good—bikes and brews— came more than 10 years ago. I had just landed my first "real" job and had money. Lots of money. This, of course, meant two things to me: I could now afford to buy my first mountain bike, and I had more money to spend on beer.

My roommate at the time worked at a bike shop and set me up with a deal that, even to this day, seemed too good to be true. A 1990 Raleigh Tangent equipped with LX components for only $320 dollars. A steal. But more important, a mountain bike for only $320 meant even more money for beer, which brings me back to my earlier statement connecting the two.

About a month later, a buddy and I were sitting in a bar staring with much envy at a menu that listed over 300 very expensive beers from around the world. A menu so novel it even listed American beers that were not brewed by Coors, Anheuser-Busch, or Miller Brewing Company. Remember, this is back in 1990.

"I'm gonna have an Anchor Steam," Sean says, closing the menu.

"What's that?" I ask, still trying to decide between a Molson and Labatt.

"It's a beer from San Francisco—you probably wouldn't like it," he says, sounding a little smug.

What? "Why not?" I ask, feeling slightly challenged.

"Well, it's pretty bitter, . . ." and so my indoctrination to what beer really is all about began as we proceeded to drink our way around the world that night.

My mountain biking was sporadic for a few years, but fortunately, I was still able to hone my beer-drinking skills and knowledge. I also developed some brewing abilities until I was a self-proclaimed finely tuned beer connoisseur.

As brewpubs gradually proliferated across the landscape—and I quit said job—I was able to spend more time on my Raleigh and less time in the kitchen boiling wort, weighing hops, measuring specific gravity, and sanitizing bottles, forever in search of the perfect pint of barley and hops. Yes, I was effectively put out of the homebrewing profession. But on the bright side, I now had access to great locally brewed beer just a stone's throw from a hard day on the trails.

More time in the saddle improved my biking skills, and I began traveling farther and farther from home in search of sweeter singletrack, bigger hills, and, yes, better beer. Fortune has smiled upon me more than a few times, and I've managed to sample some of the best riding and finest brews North America has to offer. I'm trying to ride it all, from the great Florida swamps to the Rockies of Colorado, from the red sands of Moab to the top of Mount Tamalpais. Along the way, I'm also trying to drink it all. From nitrogen taps in Seattle to hand-pumped brews in Michigan, from cask-conditioned ales in Kansas to unfiltered hopfests in Boulder. I've braved alcohol-starved Utah only to get blasted by a Trappist Tripel–style ale in Missouri boasting an alcohol content of 12%! Through all this, only one truism has remained constant: no matter where I travel there is always prime singletrack and quality handcrafted beer—you just need to know where to look.

And now, as a new millennium begins, it is high time to share this hard-won knowledge with you—the millions of mountain-biking, beer-loving kindred spirits out there.

Bike & Brew America: Midwest Region is the second in a series of mountain-biking, beer-drinking guides to the sweetest, most heroic, or just plain twisted, nasty, sicko singletrack rides you could ever find yourself on, followed by the best brewpubs you could ever find yourself in.

There's always fine print, so here's some to let you know where I'm going. *Bike & Brew America* outlines the best mountain-bike trails in the country that are situated within a 30-minute (or so) drive of the best brewpubs in the country. Sometimes a pub is on the way to great riding or a trail is on the way back from some place where there was great beer. Understand that you have to get to and from the trail somehow, and, unfortunately, brewpubs are usually not located right at the trailhead. Although, sometimes they are, as you will soon see.

Also, because I happen to like quaint, old-fashioned stuff, buildings with some character, and downtown areas with a lot of history, that's where I envision Bike & Brew travelers to be spending most of their evenings. In other words, if it became a choice between hitting the strip mall for a chain brewery or driving a little farther into town for a nineteenth-century building and cool downtown aura, I invariably drove the extra five minutes. I believe that just as the scenery makes up part of a good mountain-bike ride, your surroundings, while drinking the fruits of your daily labor, make for a better beer.

And now, without further ado, let's continue our search for the perfect Bike & Brew experience in perhaps the most underrated of all locales, the tree-covered, and freshwater-endowed, Midwest region.

INTRODUCTION

Bike & Brew America is a comprehensive series of guidebooks to America's best mountain-bike trails and best brewpubs. But why mountain bikes and brewpubs? What is the attraction mountain bikers feel toward micro-brewed beer in general and brewpubs in particular? Beyond the obvious answer—both mountain biking and brewpub frequenting are great fun and offer endless hours in the company of good friends—what pairs these two seemingly random activities together is called *character*.

Mountain biking and brewpubs say something about a person's character. They speak of a person who enjoys freedom and following a path less traveled. They speak of individuality, someone who likes trying new and different things. One who enjoys the atmosphere, the experience, and the trip—not just the destination. Not to mention someone who likes to ride bikes and drink good beer.

And just as mountain biking and drinking real beer offer a glimpse into a person's character, so too do they open a window into a region's character. Each trail and each brewpub tell something about the area where they are located. A trail tells about the outdoors, the wilderness, the area's geography, and its flora and fauna. A brewpub tells a tale of history, philosophy, local pastimes, local cuisine, and age-old beer styles. What better way to sample a town's character than by exploring its historic streets and stopping in at the local brewpub for a taste that can be found no other place in the world?

As mountain bikers know, every trail—no, every *ride*—is different. Terrain, elevation, distance, climate, companions, and weather—all add up to make each ride new and exciting. As each trail is unique, molded out of the local

geography, each brewpub is also a creature of its environment. Different architecture, atmosphere, food, people, and, of course, beer give each brewpub a character all its own. This individuality is what having a pint at the local brewpub is all about.

So I ask you, what better way is there to explore an area than by biking its trails and drinking its ales? And, what better way to find out about the breadbasket of our nation, the Midwest's trails and ales, than by reading this book?

How to Use This Book

This book does not describe random collections of trails and brewpubs. Rather, it presents carefully researched selections of the best trails that are located near great brewpubs. Each entry guarantees its readers a great day of biking and a great night of eating and drinking. It effectively eliminates the guessing game all traveling bikers encounter at one time or another.

No longer will mountain bikers planning a vacation spend hours trying to locate that barely remembered article detailing a great ride. Worse, the trail may not turn out to be even near where the bikers are headed. Readers will now find all rides in a particular geographic region of the United States between two covers.

Each chapter begins with an introduction to the state's overall Bike & Brew (B&B) character and a locator map marking the places to be covered. The section then proceeds to detail each featured trail and brewpub in a fun, conversational style. A road map showing both trail and brewpub locations, as well as the local bike shop and additional trails and watering holes, accompanies each trail and brewpub pairing.

Online Web Site

In order to combat the greatest problem with all guidebooks, that of its information becoming dated, Bike & Brew America maintains a web site at www.bikeandbrew.com. This site continually offers trail and brewpub updates, which will allow your copy of *Bike & Brew America* to remain up-to-date until a complete revision is required. Reader input, comments, and suggestions are welcomed for online posting and future editions.

Descriptions of Rides and Brewpubs

I have methodically organized the descriptions to assist you in finding specific aspects of each ride and brewpub. Thus, for each city, town, or area for which I endorse a Bike & Brew pair, I offer brief teasers covering the attractions and scenery and then full descriptions in the following format:

TRAIL NAME: Well, its most common name anyway.

THE SCOOP: What to expect on the trail in about ten words or whatever it happens to take.

RIDE LENGTH AND TYPE: The ride's distance in miles and what kind of ride it is—out-and-back, loop, town-to-town, balloon-on-a-string, or "variable." Variable trails are part of a large trail network and are rarely ridden the same way twice.

THE BIKE: Details covering what the ride is like including terrain, elevation, trail conditions, scenic opportunities, trail highlights, and directions, when appropriate.

DIFFICULTY: A general rating of novice, intermediate, or advanced and a short explanation of why this rating was applied. Although I didn't intend to restrict the trails in this book to a particular difficulty rating, most trails I selected are intermediate and intermediate to advanced because this level just happens to be the difficulty most people consider makes for the best or most "classic" of rides.

AEROBIC DIFFICULTY (1–5): A subjective rating used to describe the physical conditioning needed to successfully complete a trail with a smile still on your face. The easiest trails are rated a 1 and the hardest, steepest, highest-elevation trails are rated a 5. Most Bike & Brew trails fall in the 2–4 range with 3 being the most common.

TECHNICAL DIFFICULTY (1–5): Another subjective rating used to describe the technical skill needed to successfully complete a trail without having to dismount and walk over

or around obstacles—not to mention making a face plant, hitting a tree, or falling off a cliff. The smoothest trails are rated a 1; the most twisted, gnarly, rocked-out, rooted, off-camber mountaintop trails are rated a 5. Again, most Bike & Brew trails fall in the 2–4 range, and a technical difficulty of 3 is the most common.

MIDWEST TECHNICAL DISCLAIMER: How hard can mountain biking be in the Midwest? Plenty hard. Granted you're not gonna be climbing many mountains in the Midwest, but that doesn't mean the riding is not difficult. Often, in places of extreme terrain like the Rocky Mountains, by necessity trails deliberately follow the easiest route to their conclusion, be it the top of a mountain, an alpine lake, a scenic vista, or the brewpub. Not so in the less-endowed lands of the Midwest. Trails are deliberately made more interesting by taking advantage of every obstacle nature places in the way as well as a fair amount that bikers purposefully create. Put another way, expect winding, tight, hilly singletrack through trees, rocks, roots, log piles, elevated narrow bridges, ramps, and just about anything the local trail builders can come up with. If you're not from the Midwest, or areas like it, let's just say, you've been warned.

DIFFICULTY DEFINITIONS: Although all systems of rating difficulty are subjective, the following descriptions should give you a way to measure where you stand, understanding you may fall into one category technically and another aerobically.

DIFFICULTY LEVEL 1: You definitely enjoy your beer more than your bike. Rarely have you ridden on singletrack trails. Perhaps until recently you have preferred to lead an inactive lifestyle.

DIFFICULTY LEVEL 2: You are a "social cyclist" who rides singletrack occasionally. You lead a fairly active lifestyle and are interested in seeing what adding a little more mountain biking to your routine has to offer.

DIFFICULTY LEVEL 3: You are comfortable rid-

ing singletrack, train regularly, and are looking to improve your skills. You may even race
occasionally just to see where you stand
among your peers.

DIFFICULTY LEVEL 4: You're a good rider. You
know it, your friends know it, and your mom
and dad know it. You train regularly and do
well when you race.

DIFFICULTY LEVEL 5: When you race, other
racers know your name. You regularly clear
obstacles other accomplished cyclists only
dream of. Basically, you're the mountain
biker everyone else wants to be.

WARNINGS: Under this heading are spelled out any trail-
specific warnings—those beyond the standard "wear your
helmet, keep your eyes open at all times, carry food and
water, carry tools, know how to use those tools, maintain
your bike regularly, and know how to get back to your
car." Examples of what may be included are crowded trail
conditions, extreme weather conditions, dangerous animals or other critters known to inhabit that particular part
of the country, fragile environmental areas, and hazards
such as flat-causing thorns and cactus needles, poison ivy
infestations, complicated trail intersections, and pretty
much anything else that may make your day uncomfort-
able. However, all the warnings in the world won't help if
you don't heed them, take the proper precautions, and use
common sense wherever you ride.

MIDWEST WARNINGS: In addition to the blissful opportunities to ride near-limitless singletrack through tall
shady stands of pine, oak, maple, poplar, and birch, there
are a few unpleasant aspects particular to the Midwest
that should be discussed. Chief among these are humidity, poison ivy, and bugs. First humidity. The months of
July and August throughout the Midwest will have you
sweating through that Lycra jersey before you even reach
the trailhead. Be aware of the heat index and drink water
accordingly. Second, poison ivy, poison oak, poison
sumac—whatever it happens to be called in the region

you're visiting. Without going into a botany lesson on
these pages, find out what these more common varieties
look like and avoid their leaves, stems, flowers, and
berries at all costs! However, if you happen to kneel in
some while fixing those flats, don't panic. When you finish your ride (or within 6 hours), either shower repeat-
edly using coarse brown soap or wipe down any area
that might be infected with a cloth soaked in rubbing
alcohol. Yes, believe it or not, rubbing alcohol is the
equivalent of six soapy showers when it comes to removing the insidious oil found on poison ivy in all its forms.
Third, mosquitoes and biting flies. Like most places, the
Midwest has them all—and the deeper into the forest you
get, the more of them there are. Your weapon is an insect
repellant containing the almost-banned substance known
as DEET. Find a little bottle and keep it in your pack.
There's no outrunning them and nothing worse than trying to climb a hill while getting bit in the shorts. And
finally, on occasion (mostly during the spring rainy season), a tornado or two may rear its ugly head somewhere
in the Midwest. If the sky looks threatening, turn on the
trusty Weather Channel and see if the conditions in your
area are prime for a twister. You don't want to start out
biking in Kansas and end up in Oz. Or maybe you do. . . .
OTHER TRAILS IN THE AREA: Summary of at least two
other rides, of varying difficulty, located in the area.
CONTACTS: The local land managers' addresses and
phone numbers. When these folks are also the ones with
the all-important trail map, their location is noted on the
map of the area. Otherwise, it's always a good idea to give
them a call before your visit to learn about other vital
information such as current trail status, camping opportunities, or more detailed directions. Also included is a general contact such as the Chamber of Commerce or Tourist
Information Center just to make sure all travelers' ques-
tions will be answered. The general contact follows the
local land managers' information.
MAPS: Where you can get the most current maps of the
trails described. Frequently the maps are free, created by

the local bike shop for out-of-town riders such as your-self. Sometimes, in popular mountain-bike destinations, an enterprising individual has created a detailed map of many local trails (or a narrative guide) that is available at a nominal cost. Unless you enjoy exploring on your own and don't care when you get home, such maps are very useful and worth a stop to pick one up.

BIKE SHOP: Source of the local knowledge for all traveling bikers and where all riders new to an area should begin their day. The shop proprietors and/or employees are the experts on the trails. Besides being where the free maps are usually located, bike shops are the place to check on trail conditions, get directions, or score any last-minute purchases or repairs.

BREWPUB NAME: The official name.

BREWPUB INFORMATION: The address, phone number, and web address (if available).

THE PUB: A description of the brewpub's atmosphere, his-tory, setting, features, surroundings, feel, and character.

THE BREW: A detailed account of the brewpub's lineup of unique beers, including the year-round selections, crowd pleasers, employees' favorites (usually a great way to pick your first pint), and some of the more memorable seasonal and brewer specialties.

PRICE OF A PINT: How much a pint of beer costs regularly and, more important, the ifs, ands, and buts of the almighty happy hour.

OTHER BREWS IN THE AREA: Just as there is always more than one good trail in an area, there is always more than one good place to get a brew. This section summarizes other brewpubs, microbreweries, or local bars that serve good beer and attract the mountain-bike crowd.

QUOTE: An original, insightful, or humorous quote or fact overheard on the trail or at the brewpub is included in most B&B pairings.

A WORD ABOUT THE MAPS PRINTED HEREIN: The maps included in this book are artistic renderings of the states and cities, towns, and areas described. That's not to say the maps are inaccurate, just that distances may be longer,

or shorter, than they appear. Not to worry, the street names are correct and directions are straightforward, so rest assured that you will arrive at the primary trail, brewpub, and bike shop. With all that stated, please be aware that in some instances, the maps will point you to trails or breweries off the page. When this is the case, it is because it was not practical to fit all secondary details on the map. Please obtain detailed directions from the maps described in the map paragraph of each Bike & Brew section.

LEGEND FOR MAPS

 Pint Glass & Fat Tire ~ Bike & Brew America destination

 Single Fat Tire ~ Trail or trailhead location

 Full Pint Glass ~ Brewpub or microbrewery location

 Double Fat Tires ~ The all-important bike-shop location

 Star ~ Other important locations such as landmarks, land manager, tourist information, or beer joint that is not a brewpub or microbrewery

BIKING ADVICE FROM THE INTERNATIONAL MOUNTAIN BICYCLING ASSOCIATION (IMBA): Have fun out there, but please don't forget to live by the International Mountain Bicycling Association's Rules of the Trail:

1. Plan ahead.
2. Always yield trail.
3. Never scare animals.
4. Ride on open trails only.
5. Control your bicycle.
6. Leave no trace.

IMBA works to keep trails open for mountain bikers by encouraging responsible riding and supporting volunteer trail work.

BIKING AND DRINKING ADVICE FROM BIKE & BREW AMERICA: Always wear your helmet! And remember, please drink responsibly and NEVER drink and drive OR ride. See you on the trail, in the brewpub, and maybe even at the bookstore!

CHAPTER ONE

ILLINOIS

As the sixth most populated state in the country, nearly twelve million people work to support the five microbreweries and twenty-seven brewpubs in Illinois. However, given the Illinois population and the fact that manufacturing leads its economy, you might be surprised to learn that mountain bikers need not travel far for some time in the saddle. In addition to the obvious urban riding potential Chicago offers (see the appendix), the metro area is also blessed with an extensive trail network not more than 8 miles from the Chicago city limits!

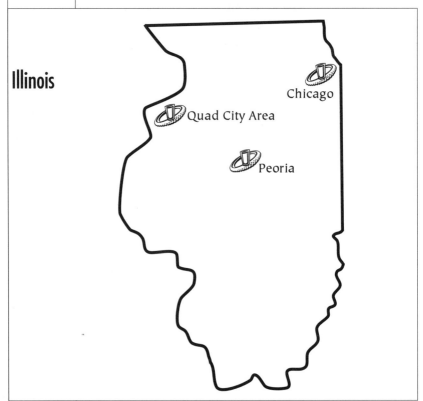

Illinois

Chicago

Quad City Area

Peoria

Singletrack through towering trees at Loud Thunder Forest Preserve near Andalusia, Illinois.
(Photo by Quinn Kirkpatrick)

More than two-thirds of the Illinois population is centered in and around the Chicago area and its high concentration of brewpubs. This puts the remainder of the state right on par with the rest of the Midwest as far as the amount of open prairie and forestland left to enjoy. True, the riding won't be what anyone can call mountainous, or even hilly (having pretty much been leveled by the last couple of Ice Ages), but it will be in deep green forests, it will be singletrack, and it will be fun.

Perhaps the best aspect of Illinois, in terms of Bike & Brew America, is its central location to the rest of the Midwest region. In addition to the two stellar destinations

ILLINOIS

in Illinois itself, there are no less than eight Bike & Brew pairs within reach of a little dedicated driving to neighboring states. Indiana, Iowa, Michigan, Missouri, and Wisconsin all offer prime destinations worthy of a weekend or more of superb biking and fresh local beer. And all you Illinois Bike & Brew travelers, be sure and check out the section on Davenport and the Quad City Area in Iowa's chapter for more in-state riding.

Chicago

   Located on the southwest shore of Lake Michigan, Chicago is a city rivaled by few and serves as the Midwest's transportation, finance, industrial, and commercial hub. With five major universities and countless museums, Chicago is also the cultural destination for the country's midsection.

   Interested in a little intellectual enlightenment after your ride? Grant Park, located on Lake Michigan's shores, is the place to go. You'll find the Art Institute of Chicago with its

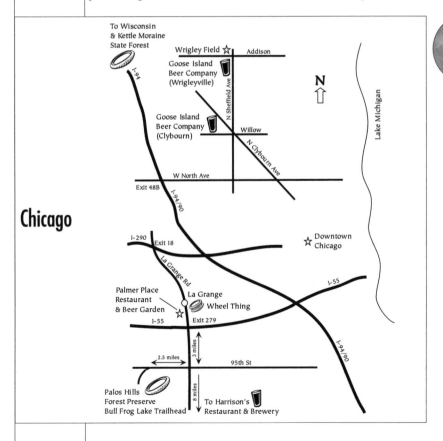

Chicago

To Wisconsin
& Kettle Moraine
State Forest

I-94

Wrigley Field ☆ Addison

Goose Island
Beer Company
(Wrigleyville)

N Sheffield Ave

Goose Island
Beer Company
(Clybourn)

Willow

N Clybourn Ave

N
⇑

Lake Michigan

W North Ave

Exit 48B

I-94/90

I-290

Exit 18

La Grange Rd

☆ Downtown
Chicago

I-55

Palmer Place
Restaurant
& Beer Garden
☆

I-55

La Grange
Wheel Thing

Exit 279

I-94/90

2.5 miles

3 miles

95th St

Palos Hills
Forest Preserve
Bull Frog Lake Trailhead

8 miles

To Harrison's
Restaurant & Brewery

fabulous Impressionists collection; the natural history Field Museum, which is home to Sue, the largest and most complete *Tyrannosaurus rex* fossil ever discovered; Shedd Aquarium, the world's largest (by the way); and the Museum of Science and Industry, which features a captured World War II U-505 German submarine, a Boeing 727 airplane, and a coal mine. This place may be even more fun than a well-stocked bike shop.

And, of course, there is always the Magnificent Mile to entice shoppers to Chicago's downtown. This stretch of Michigan Avenue, from the Chicago River to Lake Shore Drive, features enough upscale shopping to satisfy even Donald Trump's latest girlfriend. This lineup of department stores, exclusive shops, plush hotels, theaters, restaurants, and various tourist attractions actually sees in excess of 22 million visitors each year.

Still looking for more? Well this place has it. Most notably, Chicago has an incredible amount of outdoor recreation opportunities. The entire lakefront is almost completely devoted to outdoor activity with bike paths, running paths, beaches, harbors, and parks throughout. Or take an architectural tour along the Chicago River. You'll learn about the historic buildings and architectural styles of the past and may even get lucky and see one of the river's drawbridges in action. Truly a sight in such a busy downtown. And, although there are no mountains here, you can still take in the city's magnificent skyline along with sneaking a peek at the surrounding states of Indiana, Michigan, and Wisconsin from the Skydeck observatory of one of the world's tallest buildings, the 1450-foot Sears Tower.

Not here to see the sights? No problem. At last count there were over 20 brewpubs in the Chicago area to slacken a traveling mountain-biker's thirst. And, even though it may be hard to believe mountain biking could be found anywhere near a city the size of Chicago, believe it. Make sure you bring your bike the next time you visit the Windy City.

Palos Hills Forest Preserve

THE SCOOP: Over 50 miles of singletrack just 8 miles—or about 20 minutes—from Chicago's city limits.

RIDE LENGTH AND TYPE: Variable—come and explore for a day, a weekend, or a week and you still will not have ridden all the trails in this incredible metro-area trail network.

THE BIKE: The **Palos Hills Forest Preserve** is 6500 acres of outdoor sport within sight of downtown Chicago's skyline. How can such an immense stretch of undeveloped land still be this close to the third-largest city in America? The fact that the first nuclear chain reaction took place at the University of Chicago in 1942, which led to nuclear weapons being developed here during World War II as part of the Manhattan Project, may have something to do with it. However, this is a case of making a good situation out of bad, and, as long as you don't bring your shovel and start digging, you'll be fine.

What quality of trail will you find this close to urban America you ask? Impressive, that's what. And the locals know it too. On a sunny Saturday or Sunday, the **Bull Frog Lake Trailhead** parking area is a truly awesome spectacle with dozens of bikers filling the three lots, prepping their bikes, and riding off into the woods.

Still, this is Illinois so you won't find any real elevation changes—or significant hills for that matter—but you will find lakes and hardwood forests, short steep climbs, plenty of roots, rocks, log piles, and tight twisty singletrack. Although there are many miles of trails here, there are no clearly defined loops. Widetrack paths around Bull Frog Lake lead to singletrack spurs in all directions. These trails intersect frequently, and often it is difficult to tell if you are riding on legal or illegal trails—although a good

indication of a closed trail is a big pile of brush blocking the entrance. Just don't go there even though you may see where others have gone around the obvious blockage.

Still, come early and plan on spending the entire day exploring the trails here. You will have fun, but because the trails are poorly marked, you will get lost, and then you will find someone who will direct you back to the trailhead.

DIFFICULTY: Beginner to intermediate. By sticking to the wide gravel paths, beginner riders will find this area to be perfect as the terrain is gentle and there is little chance of getting lost on these paths. Start exploring and you had better be at least intermediate, as you will encounter tight singletrack and stand a good chance of getting lost.

AEROBIC DIFFICULTY (1–5):

3 (2 on the gravel widetrack)

TECHNICAL DIFFICULTY (1–5):

3 (2 on the gravel widetrack)

WARNINGS: A lot of the credit for the fact that the trails in this preserve are even open to mountain bikers should go to the Chicago Area Mountain Bikers (CAMBr) and other trail volunteers who have done a masterful job of creating and maintaining this network of trails that would otherwise be in constant jeopardy of overuse and overcrowding.

Please bring your bike the next time you come to Chicago, but also remember there are a lot of hikers, bikers, and horses out here—so be on your best behavior. Be considerate of the locals' efforts to keep these trails open, don't ride closed trails, and don't ride when it's wet.

OTHER TRAILS IN THE AREA: Chicago offers unlimited urban riding opportunities that can end at the brewpub of your choice. To see what the world of urban riding is all about and get a few ideas for your own urban ride, check out the article "Welcome to the Jungle" in the appendix. As far as opportunities in the dirt, Palos Hills is the best legal trail system this close to Chicago and should be your destination near the Windy City. In addition, about a two-hour drive north gets you to the **Kettle Moraine State Forest** in Wisconsin, an excellent Bike & Brew destination (see the section on Whitewater, Wisconsin, for details).

CONTACTS: Forest Preserve District of Cook County, 536 North Harlem Avenue, River Forest, IL 60305; (708) 366-9420 or (800) 870-3666. Chicago Area Mountain Bikers, CAMBr/TURF, P.O. Box 444, Oak Forest, IL 60452; www.cambr.org. Chicago Chamber of Commerce, 2457 West Peterson Avenue, Suite 3, Chicago, IL 60659; (773) 271-8008.

MAPS: Currently the map situation is a little sparse at Palos Hills. There are rather limited maps available at Bull Frog Lake Trailhead's map kiosk, and CAMBr is working on more detailed maps of the area. Until such a time as these are ready, your best bet is to find someone riding at about your speed and ask to be shown around. Learn the trails and make a new friend all at the same time.

BIKE SHOP: Wheel Thing, 15 South La Grange Road, La Grange, IL 60525; (708) 352-3822. A very solid shop and probably the easiest one for a Windy City visitor to find coming from, or heading to, Palos Hills.

Goose Island Beer Company

1800 North Clybourn Avenue
Chicago, Illinois 60614
(312) 915-0071
www.gooseisland.com

THE PUB: Hardwood floors, brick walls, and a community bar set you up for the perfect brewpub experience in the place that started the Goose Island brewing experience: **Goose Island Beer Company** on Clybourn Avenue. True, there may be a brewpub a little closer to the trailhead but, quite frankly, none compares to the legendary Goose Island.

Set in downtown Chicago, this brewpub is also not the easiest place to find, but the trip will be worth it. With at least 10 different beers on tap at any time, there is something for everyone here, and any trip to the Windy City would be a disappointment without at least a brief visit to this Midwestern brewing legend.

Since 1988, Goose Island has been pumping out fresh beer from its Clybourn Street location. More recently, the company has added a microbrewery on Fulton Street and another brewpub within walking distance of Wrigley Field. The Fulton Street microbrewery handles their bottling and distribution, and the Wrigleyville brewpub handles the vast quantities of die-hard Cub fans. Although some of the beers on tap at both brewpubs may have been brewed at the Fulton Street microbrewery, rest assured you're still getting genuine fresh Goose Island product in every pint whether you settle in at the bar, pool hall, or atrium.

THE BREW: The beers on tap change from time to time, but you'll always find five year-round brews, a couple of seasonals, and a couple more cask-conditioned styles on tap at either location. Of the five standards, three have taken gold at the Great American Beer Festival. The **Honker's Ale**, a 1997 gold medallist, is Goose Island's flagship beer and an excellent example of an English-style pale ale with a malty body and mild hop finish. The **Goose Island Blonde Ale** won in 1999 in the golden ale–Canadian-style ale category, and the exquisite nitrogen-charged **Goose Island India Pale Ale** took top honors in the English-style IPA category in 2000. The smooth and easy **Goose Island Hex Nut Brown Ale** and **Goose Island Oatmeal Stout** round out the regulars, and are both excellent selections.

In addition, you'll find two cask-conditioned ales on tap along with a mix of seasonals such as **Colonial Pumpkin**, **Belgian Kriek**, **XXX Porter**, and the **Summertime Kolsch**, to name a few you'll be able to choose from depending on the time of year you visit.

PRICE OF A PINT: No standard happy hour and this is the big city, so plan on at least four bucks a pint; 20-ounce imperial-size hand-pulled glasses go for $4.25.

OTHER BREWS IN THE AREA: If you happen to be going to the Cubs game after your ride, then skip Goose Island on Clybourn Avenue and head straight to **Goose Island**'s newer **Wrigleyville** location. Nine TVs and all the Wrigley Field fun you can handle line up alongside exceptional Goose Island beers.

However, if it's the closest brewpub to the trail you're looking for, then head south on La Grange Road for 8 easy miles to **Harrison's Restaurant and Brewery** at 15845 La Grange Road, Orland Park, IL 60462; (708) 226-0100. Although this is in a mall parking lot and caters to the shopping crowd, the establishment does serve good food and solid beers. Just depends if you're looking for good or the best. And speaking of close, **Palmer Place Restaurant and Beer Garden** is located almost next to the bike shop in downtown La Grange at 56 South La Grange Road, La Grange, IL 60525; (708) 482-7127. Although the concern has all the fixing's for a brewery including a full brew-house setup, don't be

fooled as there is no brewing going on here. Still, there is a nice beer garden, and the place serves microbrews from several taps. So if the rig is in the shop, you may want to think about giving Palmer Place a try.

Peoria

Sitting right on Interstate 74, the Peoria area offers a great Bike & Brew pair right smack in the middle of Illinois. This town, dating all the way back to the 1600s, when French explorers built Fort Pimeteoui on the western shore of the Illinois River, is believed to be the first permanent settlement in Illinois. Today, its location on the Illinois River between Saint Louis and Chicago allows

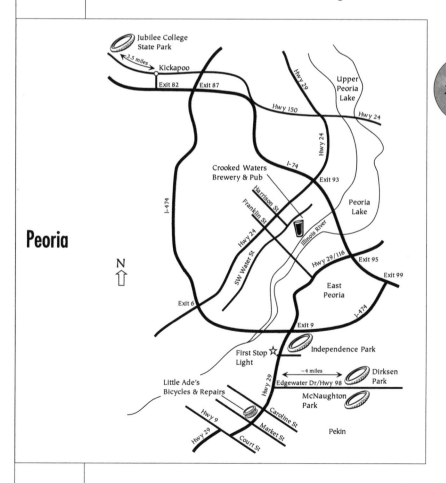

Peoria

Jubilee College State Park

3.5 miles Kickapoo

Exit 82   Exit 87

Hwy 29

Upper Peoria Lake

Hwy 150   Hwy 24

Hwy 24

I-74

Crooked Waters Brewery & Pub

Exit 93

Peoria Lake

Harrison St

Franklin St

Illinois River

I-474

Hwy 24

SW Water St

Hwy 29/116   Exit 95

Exit 99

East Peoria

Exit 6

I-474

N

Exit 9

First Stop Light   Independence Park

~4 miles

Little Ade's Bicycles & Repairs

Hwy 29   Edgewater Dr/Hwy 98   Dirksen Park

McNaughton Park

Caroline St

Hwy 9

Market St

Hwy 29   Court St   Pekin

BIKE BREW AMERICA

ILLINOIS

Peoria to serve as an important inland port between the Great Lakes and the Gulf of Mexico.

Even early on, Peoria had a bright future in brewing thanks to three things: plenty of grain from the surrounding fertile farmlands, the shipping potential supplied by barges along the Illinois River, and fresh spring water from the Peoria Mineral Springs. Since 1850 when the Peoria Mineral Springs Bottling Works opened up its doors across Seventh Avenue from the springs, various alcoholic spirits have been mass produced in Peoria. In fact, by 1900 Peoria was known as the Whiskey Capital of the World. All this thanks to the pure spring waters that have been flowing from the Peoria Mineral Springs for the past 14,000 years.

Of course, it was the arrival of the Benjamin Jolt Company, the precursor to the Caterpillar Tractor Company, in 1909 that changed Peoria's future forever. Now the world's largest manufacturer of earth-moving machines, Peoria's past and future revolve around the manufacturing giant.

The town considers itself to be a model town of America, mirroring the typical American's thoughts and ideals. True or not, the fact remains that fresh beer is once again pumping along the shores of the Illinois River, and miles of singletrack await the B&B traveler right out Peoria's front door.

Jubilee College State Park

THE SCOOP: Over 40 miles of single- and widetrack multi-use trails winding through a 3200-acre state park.

RIDE LENGTH AND TYPE: Variable—rides as long or as short as one would want with plenty of park road bailouts available.

THE BIKE: Named after the nineteenth-century college located on one corner of the immense park, **Jubilee College State Park** is located 3½ miles from the small town of Kickapoo. Although the college has long been abandoned, the park is now home to more than 40 miles of trails for higher pursuits including mountain biking. Twenty-five miles of designated horse trails and another 10 miles of hiking trails are open to mountain bikes year round, weather permitting. In addition, many miles of singletrack trails created specifically for mountain bikes wind among these 35 miles of mapped and marked trails. Now this is the heart of the Midwest, so you won't find any mountains to climb here—but you will find plenty of tight rolling singletrack making its way through deep hardwood forests with lots of deer, birds, and other small animals to keep you company.

Start exploring this central Illinois gold mine on the trails, mostly widetrack, south of the main park road. Cruise these buffed-out trails on the lookout for the singletrack spurs winding off into the trees. Designed and used by bikers, these spur trails are true singletrack sweeties and what makes Jubilee great.

The place is perfect for beginners if you stick to the well-marked wide-open multiuse trails on the south side of the park. For the more adventurous, pick any (or all) of the obvious singletrack spurs and up the ride a notch or

ILLINOIS

two with steeper hills, tighter turns, narrow singletrack, and multiple log jumps. Keep your eyes open for the 2-mile **Plank Trail** spur off of **Red Fox Run**. If you like this little diamond (you'll know you're on it when you see the planks), then be sure to check out Dirksen Park and Independence Park near the town of Pekin before leaving the Peoria area.

The north side of Jubilee is where most of the horse traffic can be found. Unfortunately, with the horse traffic comes increased erosion and reduced drainage, meaning lots of mud if there has been rain anytime during the previous week. However, if it is sheer exploration potential you're looking for, the north side of Jubilee is the place for you.

This park is great for an entire day of riding. Start out exploring the southern trails with a mandatory destination being the restored Pioneer College buildings dating back to 1839 on the east end of the park. Then, after lunch, head north and check out the horse trails up there. Now with class out of the way, you can progress to the next course in downtown Peoria at Crooked Waters Brewery & Pub.

DIFFICULTY: Beginner to intermediate. If you stick to the wide hiking and cross-country ski trails south of the main road in the park, you have about 10 miles of great beginner trails. If you venture off on one or more of the many spurs among these southern trails, raise the difficulty a notch because of the many log crossings and tighter trail conditions. To the north on the horse trails, the riding is more intermediate because of the eroded singletrack and generally rougher conditions left behind by the horse traffic.

AEROBIC DIFFICULTY (1–5):
2–3
TECHNICAL DIFFICULTY (1–5):
2–3

WARNINGS: All of the trails in the park are multiuse trails, so expect to see hikers, horses, and other bikers on these trails. Not only should you watch out for physical evidence of our four-legged friends, but be sure to be courteous and move out of the way for all equestrians.

Although it would be hard to get lost on the main park trails, the singletrack spurs are not mapped and could pose a problem if you don't maintain at least a little awareness of your surroundings.

OTHER TRAILS IN THE AREA: Right next to Peoria, the small town of Pekin is a mountain-bike destination waiting to explode. First off are two neighboring city parks, which together offer about 17 miles of intermediate to advanced riding. Run by the Pekin Park District, and maintained with the help of Little Ade's Bicycles in downtown Pekin, **Dirksen** and **McNaughton Parks** both offer sections of smooth singletrack, a few Midwestern climbs, multiple bridge crossings, and a section of trail in Dirksen known as **Broken Eggs**, a short North Shore–style loop (see glossary) with seven or eight technical obstacles such as elevated trails, ramps, and jumps—one with a 7-foot drop! Of the two, Dirksen contains about 10 miles of trails and is considered the more mountain bike friendly of the two parks as McNaughton allows horses and lacks in the maintenance department. Pekin's newest development endeavor is **Independence Park** in the nearby town of Marquette Heights. A 12-mile loop having much the same feel as Dirksen with plenty of built British Columbia–style obstacles to test your mettle against, this trail is right off Interstate 475 and easy to find.

CONTACTS: Jubilee College State Park, 13921 West Route 150, Brimfield, IL 61517; (309) 446-3758. Pekin Parks and Recreation Department, 1701 Court Street, Pekin, IL 61554; (309) 347-7275. Hot and heavy in the area and worth checking out is the Peoria Area Mountain Bike Association (PAMBA) web site at www.pambamtb.org. Peoria Chamber of Commerce, 124 Southwest Adams Street, Suite 300, Peoria, IL 61602; (309) 676-0755.

MAPS: You can pick up a map of Jubilee College State Park at the park headquarters building (8:30 A.M. to 4:30 P.M. Monday through Friday). Even if the headquarters is closed, maps are still available outside the entrance. The mountain-bike singletrack trails are not on these maps but are fairly easy to find if you keep your eyes open. All trails

"Some of the obstacles you'd be better off hitting with authority."
—Brian from Little Ade's Bicycles & Repairs talks about a few of the obstacles on Broken Eggs.

25

eventually lead back to the mapped main trails, which have signposts at most intersections, making it very difficult to get lost on this one. Also, PAMBA's web site at www.pambamtb.org has maps of both Jubilee College State Park and Independence Park for those so inclined to do a little preride net surfing.

BIKE SHOP: Little Ade's Bicycle & Repairs, 305 North Fifth Street, Pekin, IL 61554; (309) 346-3900. This shop is very involved with local trail creation and maintenance and has the maps and directions to Jubilee College State Park and the Pekin area trails.

Crooked Waters Brewery & Pub

330 Southwest Constitution Avenue
Peoria, Illinois 61602
(309) 673-2739
www.crookedwaters.com

THE PUB: Located on the banks of the Illinois River in downtown Peoria's Riverfront District, **Crooked Waters Brewery & Pub** finds its home in a former Central Illinois Light Company substation. Killer views of the Illinois River are available inside behind large windows or outside on the deck, which is situated directly above the flowing river. Built in 1926, the two-story red brick building has been completely renovated and now features a wooden wrap-around deck for great ambiance and outside entertainment poten-

tial. Thrusting out high over the river and offering views of the water, the neighboring park, two bridges, and all the river activity that goes with such a prominent location, the deck offers the ideal setting in which to enjoy your well-earned rewards.

Inside you'll find casual bar

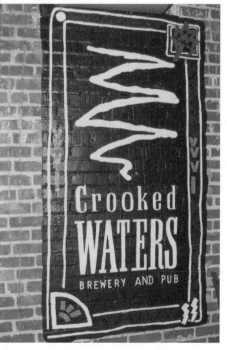

Located on the edge of the Illinois River, Crooked Waters Brewery & Pub's riverside patio is the perfect place to enjoy a little late afternoon sun.

seating with the brew house to the side and fermentation tanks behind the bar. This downstairs bar area offers a relaxed and slightly upscale atmosphere with cement floors crafted to look like large flagstones and a long marble-topped bar. Upstairs is more secluded with dining, another bar, and even better views of the river and surrounding cityscape beyond.

THE BREW: Open since October of 1996, Crooked Waters keeps five regulars on tap and two seasonals. The best seller ranges between the typical **American Waterfront Wheat,** the much more interesting German-style wheat—the **Blue Heron Hefeweizen**—and the truly outstanding **Powerhouse Amber Ale.** The Powerhouse is an excellent, full-bodied, malty session beer that will easily keep you happy all afternoon. However, if you're looking for a little bigger beer, the **Steamboat Oatmeal Stout** is a sweet creamy version worthy of the name.

There's no telling what seasonals may be waiting when you get there, but on the basis of the overall quality of Crooked Water brews, you won't be disappointed by trying a few while sitting over the Illinois River and taking in the views.

PRICE OF A PINT: No standardized happy hour here, but the brewpub plays with various drink specials regularly so you may get lucky. Just to be safe, come in expecting to pay $3.25 for an 18-ounce pint or $3.75 for a 23-ounce hefeweizen, and you won't be disappointed.

OTHER BREWS IN THE AREA: The **Illinois Brewing Company,** 102 North Center Street, Suite 111, (309) 829-2805, is located in Bloomington, Illinois, about 30 miles east of Peoria. Illinois Brewing Company was a bit ambitious and got up and running before it obtained the license needed to actually brew on premises. I can only hope that by the time you have this book in your hot little hands, the brewpub will be turning out fresh product. Give a call to be sure. The Bloomington area is also loaded with mountain biking, and the two areas will someday make for an excellent extended Bike & Brew America vacation.

CHAPTER TWO

INDIANA

Perhaps known best for its undying love of basketball, the Hoosier State embraces all that is hoops. From the high school season phenomenon known as "Hoosier Hysteria" to the infamous Bobby Knight and his former team, the Indiana University Hoosiers, all the way to the legendary collegiate and National Basketball Association former Celtics player and former Indianapolis Pacer's coach Larry Bird, Indiana is basketball. With this in mind, don't be surprised to see basketball courts wherever it's

29

Indiana

Indianapolis

Bloomington

Evansville

A view of southern Indiana's "Uplands" at the peak of the fall colors. (Courtesy of Upland Brewing Company)

not against building codes to put up a hoop. Yards, parking lots, driveways, and city parks—it's as common to find a perfectly measured and lined blacktop court in someone's backyard as it is to see a lopsided netless rim hanging over a patch of hard-packed dirt. If it's basketball, it's Indiana. But the Hoosier State does have more to offer than just basketball, including some of the best mountain biking and best beer in all of the Midwest.

First, however, there must be some commentary on the nickname "Hoosier." The source of Indiana's beloved namesake is shrouded in mystery. One of the more plausible origins of the word Hoosier is that it comes from the word "hoozer," a dialect word from northwestern England that eventually came to mean "hill dweller." Ironically, Indiana is generally known for its flat farmlands and agricultural base. The last Ice Age, which ended about 10,000 years ago, glaciated much of Indiana into flat and fertile land ripe for farming.

However, Indiana's saving grace comes in the form of a hilly wedge that begins in the middle of the state around the town of Bloomington and gradually spreads down to Evansville and New Albany, on Indiana's southern border, forming an arrowhead pointing north. This region was spared the flattening ravishes of the glaciers and today is filled with sharp ridges, exposed limestone bedrock, deep gorges, and many scenic views. This part of the state is also where those first Hoosiers settled—thus the name. Actually, you can visit many historical parks in this area to learn how these early settlers lived.

It's here in this rugged area—sometimes called the "Uplands" or "Little Smokies"—that the Hoosier National Forest dominates and provides perfect destinations for the Bike & Brew traveler. And, since Indiana is the "Crossroads of America," everyone does eventually come here. The next time you do, plan on doing some biking.

Bloomington

Who would have expected hills in Indiana? Well just don't expect them—ride them! Starting about 20 miles south of Indianapolis, the glaciers of the last Ice Age took

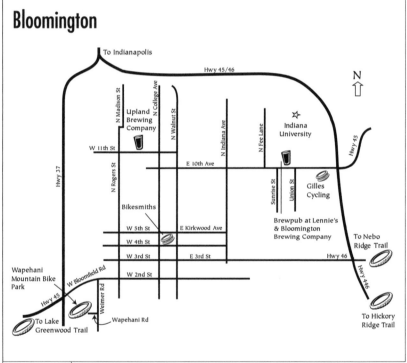

Bloomington

a sabbatical, and the flat farmlands of northern and central Indiana give way to the Indiana Uplands—rolling foothills, beautiful ridges, and breathtaking valley vistas.

Smack in the middle of this rough terrain is the college town of Bloomington—home of Indiana University and gateway to the Hoosier National Forest and the Hickory Ridge Trail System. Surrounding Bloomington is Brown County, an area known for its beauty and popular for its covered bridges and fall colors. While in town be sure to check out the buildings on Indiana's campus. When Bill Gates was building his castle up in Washington, he wouldn't settle for anything less than the best and carted out a few truckloads of Indiana limestone for his new digs. And, when the grand old Empire State Building needed a face-lift after all those smog-filled New Yorker years, how did the stone masons match the originally glorious exterior? They reopened the quarry that produced the flawless rock the first time at—yes, Empire Quarry located right here in southern Indiana. In fact, this region of Indiana is peppered with quarries—remember the quarry scene from the biking-film classic *Breaking Away*? Yep, filmed right here in the Uplands of Indiana. Now that's biking heritage!

Bloomington offers tremendous road-biking opportunities. Consistently ranked as one of the top 10 places in the country to ride, Bloomington is probably known for its roadie potential more than for its mountain-bike trails. Still, you're gonna be impressed by what the Uplands of southern Indiana have to offer mountain bikers. You'll feel like you're in the foothills of the Smokies when you're really only 1½ hours from Indianapolis.

National forests are always great destinations, and the Hoosier National Forest is no exception. So come for the riding and stick around for the beer at Upland Brewing Company. The beer is fantastic and an absolute must when shopping the beer shelves in Indiana.

Hickory Ridge Trail

THE SCOOP: Ahhhhh! National forest with miles of hilly singletrack, widetrack, and doubletrack to explore!

RIDE LENGTH AND TYPE: Variable—various well-marked loops make up this magnificent trail system.

THE BIKE: The **Hickory Ridge Trail** system itself was originally created, and is still used, for horseback riding. Not to worry, with over 40 miles of mapped and excellently marked trails, there is plenty of room for everyone. Characterized by singletrack-covered ridges mixed with plenty of dips into the surrounding ravines, it's all about fast downs into the river valleys and short, but very steep, climbs back onto the ridges. The trail is well laid out and maintained almost to a fault.

DIFFICULTY: Intermediate. There is nothing death defying here, but you won't go home without a workout either. Expect some tough technical climbs and a few water bars. Nothing adventurous novices can't handle if they don't bite off a bigger hunk than they can chew. Advanced bikers will love the many miles available for exploration.

AEROBIC DIFFICULTY (1–5):

3

TECHNICAL DIFFICULTY (1–5):

3

WARNINGS: The Hoosier National Forest requires all bikers to buy permits before using "your" trails. An annual pass costs $25, and a daily pass is $3. If you are headed to the Nebo Ridge Trailhead via Story (see under Other Trails in the Area), then you pass right by the Story Inn, which does a brisk business selling passes to fellow bikers on their way to the popular trail. Otherwise, stop in at Gilles Cycling & Fitness or call the Hoosier National

Forest, (812) 275-5987, to learn the nearest location that is selling the passes. Other than the entry fee, the next most serious obstacle is horse droppings. Just make sure to keep your mouth shut, watch where you're going, and you should be fine. Remember this is primarily a horse trail, so be sure to stay on the lookout and give way to equestrians when you happen upon them.

OTHER TRAILS IN THE AREA: Add a little map savvy and about 2 miles of pavement, and you can link the popular **Nebo Ridge Trail** to your Hickory Ridge ride. Nebo Ridge bounds the north side of Hickory Ridge. By itself, Nebo offers a 16-mile out-and-back of fast, fun, ridge-riding excitement. Don't miss it! It's a "happy ride" that will leave a smile on your face. But don't limit yourself to Nebo either because Hickory Ridge offers similar terrain, only much more of it, and you're less likely to run into other bikers who are on their way out when you're coming back. The Nebo Ridge Trail is most often approached independently of Hickory Ridge from the direction of Story

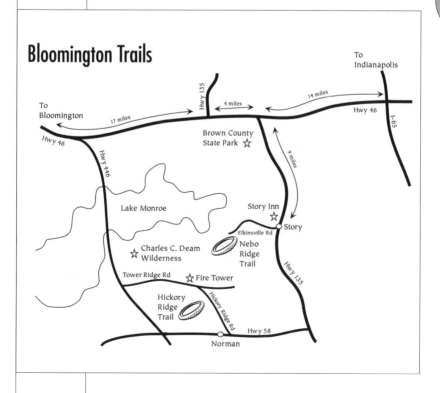

Bloomington Trails

for a 16-mile out-and-back total. A blast of a ride and Hoosier favorite to be sure. Just take Elkinsville Road southwest from Story approximately 3 miles. Shortly after the second bridge, the road makes a dramatic uphill turn to the right. The trailhead is on your left.

Is the 30 minutes from downtown Bloomington over to Hickory Ridge or Nebo Ridge too far to travel for some great riding? Well, if you don't have time to make a full day of it, try the **Wapehani Mountain Bike Park,** Indiana's only park devoted solely to mountain bikes. Located right inside Bloomington's city limits, you can't get much closer to the beer. Here you'll find between 5 and 7 miles (no one really knows exactly) of winding, intertwined, twisty, turny stuff that will have you guessing and turned around the whole time. Not technical, not real hilly, but it's there and only five minutes from a pint at Upland Brewing Company.

Ever wonder what the BEST singletrack ride in Indiana is? Well, if you don't mind technical and you're willing to make some preparations, then the **Lake Greenwood Trail** at the Crane Naval Surface Warfare Center is for you. Located about 30 miles southwest of Bloomington, 17 highly technical singletrack miles surround Lake Greenwood within this government facility. However, to get access to this unheralded diamond (and hands down, Indiana's best slice of singletrack), you have to be a U.S. citizen and obtain clearance by calling (812) 854-1165 at least 24 hours in advance of your ride. After you get in, be sure to pick up a map at the Visitors' Center—ask the guards for directions there. The trail begins behind the Visitors' Center.

CONTACTS: Hoosier National Forest, 811 Constitution Avenue, Bedford, IN 47421; (812) 275-5987. Bloomington Chamber of Commerce, 400 West Seventh Street, Suite 102, Bloomington, IN 47404; (812) 336-6381.

BIKE SHOP: Gilles Cycling & Fitness, 2530 East Tenth Street, Bloomington, IN 47408; (812) 336-0241. Gilles is just a few blocks east of Bloomington Brewing Company and right on the way to both Nebo Ridge and Hickory

Ridge. Plus, Gilles sells the necessary Hoosier National Forest Passes, so be sure to stop by and pick one up along with whatever else you may need. Another great shop located right in the mix of downtown is Bikesmiths, 112 College, Bloomington, IN 47404; (812) 339-9970 or (800) PRO-BIKE; www.bloomington.in.us/~bicycle. This shop is friendly, it has those bargain bins for gear hounds to sort through, and it's open on Sundays. However, because Bloomington consistently ranks as one of the top 10 places in the United States to road bike with its nice new roads, good shoulders, the hills already talked about—and drivers who give you some room—be prepared to talk to mostly roadies here.

"Not here!"
—IU Mountain Bike Club rider's response when asked if there was some good riding, while standing in the parking lot of the Wapehani Mountain Bike Park. The club was there preparing for a ride. Hmmm. Trying to keep the crowds away from the trails?

Upland Brewing Company

350 West Eleventh Street
Bloomington, Indiana 47404
(812) 336-2337(BEER)
www.uplandbeer.com

THE PUB: Just north of Bloomington's Downtown Square sits **Upland Brewing Company.** With loading docks and bay doors, Upland looks more like a microbrewery than a brewpub. This is not a coincidence. When Upland opened in the spring of 1998 as a microbrewery with an eye toward distribution, that's exactly what the outfit was. An idea to add a small tasting room got the city of Bloomington involved, and things soon got out of hand. City codes started adding up the square-footage require-ments for the taproom to the point where it made financial sense to turn the place into a full-fledged brewpub. A great big Thank You goes out to the city of Bloomington. Now, not only does Upland brew, distribute, and sell some

Upland Brewing Company's brick exterior as seen from Eleventh Street in downtown Bloomington.
(Courtesy of Upland Brewing Company)

of the best unfiltered beer in the state, it also has a great pub and patio where you can get some excellent food while you're enjoying a pint or two.

Although the outside says microbrewery, the interior welcomes thirsty guests with a wooden bar, dining area, and genuine cork dartboards. And, in the summer months, a patio overlooking the city is open for those so inclined.

THE BREW: Do not miss a beer here. Start with the **Upland American Pale Ale** and work your way through the **Upland Wheat, Upland Amber,** and **Upland Porter.** Never filtered, always natural is the creed here, and it shows—only the pale ale is clear enough to allow you to see your hand on the other side of the pint! The latest addition to this all-star lineup is the **Dragonfly India Pale Ale.** If you're a hop-monger, go straight here and you'll be in for the ride of your life.

PRICE OF A PINT: The steep, but typical, $3.50 a pint can be offset if you have the "Beer of the Day," which knocks a buck off the top. Hey, it's like buy three and the fourth one is on the house!

OTHER BREWS IN THE AREA: The **Brewpub at Lennie's and Bloomington Brewing Company,** 1795 East Tenth Street, (812) 323-2112, pumps fresh beer into Lennie's Restaurant right next door. Truly a partnership made in heaven. Even though it is located in a strip mall near campus, the food at Lennie's is outstanding, and the beer served both in the brewpub and restaurant is close to perfect. You're looking at a little more refinement here (the restaurant has been in business since 1989 and the brewery since 1994), but if you can stomach a fresh change of clothes and a strip mall, this place is worth a stop.

Evansville

Located on the Ohio River near the southwest extremity of the Indiana Uplands and only 383 feet above sea level, Evansville does not enjoy the rugged landscape so prevalent farther north. As a busy port on the Ohio River, Evansville has had significant industry involving woodworking, iron, steel, oil, coal, and manufacturing in the past.

Evansville

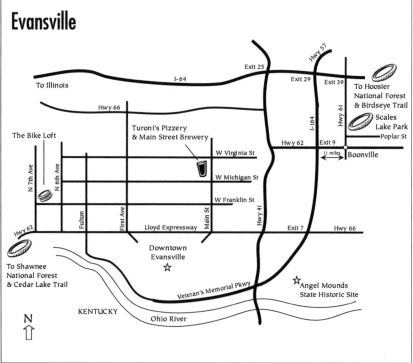

Thanks to the steamboats and barges of the Ohio River, early wealth provided Evansville with what is now a historic downtown boasting late-nineteenth- and early-twentieth-century architectural styles. Today, as businesses begin the migration back into downtown Evansville, this elegance can most thoroughly be enjoyed by visiting the 1891 restored Beaux Arts–style Old Vanderburgh County Courthouse and by strolling along the Downtown Walkway, a pedestrian-only redevelopment of old Main Street's business district. Various trolley and walking tours are also a popular way to explore the city's historic districts and buildings.

Another gem is the Angel Mounds State Historic Site located on the Ohio River just south of Evansville. This "historic" site is really a prehistoric site constructed by an ancient culture of mound builders who inhabited the area between A.D. 1250 and A.D. 1450. The site features a burial mound that is one of the largest prehistoric structures in the eastern United States.

History aside, what really puts Evansville on the Bike & Brew America map is its proximity to both the Hoosier National Forest in Indiana and the Shawnee National Forest in Illinois. And although the drive is over 1 hour to the Birdseye Trail in Hoosier National Forest and 1½ hours to the Cedar Lake Trail in Shawnee National Forest, the fact remains that Evansville will likely be your launching point for either.

Scales Lake Park

THE SCOOP: A fun singletrack excursion minutes from Evansville.

RIDE LENGTH AND TYPE: 5-mile singletrack loop.

THE BIKE: While a Bike & Brewer is visiting Evansville, **Scales Lake Park** is a must ride even though it's only 5 miles around the lake. You'll just have to do it once in each direction if that's not long enough for you. Though not a large area by any means, the trail builders at Scales did a fantastic job of taking advantage of every inch of the intricate terrain. Strip-mined back in the 1920s and 1930s, the spoils of the digging make the terrain look like a crumpled-up piece of corrugated cardboard. Long since revegetated with pines and various hardwoods, the park's landscape has completely reverted to a natural state with the centerpiece being the 66-acre Scales Lake, which the trail loosely circumscribes.

Now back to the cardboard. The trail takes you on fast downhills into the crevices and back up quick little hills, which land you on the smooth and fast ridgelines until

INDIANA

The "swimming hole" along Cedar Lake Trail gets some use.
(Photo by Quinn Kirkpatrick)

your next dip into the depths. This up and down is a complete rush as long as you get up enough speed on the downs to give you a push on the next up. Scales Lake is definitely a trail you'll enjoy.

DIFFICULTY: Intermediate. Only 5 miles long means you won't be destroyed aerobically out here, at least on one lap, but the terrain does supply a workout. The technical part involves the steep dips and climbs as the trail traverses the strip-mine diggings and takes you up and down some steep, but short, hills.

AEROBIC DIFFICULTY (1–5):
2

TECHNICAL DIFFICULTY (1–5):
3

WARNINGS: This is a county park, so not only is there a $2.00 vehicle entrance fee (or 50 cents per biker) but also be prepared for hikers. Also, since the trail is only 5 miles, many riders make it a destination by doing the trail in both directions, so watch for oncoming traffic.

OTHER TRAILS IN THE AREA: Okay, now on to the national forest goods. The favorite trail (and easiest to reach from Evansville) in the southern reaches of the Hoosier National Forest is the **Birdseye Trail.** Here, a 12-mile intermediate loop awaits. A mix of singletrack and fire roads takes you around lakes, through creeks and stands of hardwood and pine. However, if you're headed west, or don't mind a little more time in the car, then drive across the border to the Shawnee National Forest where the trail to hit is **Cedar Lake Trail.** Commonly considered the best trail in Illinois, Cedar Lake will hand out a more technical ride with rocks, roots, multiple creek crossings, and even a section of slickrock along with plenty of air on the multiple whoop-de-dos the trail has to offer.

CONTACTS: Scales Lake Park, Department of Parks and Recreation, P.O. Box 58, Boonville, IN 47601; (812) 897-6200. Hoosier National Forest, 811 Constitution Avenue, Bedford, IN 47421; (812) 275-5987. Shawnee National Forest, 901 South Commercial Street, Harrisburg, IL 62946; (618) 253-7114. Evansville Chamber of

BIKE BREW AMERICA

INDIANA

Commerce, 100 Northwest Second Street, Suite 100, Evansville, IN 47708; (812) 425-8147.

MAPS: Scales Lake Park has maps at the entrance hut, so as you're paying your fee, ask for a map. The best place to park is at the lake's beach parking lot. Pick up the trail across the park road at the outside shelter. That way when you've finished your ride, you can wash some of the dust off in Scales Lake's refreshing waters.

BIKE SHOP: The Bike Loft, 1731 West Franklin Street, Evansville, IN 47712; (812) 425-7799. Also known as Westland Honda, this is the place the bikers in Evansville call home, and you should too when you need to get any last-minute accessories. If you're headed to Birdseye, try REM Bicycle Center, 804 Main Street, Jasper, IN 47546; (812) 634-1454. For Cedar Lake, be sure and get the scoop from the Carbondale Cycle Shop, 303 South Illinois Avenue, Carbondale, IL 62901; (618) 549-6863.

Turoni's Pizzery & Main Street Brewery

408 North Main Street
Evansville, Indiana 47708
(812) 424-9873

THE PUB: Dark with an aroma of garlic, you can almost feel the Italian as you walk into this large brick building just north of Evansville's Historic Downtown District. Tin ceilings, dark-stained wood trim, wooden tables, and private booths offer dining and conversation options in both the bar and restaurant sides of this establishment.

A pizza tradition since 1963, **Turoni's Pizzery** added the **Main Street Brewery** in 1996, and what a nice addition it was. The early-twentieth-century building suits this restaurant, bar, and brewery perfectly.

Turoni's has always been a pizza joint by nature, and thin-crust pies are the specialty—what a perfect carbo-reload after a day at Scales or in the national forests. Extra hungry? Then check out the 29-inch version, which is equal to four large pies and can run you over $50. Not in the budget? Then check out the Cheapo-Special, which is a thin slice of baloney on day-old bread and runs you only 50 cents. It's all available here at Turoni's . . . including a good sense of humor and freshly brewed beer.

THE BREW: As for the beer, Turoni's is one of those rare establishments where the lighter brews actually taste good enough to order. Not overly hopped and not overly carbonated, both **Turoni's Honey Blonde Ale** and **Turoni's Light Lager** are very good beers. Turoni's Light Lager is actually a rice and barley mix, but the fact that it's a true lager and not an ale wannabe makes this a very drinkable beer, and the fact that it's always on special doesn't hurt a bit.

"It's all about the water."
—Brandon Erny, mountain biker and brewer at the Main Street Brewery, discusses the secret of his impeccable Turoni's Light Lager.

On the darker side of the beer menu, the **Thunderhead Red** is malty and an easy step up from the lager, whereas the **Blue Eyed Moose IPA** (India pale ale) is excellent even though it tastes more like a big pale ale than an IPA. The darkest of the bunch, the **Ol' 23 Cream Stout** is also very memorable with such a smooth and flavorful cream taste it's hard to believe it's not served via nitrogen.

PRICE OF A PINT: Turoni's runs a beer special every day of the week in addition to Turoni's Light Lager always being on sale at $2.00 a pint and $6.50 a pitcher. The prices of other house beers rotate through each day of the week so that the daily special beer's price per pint drops from $2.75 to $2.00.

OTHER BREWS IN THE AREA: No other brewpubs in Evansville, although the **Firkin Brew Pub**, 329 Main Street, (812) 422-9700, located in the historic downtown, was once and still claims to be, but isn't. The new owners still have a nice selection of imports and micros on tap but are without the knowledge to brew, and no way to get the kettles out of their basement location without cutting them to pieces. So the kettles sit and wait to be turned back on. Hopefully someday they'll find themselves a brewer or a way is discovered to move the equipment to a good home.

Indianapolis

Indianapolis has managed to accomplish what most Midwest cities can only dream about. A number of downtown development projects have spurred the revitalization of the state's capital city that was little more than a ghost town after dark during the 1970s and 1980s. Now, Indianapolis is home to two major sports franchises, the National Basketball Association Pacers and the National Football League Colts. These join the Indianapolis Motor

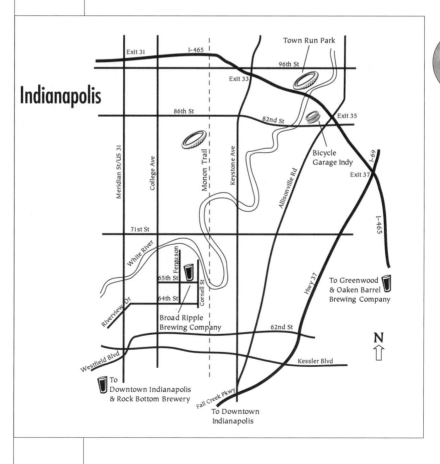

Speedway—which hosts the two largest single-day sporting events in the world: the Indianapolis 500 each May and the Brickyard 400 each August—and a multitude of museums, theaters, and parks such as you would expect from a city of this size.

The self-proclaimed Amateur Sports Capital of the World, Indianapolis is now home to the National Collegiate Athletic Association (NCAA). World-class swimming, track and field, and tennis facilities at Indiana University–Purdue University at Indianapolis (referred to as IUPUI and with Hoosier flare pronounced "ou-eey-pou-eey") allow Indianapolis to host multiple Olympic trials and NCAA championships.

Of course, no Amateur Sports Capital of the World would be complete without a velodrome, and Indianapolis has one of the country's finest. The Major Taylor Velodrome was named after Marshall Taylor, a world-champion cyclist from the turn of the twentieth century who was born and won his first race here in Indianapolis. His story is all the more astounding because he was able to excel to such great heights even while restricted by the limited opportunities allowed a black man in early twentieth-century Americia. Today, the velodrome and surrounding park bearing his name host weekly events including track, bmx, and cyclocross races.

With this kind of a bike scene going on, it's not surprising to find plenty of biking opportunities here even in the flat confines of central Indiana. Thanks to strong advocacy from the local mountain-bike club, you don't even have to leave the city limits to find some time in the dirt here in Indianapolis.

Town Run Park

THE SCOOP: A river trail with plenty of short hills and thrilling descents mixed in with the well-buffed singletrack.
RIDE LENGTH AND TYPE: 7½-mile loop with an optional trailhead behind the local bike shop that will add another 4 miles to your total.
THE BIKE: Although river trails usually don't offer the type of terrain usually associated with classic mountain biking, the Indy Spoke Breakers mountain-bike club and Indy Greenways have teamed up to create an excellent little river trail right on the northern edge of Indianapolis.

Taking advantage of every ounce of the rippled terrain, **Town Run Park** is a long skinny singletrack loop through surprisingly heavy forest following the White River for most of the trail's 7½ miles. Hugging the White River Greenway, with several refreshing views of the river itself, the trail travels south of Ninety-Sixth Street and crosses under Interstate 465. If you do the complete loop (with the Interstate 465 underpass as your only bi-directional section), you're looking at 7½ miles from the trailhead parking lot.

A way to increase this mileage is by beginning your ride at the bike shop, not the trailhead. The Bicycle Garage Indy (BGI) bike shop sits about 2 miles south of the trailhead and has built a singletrack trail leading to the park on the other side of the river. Not only is BGI convenient to the trail, paved parking is plentiful, and the folks there have maps and directions to assure that you make it to the trailhead via as much dirt as possible.

Excellently maintained by the Indy Spoke Breakers, Town Run Park makes for a fast, fun afternoon. Maybe not a destination ride, but the challenging hills, short, fast

descents, and buffed-out singletrack still make this trail a must when you are in the Indianapolis area. However, perhaps most important is this trail's proximity to the Broad Ripple Brewing Company, a true Midwestern classic.

DIFFICULTY: Beginner to intermediate. This is a great trail for the adventurous beginners to polish their off-road riding skills. Indy Spoke Breakers even hosts an annual Dirt Day at the park when local bike shops and bike manufacturers bring out mountain bikes for anyone to try the sport free of charge.

AEROBIC DIFFICULTY (1–5):
2

TECHNICAL DIFFICULTY (1–5):
2

WARNINGS: This is a city park in a populated area, and although it was created for mountain bikers, it is also open to hikers, so be on the lookout. It seems impossible that such a thin strip of land along the river is actually a loop, but it is—so please abide by the directional arrows and ride in a clockwise direction. Also, before there were mountain bikers riding the Indy Greenways paths along the White River, there were motorcyclists. They can still be a problem even though motorcycles are now against park rules. Call (317) 327-PARK to report any illegal activity, including motorcycles on the trail.

OTHER TRAILS IN THE AREA: Not exactly singletrack, the **Monon Trail** is part of the Indy Greenways trail system and bears mention because it passes within a block of the Broad Ripple Brewing Company. A paved rail trail currently 7 miles long with plans for expansion, the Monon is a great way to tour the north side of Indianapolis. By using the Monon Trail to connect to the **Central Canal Towpath** (5 unpaved miles) and the **White River Trail** (7 more paved miles), another 12 miles can be added to your Tour de Indy. For more singletrack riding, your best bet is to head about 1 hour south to the Hoosier National Forest covered in the Bloomington, Indiana, section of this book.

CONTACTS: Indy Greenways, 900 East 64th Street,

Indianapolis, IN 46220; (317) 327-7431. Indianapolis
Chamber of Commerce, 320 North Meridian Street, Suite
200, Indianapolis, IN 46204; (317) 464-2200. If you're
local and interested in mountain-bike advocacy in central
Indiana, you can contact the Indy Spoke Breakers via their
web site at www.spokebreakers.com.

MAPS: The trail is well marked, and plans are underway
for a map kiosk at the trailhead. Bicycle Garage Indy
keeps maps at the 82nd Street store; however, even
without an actual map, the trail is easy to follow. Plus,
the fact that the trail is hemmed in by Ninety-Sixth Street
to the north, the barrier of the White River to the east,
and Interstate 465 right through the middle makes it very
difficult to get lost.

BIKE SHOP: Bicycle Garage Indy, 4130 East 82nd Street,
Indianapolis, IN 46250; (317) 842-4140; www.bgindy.com.
This is the place to get a map and the place to park and
increase your ride to nearly 12 miles. A well-appointed
shop, BGI is also a great place to outfit yourself before
and after your ride.

Broad Ripple Brewing Company

842 East Sixty-Fifth Street
Indianapolis, Indiana 46220
(317) 253-2739

THE PUB: Located in the eccentric arts and entertainment district of Indianapolis known as Broad Ripple Village, this seemingly authentic English pub houses some of the best beer in the Midwest. From the moment you walk in to the **Broad Ripple Brewing Company,** you'll feel like you're in England with dark Victorian woodwork, glass French doors, and stained glass windows above the glass walls looking into the brew house. Invitingly undersized and cozily disjointed rooms mix with a small and cluttered bar area and create the feeling of a local English tavern.

A dining atrium, sidewalk patio, and real dartboards offer sport and the great outdoors, but this place is at its best with good friends and lively conversation. Settle into the special Pub Snug area—an English tradition where you place your order at the bar and no one bothers you. The Pub Snug even comes complete with a fireplace and finely carved mantle. In short, you'll find it impossible to believe that prior to opening in 1990, this place was a NAPA auto parts store.

THE BREW: With décor this English, it stands to reason that the pub is known for its **Broad Ripple ESB** (extra special bitter). Close your eyes, take a sip, and you'll taste a part of England. Fortunately, this is not a one-beer establishment so the beers don't stop there. Every regular who walks through the door has a different favorite and rarely wavers in ordering it up. The **Broad Ripple IPA** (India pale ale) and **Broad Ripple Porter** have the staunchest followings after the insanely popular ESB, but keep a look out

"Bet you a dollar you can't climb that pole."
—And the gauntlet is thrown barely a pint into the night.

Once a NAPA Auto Parts store, Broad Ripple is now a comfortable English pub located in the eclectic arts and entertainment district of Indianapolis known as Broad Ripple Village.
(Photo by Bill Baetz)

for rotating seasonals as well as what beer they're currently serving via hand-pump.

PRICE OF A PINT: No happy hour, but pints are 20-ounce Imperial English pints and range from $3.50 to $3.75 depending on what flavor you order.

OTHER BREWS IN THE AREA: Downtown Indianapolis is in the middle of a very successful renaissance with shopping, sports, theater, and museums all adding to the festive horse and carriage atmosphere. In the center of the city, you'll even find a mall cleverly concealed behind the restored facades of the original nineteenth-century buildings. In the midst of this activity, the **Rock Bottom Brewery** at 10 West Washington Street, (317) 681-8180, makes a popular destination with great food and decent beer, including one or two hand-pumped ales on tap at any time. Too bad it's a chain, and the beers are fairly structured. If it's fresh original beer you're looking for, after Broad Ripple, the next best local brewpub is actually south of Indianapolis in the town of Greenwood. Located in a strip mall, the **Oaken Barrel Brewing Company** at 50 North Airport Parkway, (317) 887-2287, serves up outstanding beer in a sports bar atmosphere. Go for the **Gnaw Bone Pale Ale** and you'll be set all night.

CHAPTER THREE

IOWA

Anne Kirkpatrick rides the smooth single-track of Scott County Park in Long Grove, Iowa.
(Photo by Quinn Kirkpatrick)

Once again the repeated glaciations of the last Ice Age strike, and this time it's in Iowa. As the third most productive agricultural state in the country behind the California and Texas giants, it's easy to see how the glaciers not only ground off the once prominent hilly and rugged terrain on their way south but left behind plenty of very fertile till on their way back to Canada. And even though this fertile prairie land is good for growing, it doesn't always promise much in the way of mountain biking.

But that's not to say that Iowa is not bike friendly. Thousands of miles of rural roads offer unlimited road-riding potential including the well-known Des Moines Register's Annual Great Bicycle Ride Across Iowa, more commonly known simply as RAGBRAI. This seven-day, almost 500-mile event started in 1973 when a few friends got together and decided to ride their bikes across Iowa.

Now it's the largest, longest, and oldest bicycling touring event in the world. Can you imagine the size of the truck it would take to haul around enough beer for that group?

However, with the exception of the many well-developed rail trails throughout the state, most of Iowa is privately owned and farmed, leaving far less room for mountain biking to hold a position of such prominence. And, therefore, Bike & Brew America only features one trail actually in Iowa. But that one trail is truly exceptional. Two other trails, one in Illinois and one in Nebraska, border the state and actually pair up with Iowa brewpubs (no one doubts that there's beer in Iowa, it's just that there isn't much riding close to it). Additionally, three more destinations in Nebraska, Minnesota, and Illinois are within an easy drive of Iowa's borders. Thus, a dedicated Iowan mountain biker does not have to drive far to reach prime trail and even primer suds.

Iowa

Sioux City

Cedar Rapids

Davenport

Cedar Rapids and Solon

Sugar Bottom Recreation Area, commonly considered the best trail in Iowa, is located just 25 miles from the thriving college town of Iowa City. The pairing of the two looked like a proverbial Bike & Brew slam-dunk. Unfortunately, the only brewpub in Iowa City serves barely drinkable beer. However, just when things look bleakest, the small, beer-friendly town of Solon appears. Actually closer to the trail than Iowa City, Solon supports a 16-barrel microbrewery with a small taproom serving great unfiltered beer and is the perfect place to stop before heading to Iowa City or Cedar Rapids for the full-blown brewpub thing.

Cedar Rapids is the second largest city in Iowa behind the state capital, Des Moines. The area offers many diverse cultural opportunities including the Czech Village and the nearby Amana Colonies National Historic Landmark. The Amana Colonies are just southwest of Cedar Rapids and offer seven preserved German villages founded over 150 years ago. Known for its family-style German meals, Amana is one of the longest-lasting communal societies in the world. Not only is this THE place to spend the first weekend of each October for the most authentic Oktoberfest in Iowa, it's also home to Iowa's oldest brewery, the Millstream Brewing Company. The Amana Colonies are worth the full day it would take to properly experience them.

Cedar Rapids itself is rightfully proud of its collection of museums and historic places including the Cedar Rapids Museum of Art, the Iowa Children's Museum, and the nineteenth-century Queen Anne–style Brucemore Estate as well as various cultural museums. Cedar Rapids is also overflowing with theater and music including the Cedar Rapids Symphony Orchestra, Paramount Theatre for the Performing Arts, and the historic Theatre Cedar Rapids, to name just a few.

Cedar Rapids and Solon

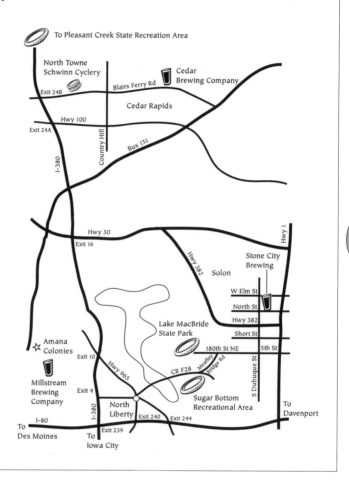

Sugar Bottom Recreation Area

THE SCOOP: Masterfully designed and maintained trails through stands of pine, hardwoods, and open fields.
RIDE LENGTH AND TYPE: 10 miles if all the longer loops are taken.
THE BIKE: If you only do one trail in Iowa, make sure it is Sugar Bottom. Overlooking Coralville Lake, the **Sugar Bottom Trail** was designed specifically for mountain-bike use. And it shows. The trail itself is like a big and funny-looking crazy eight: the novice trail makes the eight, and various intermediate and expert loops branch off and, even more important, return to the main trail. No more backtracking and searching for the good stuff here—careful planning has resulted in a trail that flows well and allows the whole thing to be ridden without circling and backtracking to try to pick up pieces that were missed the first time around.

The "easier" trails are smooth and mostly flat with wide-open sections of gloriously smooth singletrack. The "more difficult" sections will get you into some more significant terrain and have you winding among the trees. The "most difficult" trails tighten up the turns and give you steeper hills and a few log obstacles. And although these so-called "expert" or "most difficult" trails may be pushing the rating system a bit, as all the trails here can be handled by a dedicated intermediate rider, the fact remains that these trails are superbly laid out and maintained and a pure joy to ride.

In addition to being a great slice of singletrack, Sugar Bottom is very scenic. Coralville Lake is often visible, and many parts of the trail travel through mature pine forests where the singletrack is barely visible through the soft bed

The view along the trail at Sugar Bottom Recreation Area.
(Photo by Quinn Kirkpatrick)

of needles covering the trail. Ah, true bliss indeed, it won't take you long to figure out why Sugar Bottom is frequently called the best trail in Iowa. So, if you ever meet a member of the Iowa City Off-Road Riders (ICORR), the folks responsible for building or maintaining this trail, be sure to thank them and offer to buy 'em a beer!

DIFFICULTY: Beginner to intermediate. This is a great trail system for novices wanting to get their first taste of a real dirt trail. The excellent maps and difficulty-rating markers at all trail intersections mean novice riders will never get in over their heads, and the **Access Road** that cuts right through the middle of the trail offers the perfect bailout for a tired rider. However, at the same time, by taking all of the "more difficult" and "most difficult" side trails, intermediate and advanced riders will assure themselves an enjoyable day at the Bottoms.

    AEROBIC DIFFICULTY (1–5):
        2 (novice and intermediate trails),
        3 (expert trails)

    TECHNICAL DIFFICULTY (1–5):
        2 (novice and intermediate trails),
        3 (entire trail)

WARNINGS: These trails are directional and meant for mountain bikers, so just follow the markers and you'll be fine. No motorized vehicles or horses are allowed, although you may encounter some hikers and hunters during certain

times of the year. The real concern for you here is the weather. The trail gets closed when it's muddy, and if you ride anyway, you're looking at a $75 fine! Not only is this the reason this trail is of such high quality, it also ensures the quality of the trail will remain just like it is. The best way to avoid an unnecessary trip to the trailhead is to call the Trail Conditions Hotline at (319) 626-1160.

OTHER TRAILS IN THE AREA: If it's raining out, you're not gonna be allowed to ride at Sugar Bottom Recreation Area. Period. But you still have a few options in the area. First, you can head straight to Solon and Stone City Brewing and order up some pints. Not quite ready for that yet? Right outside of Solon is the crushed-gravel 5-mile **MacBride Trail,** a connector bike path along Lake MacBride leading to the nearby Lake MacBride State Park. In addition to the various rail trails that are so popular in this region, **Pleasant Creek State Recreation Area** offers a 10-mile off-road loop of singletrack just north of Cedar Rapids, which also just happens to makes it a perfect fit with the Cedar Brewing Company.

CONTACTS: U.S. Army Corp of Engineers, Coralville Lake, 2850 Prairie Du Chien Road NE, Iowa City, IA 52240; (319) 338-3543. Iowa City Off-Road Riders (ICORR) maintain an excellent web site at www.icorrmtb.org. Cedar Rapids Chamber of Commerce, 424 First Avenue Northeast, Cedar Rapids, IA 52401; (319) 398-5317. Amana Colonies Convention and Visitors Bureau, (800) 579-22954. RAGBRAI; www.ragbrai.com.

MAPS: There is a map kiosk at the trailhead, and every trail is perfectly marked with complete maps at all key intersections. You would have a hard time getting lost on this one. Just call to make sure the place is dry, and then show up and ride!

BIKE SHOP: In Iowa City, check out World of Bikes, 723 South Gilbert Street, Iowa City, IA 52240; (319) 351-8337. If you're headed to Cedar Brewing Company in Cedar Rapids, then right on your way is North Towne Schwinn Cyclery, 1150 Blairs Ferry Road NE, Cedar Rapids, IA 52402; (319) 393-6557.

Stone City Brewing

220 South Dubuque Street
Solon, Iowa 52333
(319) 624-1360
www.stonecity.com

Stone City Brewing, Solon's favorite neighborhood brewery, is just minutes from the Sugar Bottom Recreation Area.

(Courtesy of Stone City Brewing)

THE PUB: A cozy family-run taproom pours **Stone City Brewing** beers at a small bar in front of the brewery. Great beer and a strong local following make this place a favorite after-work hangout and the place to get a beer after an afternoon well spent hitting the trails.

This small eastern Iowa brewery is just minutes from Sugar Bottom and brews the best beer you're gonna find this side of Davenport and the other Quad Cities. Stone City Brewing doesn't serve food here; nevertheless, it's a REQUIRED stop before heading up to Cedar Rapids and the Cedar Brewing Company for the full-blown brewpub—beer and dinner—experience.

Before Stone City owners Sal and Jeff Allen went forward with building the brewery, they presented their business plan before a Solon town meeting to find out how receptive the small town would be to a brewery in their midst. They needn't have worried. The Allens were overwhelmed by the positive response they received at that meeting. Since 1996, the quiet taproom has become popular enough in a town of around 1000 people to establish regular hours six days a week. Even the town's mayor, who lives a block away from the brewery, regularly makes the walk for a pint of fresh local beer.

THE BREW: By using a homemade 16-barrel brewery cobbled together from various farm and dairy equipment, Stone City distributes eight beers throughout eastern and central Iowa, all of which are completely unfiltered and busting with a multitude of flavors. The best seller is the **Artist Colony Ale,** a big misty brown ale with a full body and lots of malty flavor. Other favorites are the **Stone City Hefeweizen** (an unfiltered true German wheat beer), the **Iowa Pale Ale,** and the **Stonemason Stout,** a stout of such creamy proportions that the head looks like it was poured off nitrogen.

PRICE OF A PINT: Stone City is technically just a brewery, and the business has relatively limited hours: Monday through Thursday, the taproom is open from 12:00 to 6:00 P.M., and Friday and Saturday it's open from 12:00 to 7:00 P.M. It is closed on Sundays. No happy hour so expect a pint to cost between $2.25 and $2.75 depending on which flavor you pick. Growlers are a very reasonable $5.00, and the brewery also sells six-packs, pigs, ponies, and kegs.

OTHER BREWS IN THE AREA: The truth be told, **Fitzpatrick's Brewpub,** 525 South Gilbert, (319) 356-6900, in Iowa City is the closest true brewpub to Sugar Bottoms. The problem is Fitzpatrick's only brews three varieties of beer, none of which is worth even the short trip. But if you find yourself in Iowa City for the night, be sure to check out **The Sanctuary** at 405 South Gilbert Street, Iowa City, IA 52240; (319) 351-5692. It's not a brewpub, but it is the best bar in town, some say in the entire state. So, although Iowa City is a very happening Midwest college town, Cedar Rapids is the place you have to go for both fresh food and fresh beer after you've had your fill of Stone City beer. The **Cedar Brewing Company** is a strip-mall brewpub on the north side of town with the spit and polished look of a chain restaurant, only it isn't. The place is a sports bar with TVs in every corner and a big screen dominating the bar area. This is the place to go to catch "the game." The beer is fresh but mostly unremarkable even though the bar does have eight or nine flavors going at once. Your best bets are the **Flying Aces Ale**, a copper-colored American pale with a malty start and easy hop finish, and the **Black Cobra Stout**, a smooth and slightly chocolate malty beer that is the closest thing a real beer lover will find in this place. If you plan on making the Amana Colonies part of your visit to the area, make sure you stop at Iowa's oldest brewery, the **Millstream Brewing Company** on Lower Brewery Road in Amana, www.millstreambrewing.com. or (319) 622-3672. Millstream has a beer garden and is open daily. Call for times.

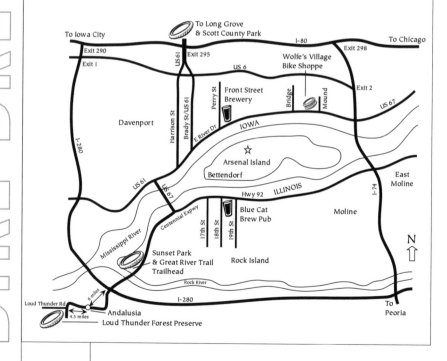

Davenport and the Quad City Area

   The four cities of Davenport and Bettendorf (Iowa) and
Moline and Rock Island (Illinois) make up a region on the
Illinois and Iowa border that is commonly called the Quad
Cities. Located directly on the Mississippi River, all have
long and rich histories in commerce and transportation on
the Great River. Today these industries are complemented
by thriving downtown districts with three riverboat casinos,
three noncasino riverboats available for Mississippi River

Davenport

FORC riders carefully cross Tree Bridge along the Extra Mile deep in Loud Thunder Forest Preserve.
(Photo by Quinn Kirkpatrick)

cruises, restaurants, bars, and no less than three brewpubs hard at work bringing the Quad Cities fresh beer.

Of the multiple art galleries and museums in the area, be sure to visit the 1833 Federal-style Colonel Davenport House located on Arsenal Island, which shows the restoration project and period artifacts. The island is also the site of a working ammunition-manufacturing arsenal, National and Confederate cemeteries, the second-largest United States–owned home, and other historic military museums including the Rock Island Arsenal Museum.

Although the Quad Cities are probably best known for the over 200 miles of converted rail trail and canal tow paths, which originate in the Quad Cities, singletrack has lately started making its presence felt in the local biking scene. Recently, the Loud Thunder Forest Preserve has been taken under the wing of the local mountain-bike club—the Friends of Off-Road Cycles, also known as FORC. Since then, the Quad Cities area has become a Bike & Brew destination in its own right, complementing, rather than relying on, the popular (and very excellent) Sugar Bottom Recreation Area between Iowa City and Cedar Rapids. Now that the Quad Cities area is a Bike & Brew player, less than one hour separates the components of a weekend of fat-tire fun.

IOWA

Loud Thunder Forest Preserve

THE SCOOP: Nicely maintained horse trails offering miles of challenging singletrack.

Snow-covered singletrack beckons at Loud Thunder Forest Preserve.
(Photo by Quinn Kirkpatrick)

RIDE LENGTH AND TYPE: 8-mile, balloon-on-a-string ride from the ranger's house trailhead or a 5-mile loop from the horse corral trailhead.

THE BIKE: The **Loud Thunder Forest Preserve** is riding proof of the value of the 48-hour rule. What is the 48-hour rule? Simple. Don't ride your horse OR your bike on the trail within 48 hours of rain. Sounds simple enough, doesn't it? Whereas horse trails are usually badly eroded and poorly maintained as far as mountain bikers are concerned, Loud Thunder is a refreshing exception thanks to FORC, the local mountain-bike club, which is affiliated with IMBA (International Mountain Bicycling Association). Currently, Loud Thunder offers over 8 miles (more miles are in the works) of well-maintained, fun, and somewhat technical singletrack weaving through the rough

terrain surrounding the 167-acre Lake George about 20 miles southwest of Rock Island, Illinois.

There are a couple of different places to pick up the trail here: across the park highway from the green ranger's house or at the horse corrals. You'll get more bang for your buck by leaving from the ranger's house as the trail is basically a balloon-on-a-string ride with the 1½-mile string leaving from the ranger's trailhead and the 5-mile balloon picking up at the horse corral. Additionally, a small loop called **The Extra Mile** offers a chance to tack on another mile to the 5-mile main track.

The first 1½-mile stretch from the ranger's house takes you down into two significant ravines and then back up again along the borders of a couple of corn fields. Eventually you will come to a narrow dirt road, which will drop you out after a quarter mile onto the northwest side of the horse corral. Two trailheads leave from the horse corral area. As the trails are bi-directional, you can take either one to begin the 5-mile loop, which will eventually return you to the corral. The horse corral also makes a perfect trailhead if you want to keep your ride down to only 5 miles.

You won't be able to get lackadaisical gliding along the tight dirt track in Loud Thunder. Plenty of fallen logs and fast dips into multiple stream crossings will assure you'll stay on your toes as you make your way through the trail. While things get a little sloppy around the stream crossings, many have bridges or log crossings to aid mountain bikers and hikers through the torn up mud fields resulting from the horse traffic.

Once across the water, the climbs out of the multiple river valleys are sharp and steep. You might be hugging your handlebars and getting to know the front of your saddle in a completely new light. Don't worry; it's completely worth it. The nice lazy singletrack on top of the ridges will keep the smile up and the heart rate down.

DIFFICULTY: Intermediate. These trails are the perfect intermediate ride. You'll have to work on occasion but between the technical river fordings and the steep climbs out of the hollows, the singletrack is smooth and fun.

AEROBIC DIFFICULTY (1–5):

3

TECHNICAL DIFFICULTY (1–5):

3

WARNINGS: Another reason the trails are in such excellent condition is because they are closed March, April, and May for the spring thaw, although sometimes they are opened early if the season was dry enough. Signs are posted at the ranger's house with the current status but, to save yourself a trip, it's often best to call the ranger directly at (309) 795-1040. Only the horse trails to the west of Lake George are open to mountain bikes, and remember, the club has worked hard adopting this trail and keeping it in top shape for all users so don't be a knucklehead and ride when the trails are closed or break the 48-hour rule. And remember, Loud Thunder was primarily intended for equestrians, which means there will be horse traffic, some choppy places in the trail, and the occasional horse residue trail hazard.

OTHER TRAILS IN THE AREA: Scott County Park is a popular destination in the Quad City area and offers over 10 miles of beginner to intermediate cross-county ski trails and singletrack. The Quad Cities area also offers two maintained bike paths, both part of the proposed 475-mile **Grand Illinois Trail** that will circle northern Illinois from the Quad Cities over to Chicago and back. The **Hennepin Canal,** (217) 782-3715, is the oldest canal in Illinois and runs 75 miles from the Quad Cities eastward to the LaSalle-Peru area where it picks up the **Illinois and Michigan Canal State Trail,** (815) 942-0796, for another 50 miles, creating a continuous off-road route all the way to Chicago. **The Great River Trail,** (309) 793-6300, is a rails-to-trails project that travels from Rock Island north along the Mississippi River 62 miles to Savanna, Illinois. It offers a mix of pavement and crushed gravel with plenty of small singletrack side trips onto surrounding public lands along the way.

CONTACTS: Loud Thunder Forest Preserve, 19408 Loud Thunder Road, Illinois City, IL 61259; (309) 795-1040.

FORC is also a great contact while riding in the area; check out the web site at www.qcforc.org or contact the group by mail at 1255 Thirty-Seventh Street, Rock Island, IL 61201. Davenport Chamber of Commerce, 130 West Second Street, Davenport, IA 52801; (319) 322-1706.

MAPS: FORC has recently completed mapping the trails at Loud Thunder. A copy of the map is on their web site (www.qcforc.org) and should also be available at the trailhead and local bike shops by the time you're ready for your ride. Maps for the maintained bike trails, such as the Great River Trail and Hennepin Canal, are available at Wolfe's Village Bike Shoppe but don't show some of the more interesting singletrack spurs. Those you're just gonna have to find on your own.

BIKE SHOP: Wolfe's Village Bike Shoppe, 1018 Mound Street, Davenport, IA 52803; (319) 326-4686. Just down East River Drive is the cool little section of town known as the Village of East Davenport. It was once a Civil War military community. Wolfe's is right on the corner and can supply you with whatever your Bike & Brew America heart desires.

Front Street Brewery

208 East River Drive
Davenport, Iowa 52801
(319) 322-1569

THE PUB: This is a snug little riverfront bar in downtown Davenport with comfortable wooden booths and tables offering the perfect place to discuss the merits of the day's trails.

Located in an old brick riverfront building, Front Street opened in 1992 only to have the big flood of 1993 shut down the place for a few months to dry things out. The water stains on one of the wooden doors still show how high the Mississippi rose during that memorable flood. Not to fear. When water again threatened in 2001, members of the local mountain-bike club, FORC, came to the rescue of their "Club House" and, in lieu of the scheduled group ride, spent the evening sandbagging the place in preparation for the spring flood. Rumor has it they were compensated accordingly. However, most important, according to Dean Mayne, FORC's front man, the "sandbag fortress" that East River Drive had held in fine fashion. By the time the Missouri had receded back to normal levels, Front Street was back in business. Now that's a bike club whose members take their duties seriously!

Walking in the front door, you cross to the pub on a small balcony where an open view of the brew house is directly below in the restaurant's basement. Kettle, mash tun, and hot-liquid tank all offer assurance of what lies beyond. Worn wooden floors and exposed brick walls then welcome you into the darkened interior of this narrow building a block away from the Mississippi. Settle at one of the small tables overlooking the brewery in the Beer

Parlor, or proceed past the bar and out the back door where you can relax on Front Street's pleasant outdoor patio and watch the Perry Street traffic go by.

THE BREW: Front Street keeps five regular brews on tap and usually rotates in an excellent seasonal or specialty. The brewpub's best-selling beer is the **Raging River Ale**, an English ale named after the flood of '93. This beer is a nice deep bronze color with hints of hops in the nose and body. The next beer not to miss is the **Bucktown Stout**, so named after Davenport's infamous Red Light District of the late-nineteenth century and where the Front Street Brewery is now located. Bucktown is smooth; it's served on nitrogen with a slight espresso flavor worked into the body. The best beer in the bunch, and what the real beer drinkers have while visiting, is the **Front Street Hefeweizen**—a true German wheat beer brewed with noble German yeast to give the beer the authentic German flair so often missing from many so-called hefeweizens. An excellent beer and the one to have if you're only having one.

PRICE OF A PINT: Monday through Friday between 3:00 and 6:00 P.M., pints go from $3.00 down to $2.00, which is just perfect for a little Loud Thunder R&R.

OTHER BREWS IN THE AREA: Directly across the Mississippi in Illinois, and actually a touch closer to Loud Thunder, in Rock Island's popular casino and entertainment district is the **Blue Cat Brew Pub**, 113 Eighteenth Street, (309) 788-8247. Blue Cat brews up some unquestionably

71

good beer, especially the **Big Bad Dog English Ale,** a big malty beer with a deep brown color. The **Honey Bee Ale** has a surprising body and uses local honey to give it some interesting character. But it's the **Guatemala Coffee Stout** that brings 'em in from all over. Made with Guatemalan coffee beans from nearby Theo's Java Hut, this is a beer for true coffee lovers. However, what really makes this place extraordinary is the food, as one of the owners is a chef. With an exotic and unique menu from catfish sate to lamb shanks, the Blue Cat serves up a cuisine much more interesting than traditional pub fare.

"Prepare for a good ass whoopin', then off to Front Street for medicinal purposes."
—Dean Mayne, aka "The Night Train," offers to show Bike & Brew America around the Quad Cities.

Sioux City

An important port on the Missouri River, Sioux City sits at the junction of the Missouri, Big Sioux, and Floyd Rivers. It's on Floyd Bluff overlooking the Missouri River where you'll find the 100-foot-tall monument to Sergeant Charles Floyd, the first U.S. soldier to die west of the Mississippi when the Corps of Discovery passed through here in August of 1804. Soon to celebrate its bicentennial, the Corps of Discovery was the name for the now famous

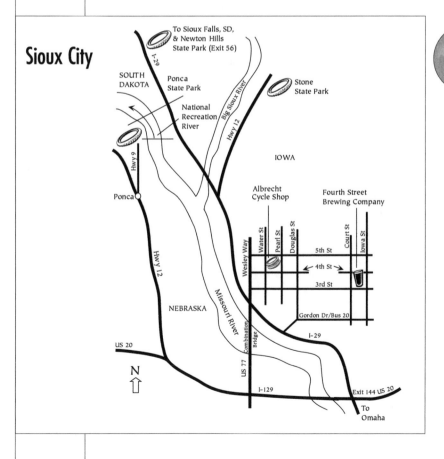

Sioux City

Lewis and Clark Expedition commissioned by President Thomas Jefferson to explore the West and possibly find a waterway to the Pacific Ocean. The monument is worth a visit for the history and for the views.

A segment of the Missouri River just west of Sioux City beginning at Ponca State Park (where you'll be heading for your ride) and traveling nearly 60 miles to Gavins Point Dam was designated a National Recreation River in 1978. This is one of only two segments of the entire Missouri River nearly untouched by humans. Thanks to the designation, even today it looks much the same as it did when Lewis and Clark made their way to the West Coast because the river here is still in a naturally flowing, undammed condition.

The majority of the riding in the region surrounds Sioux City, and it's in nearby Ponca, Nebraska, where you'll find Ponca State Park, a place worthy of an all-day excursion into the woods. Fortunately, the Sioux Falls Brewing Company folks from Sioux Falls, South Dakota, are bringing fresh beer to the masses of Sioux City (and Bike & Brew travelers) at the Fourth Street Brewing Company. Located on Historic Fourth Street, the 15 buildings (including Fourth Street's building) making up this small historic district form the most important example of Richardsonian Romanesque–style architecture in all of Iowa.

Now how's that for a cosmopolitan Bike & Brew destination? The riding is in Nebraska, the brews originated in South Dakota, and the brewpub sits in Iowa in a historically important building.

Ponca State Park

THE SCOOP: Hilly singletrack along bluffs overlooking the mighty Missouri River.

RIDE LENGTH AND TYPE: Variable—almost 20 miles of singletrack make up the diverse trails in this park.

THE BIKE: The place to ride is about 20 miles northwest of the Fourth Street Brewing Company and actually located in Nebraska at **Ponca State Park**. The park is along the eastern end of the 60-mile stretch of the Missouri River that, as mentioned, has been designated a National Recreation River.

Mountain bikes are allowed on both the hiking and horseback-riding trails (except for Memorial Day and Labor Day when the horse trails are closed to mountain bikers). The trails are rarely crowded and offer a rugged, hilly ride along the river bluffs with some climbs gaining as much as 200 feet in elevation! Remember this is Nebraska we're talking about here. It's these very climbs that return the favor by offering impressive views of the Missouri River and the valley beyond, so be sure to find the Three-State Overlook on the northeast side of **Bigleys Ravine Trail 1**. From this vantage point, you will be able to see Nebraska, South Dakota, and Iowa spread out before you. Keep your eyes open for another highlight in the park: On **Old Oak Trail 3** is a gnarled and twisted oak tree that dates back over 350 years to around 1645!

Some fairly technical singletrack loops await on the hiking paths with the more remote 3.4-mile **Buffalo Run Trail 7** being the favorite. Recently, a few more miles of trails have been added in the new park addition. These trails are north of the **Corps of Discovery Trail 6** and worth the time to explore.

The design of the park weaves the trails in and around the park roads, so there is always an easy way back to your car if things get a little tough. Just be sure to bring your suit because your daily fee entitles you to a dip in the park's outdoor swimming pool after (or during) your ride. **DIFFICULTY:** Intermediate. This trail offers about as much climbing as you'll find in eastern Nebraska and eastern South Dakota, so be prepared to suck a little wind as you spend the day exploring the many miles of trails this area has to offer.

AEROBIC DIFFICULTY (1–5):

3

TECHNICAL DIFFICULTY (1–5):

3

WARNINGS: A valid park entry permit is required to ride the trails here. Daily passes are $2.50, and annual permits go for $14.00. At Ponca State Park, you will be riding either hiking or horse trails, so give way accordingly and remember that on certain peak dates, namely, Memorial and Labor Days, the horse trails will be off-limits to bikers.

OTHER TRAILS IN THE AREA: Barely outside the city limits, **Stone State Park** is the closest riding to Sioux City and offers 6½ miles of mountain-bike trails on the bluffs above the convergence of the Big Sioux River with the Missouri River. Offering some of the best riding western Iowa has, the park dates back to the late-nineteenth century when it was a private preserve and zoo. In the 1930s, the Civilian Conservation Corps built many of the park buildings still in use today. Singletrack climbs almost 250 feet to the 1391-foot summit of Mount Lucia where you will be greeted with outstanding views of the surrounding Missouri and Big Sioux River Valleys.

Not to feel left out, South Dakota offers **Newton Hills State Park** and about 10 miles of horse-laden multiuse singletrack in the Big Sioux River Valley about 60 miles north of Sioux City and 25 miles south of Sioux Falls. **CONTACTS:** Ponca State Park, P.O. Box 688, Ponca, NE 68770; (402) 755-2284. Siouxland Chamber of Commerce, 101 Pierce Street, Sioux City, IA 51101; (712) 255-7903.

MAPS: Not only does your $2.50 day-use fee ($14 annual fee) allow you to ride the trails and use the pool, you also receive a map of the park trails with your price of admission.

BIKE SHOP: Albrecht Cycle Shop, 200 Fifth Street, Sioux City, IA 51101; (712) 258-6050. Located about 1 mile from the brewpub, the employees here will take care of all your biking needs while you visit Sioux City. If you decide to make Sioux Falls your base, check out Bike Masters, 3315 South Spring Avenue, Sioux Falls, SD 57105, (605) 334-2668.

Fourth Street Brewing Company

1107 Historic Fourth Street
Sioux City, Iowa 51101
(712) 234-1120
www.fourthstbrewco.com

THE PUB: Sioux City and Sioux Falls are about 80 miles apart, and both have brewpubs. The fact is, they're sister pubs, owned and operated by the same folks. Both are located in early-twentieth-century buildings in great downtown locations, have outdoor patios, and, well, serve pretty much the same, very solid, beer. The original brewpub is the **Sioux Falls Brewing Company**, restored and designed with immaculate care. It's the original pub in a chain (albeit a very small one), and all other things being equal, it's the place to go after your ride.

However, in this case, all other things are not equal. The riding radiates like a fat tire's spokes from the Sioux City location. Even though **Fourth Street Brewing Company** does not have quite the attention to detail as the original, it is still the logical place to end up if you plan on riding in the area.

The Fourth Street Brewing Company is located on Sioux City's Historic Fourth Street and is housed in a four-story Victorian Richardsonian Romanesque–style building known as the Bay Street Block. Built in 1890 by the Boston Investment Company, the original rough-cut Ohio gray stone columns are now covered, but the dignity and history of the building are still very much intact, as you can see as you make your way into the historic structure.

Still on the tip of restoration, Historic Fourth Street is coming along nicely and supplies the perfect setting for a classic after-ride stop. The potential is here with a new outdoor side patio offering refreshing views of the historic street beyond.

Inside you'll find a large open room with wooden floors and large glass windows overlooking the area's historic buildings. The dining area is separated from the bar by a low dividing wall, and the brew house sits behind the bar visibly pumping out dependable Fourth Street–Sioux Falls beer from behind large glass walls.

THE BREW: By sticking with a good thing and working economies of scale, Fourth Street and Sioux Falls produce mostly the same beers. Although the names have been changed to protect the innocent, basically the lineups are the same right down to the seasonals. The **Sue Bee Honey Ale** stands in for the entry-level **Midnight Star Ale** over at Sioux Falls and is a nice light ale with the slight flavor of honey. The Midnight Star won gold at the 1997 Great American Beer Festival in the Canadian-style ale category and is brewed specifically for one other bar in the world—Kevin Costner's Midnight Star Saloon in the restored gambling town of Deadwood, South Dakota. The **Famous Diving Elk Pale Ale** is a smooth-bodied ale with a mild hop finish and is named after a live act that featured elks diving into the Big Sioux River in the late 1800s. True story! A large black-and-white photograph hangs on the Fourth Street restaurant's wall depicting the event. The Diving Elk copies Sioux Fall's **Phillips Avenue Pale Ale,** which took bronze two years straight in the English-style bitter category at the 1997 and 1998 Great American Beer Festivals. A solid session beer. Two other beers without all the hardware round out the regulars. In honor of Sergeant Floyd of the Lewis and Clark Expedition, **Sergeant's Stout** replaces the **Buffalo Stout** and is rich and creamy and served via nitrogen to smooth it out. And **Spike Kelly's Red** is a well-balanced, deep copper ale, loaded with caramel flavor and stands in for the **Ringneck Red Ale.**

PRICE OF A PINT: The Brewmaster's Social is Monday through Friday from 4:30 to 6:30 P.M. when pints drop a buck and pitchers are half off—that's only $5!

BIKE BREW AMERICA

IOWA

OTHER BREWS IN THE AREA: Sioux Falls Brewing Company, 431 North Phillips Avenue, Suite 100, Sioux Falls, SD 57104; (605) 332-4847; www.sfbrewco.com. Built in 1899 for the Jewett Brothers wholesale business, the rough-hewn rock walls, exposed ceiling beams, and worn wooden floors make you feel like you've stepped into a brewery of old. Solid-wood 1½-foot columns and brewhouse equipment behind glass walls complete the picture. The nicely restored 100-year-old building welcomes you in for a pint of fresh beer. Many original features of the building have been left intact and are used to enhance the décor of the remodeled brewery, including large industrial sliding doors and an old grain silo separating the large one-room bar area from the dining and sometimes banquet room.

An outdoor patio overlooking Main Street is open in the summer and often hosts concerts and special events (like the pre-Sturgis Harley bash) with beer wagons pulling up in the parking lot to dispense cheer in an appropriate fashion. Inside, pool and shuffleboard offer diversion, which you won't be much in need of with six fresh beers on tap.

CHAPTER FOUR

KANSAS

What could be worse than the long drive through Kansas on your way to the Rocky Mountains? Not stopping for a bike ride and a beer along the way, that's what! You wouldn't know it, cruising along Interstate 70 at a cool 75 mph, but eastern Kansas is home to some of the sweetest singletrack and some of the best freshly brewed beer in the Midwest.

In the Sunflower State you'll find more than just pretty flowers. History abounds with both the Santa Fe and Oregon wagon-train trails' origins in the Kansas City–Leavenworth area. Original tracks of these historic trails are still being discovered and preserved in farms and pastures throughout Kansas. Once the Wild West, Wyatt Earp, "Wild Bill" Hickock, and "Bat" Masterson all formerly kept the peace in a younger, rowdier Kansas.

Kansas

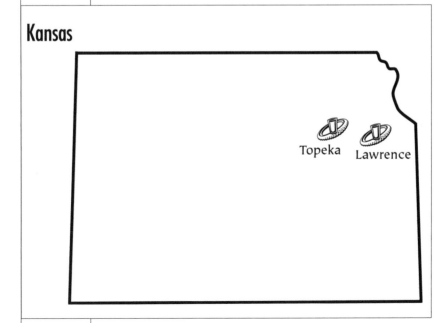

Topeka   Lawrence

Today, Kansas is home to the last of the once-dominant tall prairie grass, the three largest remaining herds of buffalo, the rolling dry hills of the high plains, and plenty of opportunities to stretch those travel-weary legs and quench your thirst before packing it in for the night. With Kansas comes a whiff of the mountains and a taste of the Midwest. Eastern Kansas trails have the exposed-rock terrain of the West and the hilly, tight, tree-covered single-track of the Midwest. Of course, no stop in Kansas (or anywhere else, for that matter) would be complete without a sample of the local wares—especially the freshly brewed beer—and once again Kansas delivers in style.

No matter why or how you got here, as long as here *is* Kansas, you'll find great riding and outstanding beer. And you don't even have to go all the way to Oz to find it!

Lawrence

If you ever find yourself traveling across country on Interstate 70, plan a stop in Lawrence, Kansas. Site of the famous abolitionist Jim Brown's fight for freedom in the 1850s and an important stop for the Underground Railroad, Lawrence played a key roll in the fight of the territory to enter the union as an antislavery state. Even today, *USA Today* cites Lawrence as one of the least-segregated communities in the entire country.

Known as the "City of the Arts," Lawrence is the only Midwest city to rank in the top 20 of "The Best Small Art Towns in America." And we're not just talking miniatures here! Nearly a dozen art galleries reside on Massachusetts Street alone! In addition to art, Lawrence offers a great historic downtown filled with theaters, shops, restaurants,

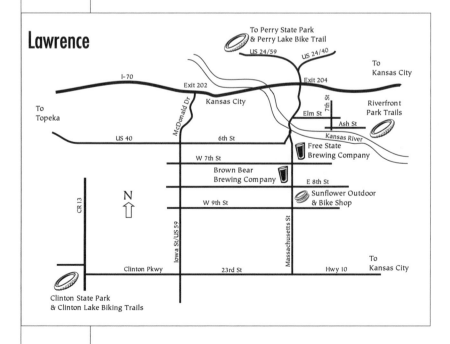

Lawrence

To Perry State Park
& Perry Lake Bike Trail
US 24/59
US 24/40
To Kansas City
I-70
Exit 202
Exit 204
To Topeka
McDonald Dr
Kansas City
7th St
Riverfront Park Trails
Elm St
Ash St
US 40
6th St
Kansas River
Free State Brewing Company
W 7th St
Brown Bear Brewing Company
E 8th St
CR 13
N
W 9th St
Sunflower Outdoor & Bike Shop
Iowa St/US 59
Massachusetts St
Clinton Pkwy
23rd St
Hwy 10
To Kansas City
Clinton State Park
& Clinton Lake Biking Trails

and cafés. Also, the presence of the University of Kansas and Haskell Indian Nations University (the only intertribal Native American university in the country) adds to the intellectual dimension of the community and helps keep the population young and diverse.

Not only has Lawrence been designated a "Biker-Friendly Community" by the League of American Bicyclists, all this culture is a mere 10 minutes from the trailhead. If you're looking for a sample of what Kansas has to offer mountain bikers, this is it. You're guaranteed to come away from this one with a big goofy grin and fond memories of a tough, classic, Midwestern-style mountain-bike ride. And, if you're looking for a sample of what Kansas has to offer the beer lover, this is it as well. Stop in and see why.

Clinton Lake Biking Trails

THE SCOOP: Technical sections; 100% singletrack!

RIDE LENGTH AND TYPE: 25-mile loop with plenty of options to shorten the ride.

THE BIKE: What pushes this ride over the edge and into the realms of the Bike & Brew Hall of Fame is its great location near the funky little college town of Lawrence. The **Clinton Lake Biking Trails** are only 1 mile outside the city limits and maybe a 10-minute drive from its cool downtown area. Of course, no trail can make it on location alone, and Clinton Lake is no exception, offering over 25 miles of well-marked and well-maintained singletrack trails . . . plenty to keep those of weak legs at home (or wishing they were) and the most advanced rider honest.

The biking trails wind along the north side of Clinton Lake, actually a reservoir of impressive dimensions with over 7000 surface acres and 85 miles of shoreline! Surrounding the lake are multiple parks, campsites, boat-launching ramps, and beaches. After (or during) a ride on a hot Midwest afternoon, there's nothing better than stopping for a quick dip at one of the many beaches mere yards from the trail. Well, maybe a quick dip and a fresh beer, but we'll get to that soon enough.

The Clinton Lake trails pretty much define what Kansas mountain biking is all about: tight technical affairs with plenty of dips, short steep rocky climbs, multiple water crossings, and hairpin turns. There are two main trails under constant maintenance by the Kansas Trails Council, a blue-blazed trail and a white-blazed trail. They interconnect at many locations and, by taking one trail out and the other one back, you can easily form a 15-mile ride or an infinite number of shorter variations. If you continue

beyond Washout Bridge at the western park boundary, the blue-blazed trail continues another 5 miles, which can bring your daily total up to an even 25 miles by the time you get back to the trailhead!

Generally speaking, the blue-blazed trail hugs the lake, and the white-blazed trail meanders outward, making it a bit longer. Just be aware of this difference if you're counting miles or planning on being in at a certain time. If you find yourself running late or just plain running out of gas, this part of the lake is surrounded by Clinton State Park so there are many opportunities to bail and ride back to the trailhead via pavement.

DIFFICULTY: Intermediate to advanced. Novice bikers will be in a little over their heads in many spots. However, if you don't mind walking up a few short hills and over a few creek crossings, there is plenty of riding here that won't leave your knuckles white.

AEROBIC DIFFICULTY (1–5):

3 (4 if you do the whole thing)

TECHNICAL DIFFICULTY (1–5):

3

WARNINGS: Poison ivy is common throughout this region. Keep on the lookout when fixing those flats!

OTHER TRAILS IN THE AREA: The Riverfront Park Trails are just across the Kansas River, a stone's throw from the Free State Brewing Company. Riverfront Park has two kinds of trails—a 10-mile recreational bike path along the top of the levee and another 5 or so miles of sometimes interesting singletrack down in the river bottoms. However, because of the trail's proximity to downtown Lawrence, it's a fast, well-worn, and often overcrowded trail. Nonetheless, the levee (as it is sometimes called) offers a good ride for the novice and dries quicker than the Clinton Lake trails after a few days of rain. Also, Lawrence is very close to Perry State Park and the excellent **Perry Lake Bike Trail.** (See the Topeka section in this book.)

CONTACTS: U.S. Army Corps of Engineers, 872 North 1402 Road, Lawrence, KS 66049; (785) 843-7665. Clinton State Park, 798 North 1415 Road, Lawrence, KS 66049;

(913) 842-8562. Kansas Trails Council; www.terraworld. net/kansastrails. Visitor Information Center, 402 North Second Street, Lawrence, KS 66044; (785) 865-4499.

MAPS: The Clinton State Park office keeps maps of the trails and is almost always staffed, even on the weekends.

BIKE SHOP: Sunflower Outdoor & Bike Shop, 802 Massachusetts Street, Lawrence, KS 66044; (785) 843-5000. This little bike shop is right next to both Massachusetts Street breweries and doubles as a wilderness outfitter's store. Definitely worth a stop between pubs.

Free State Brewing Company

636 Massachusetts Street
Lawrence, Kansas 66044
(785) 843-4555
www.freestatebrewing.com

THE PUB: Situated right down on Massachusetts Street (Lawrence's Main Street equivalent) among all the art galleries and a host of other restaurants and bars, the **Free State Brewing Company** proudly proclaims itself "The Oldest Legal Brewery in Kansas." With such a bold statement you can't help but go in and order a pint. Grab a seat at the bar or turn around and find a bench out front on the low-key and happy sidewalk patio. Free State Brewing Company has been kicking out the barley and hops since 1989 and is the best brewpub in Kansas. It has everything you're looking for in a brewpub: outdoor patio, cheap pints, and great adventurous beers. Plus, it's right downtown in an old brick building. Come as you are, biker shorts and all. You won't be turned away, and you won't feel out of place.

THE BREW: You won't be disappointed no matter what you order here. From the crisp, clean, thirst-quenching **Wheat State Golden** to the classic, dark **Free State Oatmeal Stout**, you won't find a boring beer in the batch. In addition to the brewpub's four staple beers, there's always a specialty beer or two on tap such as the cask-conditioned **Grace O'Malley's Irish Ale** (for Saint Patty's day) or one in the series of unfiltered **Hop Jack Ales**. This delightful recipe is brewed in small batches with a different kind of hops each time for a familiar but distinctly different taste.

With over 30 different beer recipes brewed since it opened back in 1989, you are sure to find one you've never had before. Oh, yeah, the food is good too. . . . What more is there to say? This place defines what a brewpub should be and so must not be missed.

PRICE OF A PINT: Because happy hours are illegal in Kansas (sheer craziness), prices are reduced all day long! Standard pints are only $2.25, and if that's not cheap enough for you, every Monday is "dollar draws" on a different beer or two featured each week, so stop in and find out what this Monday has to offer.

OTHER BREWS IN THE AREA: The Brown Bear Brewing Company, 729 Massachusetts Street, (785) 331-4338, is one block down from Free State on Massachusetts and usually has a different beer special each day and half-priced appetizers from 4:00 to 7:00 P.M. if you're on a budget. Atmospherically, the Bear has a nice, grungy, bar-like feel with live blues music five or six nights a week. Just be warned—while solid, the beers are not as unique, or memorable, as you'll find at Free State, and the Bear does not open until 4:00 P.M. on weekdays.

"Cheers, Big Ears!"

"Same goes, Big Nose."

—Overheard on the Free State Brewing Company's patio one fine spring afternoon.

89

Topeka

Topeka is the state capitol of Kansas and boasts a capitol building built to mirror the U.S. Capitol. Things to do while visiting include a variety of historic homes to check out as well as Historic Ward–Neade Park, a 5½-acre history park located on the Kansas River that includes a Victorian mansion and a turn-of-the-twentieth-century village complete with school house, log cabin, stable, general store, and depot. Stopping to smell the flowers? Then the Reinisch Rose Garden in Gage Park is notable for the more than 350 varieties of roses it contains.

Like Lawrence, Topeka played an important role in the pre–Civil War slavery battle and the entrance of Kansas into the Union as a free state. Today, Topeka is also home to the *Brown v. Board of Education* National Historic Site, which commemorates the Supreme Court Decision in 1954 that ended segregation in public schools. Also opening as a national park in 2003 will be the Topeka Monroe School cited in the landmark case. The national park will detail the case and the court's decision and how it affected the civil rights movement.

Topeka and Lawrence are closer together than other Bike & Brew America destinations. The fact that Perry Lake (near Topeka) and Clinton Lake (near Lawrence) are the sites of two of Kansas's premier mountain-bike trails constitutes special circumstances and warrants inclusion of both locales. However, please feel free to mix Topeka trails with Lawrence pubs and Lawrence trails with Topeka pubs. Whoever said the only things in Kansas were sunflowers and dogs named Toto? Whoever it was has obviously never ridden singletrack in eastern Kansas.

Perry Lake Bike Trail

THE SCOOP: Rocky and technical singletrack that seems to go on and on and on.

RIDE LENGTH AND TYPE: 14-mile loop with shorter, less technical options available.

THE BIKE: Whoever said you need mountains for mountain biking to be any good? Whoever it was never biked the **Perry Lake Bike Trail**, that's for sure. This trail—built by the Kansas Trails Council as a joint effort between the Kansas Department of Wildlife and Parks, Perry State Park, and the U.S. Army Corps of Engineers—is a mountain-bike gem. Rolling along the hills on the western side of Perry Lake, it just may be the best trail in Kansas.

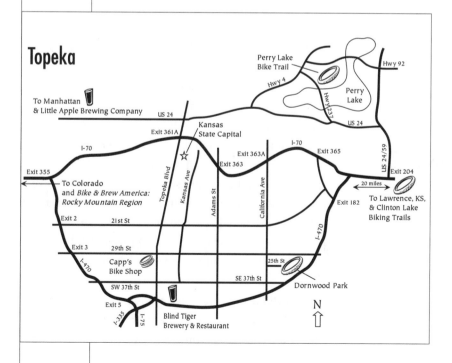

From the trailhead, the blue-blazed **Skyline Trail**, a 2½-mile loop, is the main throughway to the rest of the trail. The least technical ride available at Perry Lake, Skyline Trail is still a great singletrack experience of ravines, hills, and perfect switchback climbs and descents along with plenty of loose and jagged rocks to keep your attention focused.

By taking any of the white-blazed off-shooting loops from the Skyline Trail, you can add miles and difficulty to your ride. Proceeding counterclockwise on the Skyline Trail for about 1 mile brings you to the **Great White Trail**, a 2-mile excursion that heads down to Perry Lake and offers steeper and rougher riding. Same thing goes for the **Mad Mile** and ultimately **Logan's Run**. Logan's Run is exactly what the name implies, a 2-mile event that will take you down to the lake's shores and continue along the contours of the banks rising and falling with the terrain.

Just when you think this cannot possibly continue any farther, you arrive at the 1½-mile **Copper Head Trail**, which, if anything, is even more technical than Logan's. Once Copper Head terminates at the old Camp Road, cross the broken pavement and connect up with the somewhat milder blue-blazed **Twin Peaks Trail** and then the **Blackfoot Trail** that will return you to Skyline 4½ miles later and maybe a quarter mile from the Skyline Trailhead and completing your loop.

Someone who knows what fun is designed these trails specifically for mountain biking. And, even though no single obstacle is enough to finish you off, the trail will challenge all with its overall length and the sheer physical beating it routinely hands out to you and your bike. Technical, off-camber, with some exposed sections hanging over the lake itself, the Perry Lake Bike Trail is an advanced ride. Finish the full 14 miles of this rough and tumble ride and you will be more than ready for a Blind Tiger brew.

DIFFICULTY: Intermediate to advanced. This trail is entirely singletrack with plenty of options to make it as short or as long as you want. Stick to Skyline, Blackfoot, and Twin Peaks Trails and this is an intermediate ride. However, attempt the whole thing and this is an advanced trail.

AEROBIC DIFFICULTY (1–5):

4 (3 on blue-blazed trails)

TECHNICAL DIFFICULTY (1–5):

4 (3 on blue-blazed trails)

WARNINGS: This is a hiking and biking trail so be aware of hikers while riding here. Also, the trails are not directional, so bikers may be headed right for you around any bend.

A rider takes on the rocks and hills of Skyline Trail's singletrack at the Perry Bike Trails.
(Photo by Lyle Riedy)

OTHER TRAILS IN THE AREA: If this much technical singletrack is not your bag, then check out what **Dornwood Park** has to offer right in Topeka itself. A 7-mile loop of smooth to moderately technical singletrack meanders through this small city park. Not bad considering its close proximity to Blind Tiger Brewery & Restaurant. If you have more time in the area, then located east of Topeka are Lawrence, Kansas, and Kansas City, Missouri. Both are close and excellent Bike & Brew America destinations. Each is detailed as separate entries in this book. If you are headed west, then there are many miles of advanced

riding available at **Tuttle Creek ORV (Off-Road Vehicle) Area** near Manhattan, Kansas. Stop in at The Pathfinder bike shop in Manhattan for details on this area.

CONTACTS: Perry State Park, 5441 West Lake Road, Ozawkie, KS 66070; (785) 246-3449. Kansas Trails Council, www.terraworld.net/kansastrails. Topeka Chamber of Commerce, 120 Southeast Sixth Avenue, Suite 110, Topeka, Kansas 66603; (785) 234-2644.

MAPS: During the summer, trail maps are available at the trailhead. At other times, call ahead for a map or stop at the park office for a pamphlet, as there are no map signs on the trails even though they are extremely well marked with blue and white blazes.

Perry Lake gives way to the tree-covered home of the Perry Bike Trails.

KANSAS

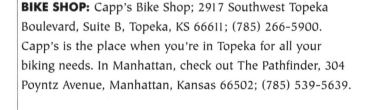

BIKE SHOP: Capp's Bike Shop; 2917 Southwest Topeka Boulevard, Suite B, Topeka, KS 66611; (785) 266-5900. Capp's is the place when you're in Topeka for all your biking needs. In Manhattan, check out The Pathfinder, 304 Poyntz Avenue, Manhattan, Kansas 66502; (785) 539-5639.

Blind Tiger Brewery & Restaurant

417 Southwest Thirty-Seventh Street
Topeka, Kansas 66611
(785) 267-2739
www.blindtiger.com

THE PUB: Built on the sprawling outskirts of Kansas's capital city, **Blind Tiger Brewery & Restaurant** is well worth a visit after a day of punishment at Perry Lake. Named after the Prohibition-era speakeasies that displayed a stuffed tiger to secretly notify potential customers of the presence of alcohol, this "Blind Tiger" no longer has to hide behind closed doors. Large and rambling with a rough wood interior, the brewery and split-level dining area are on one side of the building, and the casual bar area with outside deck overlooking two sand volleyball courts are on the other.

Interested in a quiet pint or taking it up a notch or two out on the volleyball courts? If so, this is the place to end your day in Topeka. The bar area has a large, two-sided stone fireplace to keep you warm after a brisk fall ride and TVs above to catch the news or game. Live music on Friday and Saturday nights and league volleyball with Sunday tournaments throughout the summer are all a part of the Blind Tiger's casual atmosphere.

THE BREW: Among all this commotion, you'll find a dozen freshly brewed beers on tap including six regulars and six seasonals to choose from. And, so you're not spending all night just trying to narrow down the selection to the perfect brew, here are a few tips to help you through this daunting task.

Of the regulars, things start getting interesting around the **Holy Grail Pale Ale**. Still fairly light, this beer has more body and malt than lighter beers on the menu. Next

The sprawling complex that is Blind Tiger Brewery & Restaurant.
(Courtesy of Blind Tiger Brewery & Restaurant)

up among the regulars is the **Blind Tiger Amber,** darker and fuller with just a touch of hops kicking in at the end. However, perhaps the best of the regulars is the extremely smooth and tasty **Tiger Paw Porter.**

Interestingly enough, the favorite according to the frequent customers' consensus, the **Prairie Dog Brown,** is not a regular but one of the many seasonals. It's a decent light brown ale with a full malt flavor and an easy-drinking medium body. Since the Dog is such a hit, it's pretty much always on tap, so be sure and give one a try.

If there are any complaints about the beers at Blind Tiger, it's the fact that they are served very cold and very carbonated. Although it's unusual for a brewpub to serve its beers in such a manner because cold temperature and carbonation kill much of the beers' flavor and leave a distinctive bite at the end, you can combat these effects by ordering a pint a little ahead of time and letting it sit and warm up for a bit. Sounds weird I know, but you'll definitely enjoy the experience more. Consider it the same as letting a fine wine breathe before consumption. The silver lining? If you're a growler kind of person, then this is a great time to fill one up as it will last much longer in its chilled and highly carbonated state.

With all that said, the beers are still very good and worthy; it's just unfortunate that Blind Tiger feels it has to "Americanize" its excellent product in such a carbonated, frosty-freeze fashion.

PRICE OF A PINT: Pints are regularly $3.00 and 25-ounce mugs are $4.50. On Monday, pints are only $1.50, and on Tuesdays, they ring in at $2.00. Reasonable if you happen to get lucky and visit on a school night.

OTHER BREWS IN THE AREA: Manhattan, Kansas, home of Kansas State University, is another half-hour down the road, and serving up fresh beer there is the **Little Apple Brewing Company**, 1110 West Loop Center; (785) 539-5500. Located in a strip mall, Little Apple is a popular beef restaurant as well as a brewery. Scuffed wooden floors and steer horns on the wall lend credence to the western steakhouse theme. A beer-garden awaits outside, and six homemade beers lie within. Check out the **Prairie Pale Ale**, an excellent India pale ale, very high and very dry, with a 7.1% alcohol by volume and a load of hops! The **XX Black Angus Stout** is rich, creamy, and deliciously served on nitrogen.

"We toned down the IPA a bit because people were getting arrogant and rowdy."
—Adam, the bartender, talks about the alcohol content of various Blind Tiger brews.

CHAPTER FIVE

MICHIGAN

Almost completely surrounded by four of the five Great Lakes and offering over 11,000 inland lakes, Michigan has long been considered a vacationers' paradise. Connected by one of the longest suspension bridges in the world, the Upper and Lower Peninsulas of Michigan form two separate land entities. Often referred to as the "U.P.," the Upper Peninsula is as wild, remote, and relaxed as the populated lower third of the state is a busy hub of manufacturing and fast-paced urbanization.

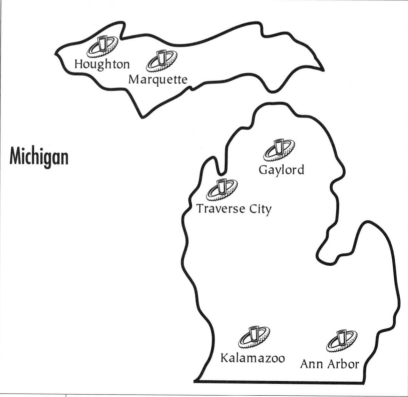

Michigan

Houghton
Marquette
Gaylord
Traverse City
Kalamazoo
Ann Arbor

This dichotomy of wilderness and population allows Michigan to lead the Midwest in Bike & Brew opportunities. With six destinations statewide, Michigan has the right combination of local advocacy and love of micro-brewed beer to make for a great Bike & Brew state. In fact, the local mountain-bike advocacy group, the Michigan Mountain Bike Association (MMBA), has even contracted with the Michigan Brewing Company for their own beer! Big Ring Ale is a big tasty brown and available throughout lower Michigan.

You won't find any mountains or very many extended climbs in the Lower Peninsula. And, because of the glaciers of the last Ice Age, you will find an unfortunate amount of sand the farther you head north. But, thanks to the strong advocacy of the MMBA, you will also find plenty of tight singletrack specifically created and maintained for mountain biking.

Although not quite the same advocacy exists in the Upper Peninsula, there is a nice bike scene there that tends toward the extreme side with a British Columbia–style renaissance taking place in Houghton and Marquette. Here, built trails are the norm with stunts and obstacles that will challenge anyone willing to make the drive. With those two exceptions, comparatively little organized trail creation and maintenance take place; thus mountain bikers are mostly led to cross-country ski trails adapted for summer biking. Beer-wise, Michigan again ranks first in the Midwest with nearly 70 small- and mid-sized brewpubs and breweries, making it very easy to find good beer near the trailhead. Almost ANY trailhead.

Ann Arbor

A rider rips the technical singletrack at Highland Recreation Area.
(Photo by Kevin Bauman)

About 45 miles west of Detroit is Ann Arbor, home of the University of Michigan. This cosmopolitan college town features many cultural attractions and festivals including the venerable Ann Arbor Art Fair, which attracts over 500,000 visitors to the town each July. Additionally, excellent specialty shops, boutiques, and a plethora of restaurants make Ann Arbor a destination for people from all over the Metro Detroit area.

Not only has Ann Arbor been rated as one of the 10 best road-cycling cities in the country, it is also a perfect place from which to launch any serious mountain-bike excursions into southeastern Michigan. Close to the Potawatomi Trail System, probably the best-known trail in the Great Lake State, Ann Arbor offers several excellent brewpubs to slacken one's thirst.

And, after you finish off The Potawatomi—but before

you pack up the car and head farther north—be sure to check out all the work the Michigan Mountain Bike Association has been putting into downstate Michigan. In addition to the Potawatomi there are many other trails within easy striking distance of Ann Arbor, further adding sparkle on this B&B diamond.

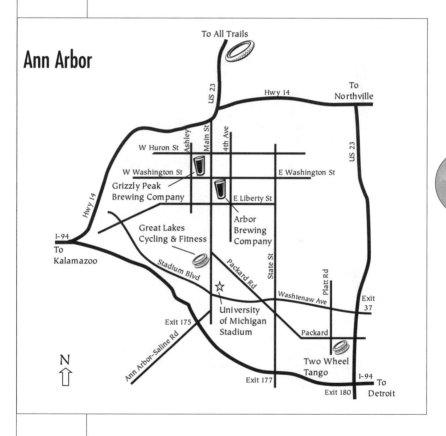

Ann Arbor

Pinckney Recreation Area and Potawatomi Trail System

A long plank boardwalk signifies you've almost reached the end of the mighty Potawatomi Trail.
(Photo by Kevin Bauman)

THE SCOOP: Often crowded and over-used, but still a great singletrack escape near Detroit.

RIDE LENGTH AND TYPE: 17½-mile loop with shorter variations possible.

THE BIKE: The **Potawatomi Trail System** is the original granddaddy of mountain-bike trails in southeastern Michigan. Its length, grueling hills, technical roots, rocks, and tight turns made it almost holy in mountain-bike circles and only spoken of in reverential tones. Unfortunately, because of its proximity to Metro Detroit, overuse has become a major problem in recent years. Although the hills are still techni-cal—mostly owing to the use of rubber mats and water bars to prevent erosion—no longer are the turns tight and fresh. What was once little more than a deer trail is now in many spots over 6 feet wide with a touch more sand than some might like.

On the bright side, the views from many locations are still wild and breathtaking. Also, thanks to the work of the Potawatomi Chapter of the Michigan Mountain Bike Association, the trail remains open to bikers and in the best shape possible given the overuse issues.

So, although the Potawatomi (known as "The Poto" to locals) may have lost some of its technical teeth, it has made up for this with an overall smoother—and faster—ride, which many people prefer anyway. If you ride a mountain bike in southeastern Michigan, this trail is still a must see and do. Having the trailhead located right at Silver Lake Beach makes for great barbecuing, swimming, and sand-volleyball after a couple of hours on the trail.

DIFFICULTY: Intermediate. Novice and intermediate bikers still regularly get beaten by The Poto. The length can be very deceiving, but there is a great bailout at mile 9. If taken, you can keep your ride down to 13 miles as opposed to the full 17. The **Crooked Lake Trail** is a 5-mile version, which incorporates the beginning and end of the main trail and is a good way to test the waters out here.

AEROBIC DIFFICULTY (1–5):

3

TECHNICAL DIFFICULTY (1–5):

3

WARNINGS: Bikers travel clockwise, and hikers travel counterclockwise, so they'll always be facing you. Please smile and give way when you encounter them. Don't be fooled thinking this is southeastern Michigan, and there isn't enough forest around here to get lost. Many hiking trails, horse trails, and dirt roads intersect the biking trails so be careful. Also bring lots of water. Make sure you pick up a map at the park entrance or ride with someone who has been here before. And this is a Michigan State Park, so plan on buying a season pass or paying the $4.00 day-use fee.

OTHER TRAILS IN THE AREA: Southeastern Michigan is a busy place—busy at building mountain-bike trails so there are plenty of singletrack miles to go around. For 18 of the best technical riding miles anywhere, go to

Highland Recreation Area about 40 minutes north of Ann Arbor. If you can do all four loops without putting your foot down here, you deserve a free beer. Not interested in that much riding? Then **Island Lake Recreation Area** has two mountain-bike loops perfect for the first-time trail rider all the way to seasoned professionals. All told there are 13 miles of well-marked directional trails making up the two loops. And you're not done yet! **Brighton Recreation Area** has two loops ready to go with more being cut as you read this. The 5.6-mile **Torn Shirt Loop** is an advanced ride that fits its name, and the **Murray Lake Loop** is another 6.6 miles of intermediate singletrack riding just waiting to be explored.

CONTACTS: Pinckney State Recreation Area, 8555 Silver Hill, Route 1, Pinckney, MI 48169; (734) 426-4913. Ann Arbor Chamber of Commerce, 425 South Main Street, Ann Arbor, MI 48104; (734) 665-4433.

MAPS: Maps are available at the park entrance, thanks to your $4.00 admission fee, and there is also a map kiosk at the trailhead.

Ann Arbor Trails

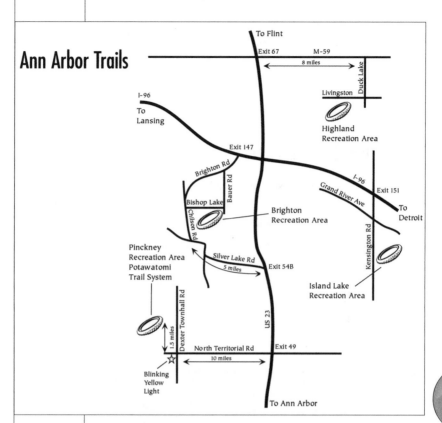

BIKE SHOP: Ann Arbor is loaded with bike shops with seven or eight in business at any given time. All carry a variety of brands and accessories. The closest and easiest to find from the brewpubs and an excellent well-appointed shop is Great Lakes Cycling & Fitness, 564 South Main Street, Ann Arbor, MI 48104; (734) 668-6576. If you don't mind driving around for a while, then check out Two Wheel Tango, 3162 Packard Street, Ann Arbor, MI 48108; (734) 528-3030. The bottom line: if you want your bike fixed right, the first time, go to Two Wheel Tango on Packard Road. This shop has some geniuses behind their stands just waiting to work on your rig.

Arbor Brewing Company

114 East Washington Street
Ann Arbor, Michigan 48104
(734) 213-1393

THE PUB: This is one of those near-perfect places that come along about once in every state. The **Arbor Brewing Company** has a great downtown location right off Ann Arbor's Main Street (yes, the one Bob Seger sang about so many years ago). The brewpub is located in a historic building with wooden floors, brick walls, and large windows looking onto the sidewalk patio and bustle of downtown life in Ann Arbor.

To pass the time while sipping on a couple of fresh, unfiltered, fantastic brews, Arbor offers regular live acoustic entertainment, garlic fries that will knock your significant other's socks off, genuine dartboards (thankfully not the machines), and shuffleboard.

THE BREW: Arbor was the first brewpub to open in the bar and restaurant mecca that is Ann Arbor, but got off to a rocky start because it was unable to maintain consistent beer quality and quantities. Opening just before the nationally acclaimed annual Art Fair weekend back in 1995 must have sounded like a good idea on the business plan. However, the thirsty fairgoers drank the place out of beer in the first week. It took Arbor Brewing over a year before it finally caught up and had enough properly fermented beer on hand to please customers and build a loyal following.

Fortunately, it was worth the wait for the perfected recipes. Even the house's lightest beer, the **Big Ben Mild**, is outstanding. And from there it only gets better. Arbor always tries to keep two beers on the hand pumps—usually the **Milestone Porter** and **Sacred Cow IPA** (India pale ale)—making both into smooth, drinkable delicacies. The **Olde Number 22 German Alt** and **Faricy Fest Irish Stout** are two seasonals to keep an eye out for. And, if you happen to be there around Christmastime (yes, The Poto is rideable almost year-round but stay off after it rains), go for the **Terminator Doppelbock**—a seasonal regular that packs a solid punch at 10% alcohol. Fortunately, the house limits you to two, so everyone makes it home okay.

PRICE OF A PINT: In addition to the regular after-work happy hour (4:00 to 7:00 P.M. Tuesday through Friday), Monday is happy hour all day long. During happy hour, pints are at the half-pint price, which will range between $2.25 and $2.50. Not an easy system to remember, but it sure beats the standard $3.50 to $3.75 a pint.

OTHER BREWS IN THE AREA: Grizzly Peak Brewing Company; 120 West Washington Street, Ann Arbor, MI 48104; (734) 741-7325. Although Arbor may have been the first brewpub in Ann Arbor, it was not always the best. Just down Washington Street, on the other side of Main, is the Grizzly Peak Brewing Company. Grizzly opened up just after Arbor and immediately started serving better beer and awesome food. Their Cheddar Ale Soup is the best you're gonna find in the Midwest, bar none. The atmosphere is a little more upscale than Arbor (so you have to wash behind the ears after your ride) and, correspondingly, a little more

expensive. Arbor gets the nod because, though Grizzly's beer is good, it's just that—good, not great like Arbor's. Catering to a more mainstream restaurant crowd, the beers stay tamer with less experimentation going on in the brew kettle.

"Beer. Just like mom used to make."
—Arbor Brewing Company T-shirt logo.

Gaylord

Near the "tip of the mitt" as Michiganders like to refer to the lower region of their state, Gaylord resides in the highest county in Michigan's Lower Peninsula, reaching just over 1300 feet above sea level. And, even though you won't get any nosebleeds at this elevation, you will find some of the best terrain the Lower Peninsula has to offer mountain bikers. The nearby Pigeon River State Forest takes advantage of the terrain and weighs in at more than 98,000 acres. Its boundaries make up the largest contiguous state forest east of the Mississippi.

Gaylord

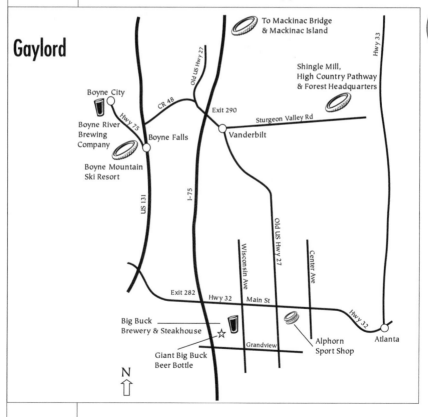

If you enjoy not just being outdoors, but being in the *wilderness*, the High Country Pathway is for you. Come, camp, and see if you can bike the whole trail in a weekend. It's truly an epic ride, and, believe it or not, it's east of the Rockies and west of the Appalachians. Either way, you'll be laughing as you head to the surprisingly close brewpub when it's all said and done.

And since you've come this far already, don't miss a chance to see the Mackinac Bridge just 45 minutes north of Gaylord on Interstate 75. Opened in 1957, the Mackinac Bridge is the longest suspension bridge in the country with a total suspension span of 8614 feet and a total length of 5 miles! Even San Francisco's famous Golden Gate Bridge, with a suspension span of a paltry 6450 feet and total length of only 1.7 miles, pales in comparison to this engineering marvel.

Of course, if bridges aren't your thing, then there is always the charming Victorian village on nearby Mackinac Island. A summer vacation destination since the mid-nineteenth century, this small island still does not allow automobile traffic. Just walking, horse-drawn carriages, and, you guessed it, bikes.

High Country Pathway and Shingle Mill Loop

THE SCOOP: Scenic overlooks, technical terrain, lots of climbing, over 70 miles, and 99% singletrack!

RIDE LENGTH AND TYPE: 12-mile and 70-mile loops.

THE BIKE: This place is really special if you're looking to get out of the mainstream "hamster cage" mountain-bike scene. The only limits are your endurance and skills. Go for a weekend and try to make it all the way around the 70-mile loop—the **High Country Pathway** proper—or spend an afternoon knocking off the 12-mile **Shingle Mill Loop** before heading over to Big Buck Brewing Company in nearby Gaylord.

This may very well be the best trail system in Lower Michigan, and it is also one of the most unknown. It typifies Michigan biking with lots of black dirt, pine forests, and glacially formed rolling hills and valleys. Hopefully, while you're there, you'll even see a member or two of the largest wild elk herd east of the Mississippi, which resides here in the Pigeon River Country Forest Area.

The Shingle Mill Loop is a well-traveled, novice, 12-mile mountain-bike and hiking loop that incorporates parts of the High Country Pathway (HCP). The loop will give you an idea of the terrain and forms a good starting point from which to launch future biking campaigns farther into the HCP.

The HCP runs through the Pigeon River Country Forest Area and was primarily built and is maintained as a hiking trail. However, bikes are allowed and, because of the light traffic, the trails remain tight and technical. The fact that it is maintained as a hiking trail also means that deadfall is often not removed from the trail, thus requiring excellent log jumping skills or many, many dismounts.

This is truly a wild place. Enjoy it as much as you can, but please ride responsibly and carefully in this impact-sensitive area.

DIFFICULTY: Novice to advanced. Novice and intermediate bikers will be better off staying on the designated biking trails around the various campgrounds scattered along the HCP, most notably the Shingle Mill Loop at Pigeon River State Forest Campground and Headquarters. Because of the unmaintained trail conditions, fallen trees, and navigational problems, only experienced bikers should venture very far on the HCP itself.

AEROBIC DIFFICULTY (1–5):

2–4

TECHNICAL DIFFICULTY (1–5):

2–4

A racer takes on the 12 Hours of Boyne Mountain Bike Race held annually at Boyne Mountain Ski Resort.
(Photo by Kevin Bauman)

WARNINGS: This place is big. As already noted, the Pigeon River Country State Forest is part of the largest contiguous state forest east of the Mississippi. Make sure you bring plenty of food and water as well as tools, maps, and compasses (and know how to use them). It's easy to get lost on some parts of the trail that have become overgrown from infrequent use or by taking a wrong turn on one of the many other trail systems that connect with the High Country Pathway.

OTHER TRAILS IN THE AREA: Abundant mountain-bike trails grace Lower Michigan. When you've finished exploring the Pigeon River Country Forest Area, head west to the **Boyne Mountain Ski Resort** where an intermediate 7½-mile loop, frequently used as a mountain-bike race course, travels in and around the mountain. After a couple of loops there, you will be more than ready to head into nearby Boyne City and have a couple of pints of Boyne River Brown Ale at the Boyne River Brewing Company. And if you decided to make **Mackinac Island** part of your vacation plans, be sure to take your bike with you. Because, even though cars aren't allowed anywhere on the island, bikes are allowed on the many miles of roads and trails. Traverse City, home of the world-class cross-country ski race, The Vasa, is also loaded with singletrack. See the Traverse City section in this book for details of the area.

CONTACTS: Mackinaw State Forest, Pigeon River Country Forest Area, 9966 Twin Lake Road, Vanderbilt, MI 49735; (517) 983-4101. Gaylord Chamber of Commerce, 101 West Main Street, Gaylord, MI 49735; (517) 732-4000.

MAPS: For your first visit, either call in advance to have some maps sent to you or visit the Pigeon River Country Headquarters. Here you can obtain maps of the HCP and the Shingle Mill Loop. The headquarters also sells a field guide to the HCP, a very, very useful book at $4.00 if you're planning on leaving the safe confines of Shingle Mill.

BIKE SHOP: Alphorn Sport Shop, 137 West Main Street, Gaylord, MI 49735; (517) 732-5616. Smash a derailleur? Get a flat? Wrap you bike around a tree? Don't worry. Alphorn Sports should have whatever the HCP took from you and your bike.

Big Buck Brewery & Steakhouse

550 South Wisconsin Street
Gaylord, Michigan 49735
(517) 732-5781
www.bigbuck.com

THE PUB: The **Big Buck Brewery & Steakhouse** was built to attract hunters, snowmobilers, boaters, fishermen, golfers, and other Detroit-area tourists coming north to play for the weekend. It is the flagship restaurant in an expanding four-brewpub chain that has the guys from Hooters on its board of directors. The billboard along Interstate 75 reads "Home of the 28-ounce steak and 23-ounce beer." The inflatable giant beer bottle outside is gaudy tourism at its finest, and if you're impressed with what you find inside, you can even buy stock in the brewery on the NASDAQ under BBUC!

On your way back to civilization from the High Country Pathway, you can't miss Big Buck and your first chance for miles at fresh beer. Once inside, an open-rafter wood décor with a raised wooden-plank bar area in the rear of the expansive building focuses attention on the large showpiece brewery.

The bar itself features an ornate, hand-carved wooden bar with otters, ducks, fish, and lily pads. Both the chandelier hanging over the bar and the tap handles behind are made from genuine Michigan white-tailed deer antlers, which, along with the other hunting paraphernalia scattered throughout, almost makes you forget that Interstate 75 is less than 100 yards away. A large-screen TV surrounded by a multitude of smaller ones assures you will not go without your favorite show or game.

THE BREW: Although **Big Buck Beer** is the outfit's self-proclaimed flagship brew, you're probably not here for the mainstream-style stuff. Ask your server for a rundown of the seasonal and specialty beers or check the chalkboard above the brewery's door. These are what really makes this place a worthy stop on any Bike & Brew tour of America.

However, of the standards, the **DOC's ESB** (extra special bitter) is the employees' favorite and probably the best of the regular brews. The **Redbird Ale** is also worthy, and the **Black River Stout** is served on nitrogen so you know it's gonna keep you happy.

All the self-promotion and big business that Big Buck represents isn't entirely hot air; it does have great food, so

The towering beer bottle alerts Interstate 75 travelers that the prospect of fresh beer is just seconds away at Big Buck Brewery.

"That's why you carry a compass."
—Mackinaw State Forest Ranger's response when told by Todd Mercer how he got lost on the High Country Pathway.

be sure to stay for one of the fabled steaks washed down with a DOC's. The combination can't be beat, and there's a satisfaction guarantee . . . on the steaks that is, not the beers.

PRICE OF A PINT: You're in Michigan on Interstate 75 so expect to pay $3.50 a pint (or $4.25 for 23 ounces) even if it seems you're in the middle of nowhere. If you're lucky enough to be there on a weekday, "naked hour" is Monday through Friday from 4:30 until 6:30 P.M. when you can score $2.00 pints. If you're there on a Tuesday, Wednesday, or Thursday, buy a growler for three bucks and get it filled for another three bucks. Now that's a good deal.

OTHER BREWS IN THE AREA: Big Buck is the closest and most accessible brewpub to the High Country Pathway. If you are thinking about heading west and trying the Boyne Mountain trail system, be sure to check out the **Boyne River Brewing Company** at 419 East Main Street, Boyne City, MI 49712; (231) 582-5588. Where Big Buck represents big business, Boyne River will make you feel like you've walked in on someone's garage sale. If only they were all like this!

Houghton

The discovery of copper in 1840 spurred the growth of this northwestern Upper Peninsula town and left behind a legacy of nineteenth and early-twentieth-century buildings throughout Houghton's downtown area. Located among hardwood forests and lakes in the middle of the Keweenaw Peninsula, a landmass surrounded on three sides by Lake Superior, Houghton is a popular resort and vacation town for all seasons. Summer is boating, swimming, fishing, camping, hiking, and biking; winter is both downhill and cross-country skiing as well as snowmobiling.

Houghton

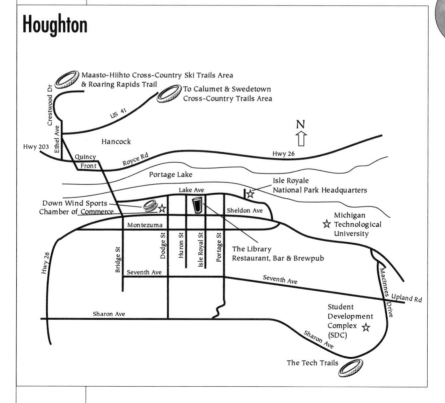

Maasto-Hiihto Cross-Country Ski Trails Area & Roaring Rapids Trail

To Calumet & Swedetown Cross-Country Trails Area

Crestwood Dr

US 41

Ethel Ave

Hwy 203

Hancock

Quincy

Front

Royce Rd

N

Hwy 26

Portage Lake

Lake Ave

Isle Royale National Park Headquarters

Down Wind Sports
Chamber of Commerce

Sheldon Ave

Michigan Technological University

Montezuma

Hwy 26

Bridge St

Dodge St

Huron St

Isle Royal St

Portage St

The Library
Restaurant, Bar & Brewpub

Seventh Ave

Seventh Ave

Sharon Ave

Macinnes Drive

Upland Rd

Student Development Complex (SDC)

Sharon Ave

The Tech Trails

During the summer months Houghton also offers ferry and air service to Isle Royale National Park, Lake Superior's largest island and home to a troubled population of moose and wolves. The moose got there the hard way by swimming in the early 1900s, and the wolves took the easier route across the ice of the rarely frozen Lake Superior in 1949. Because of the imbalance in their predator-prey relationship, and the delicate health of the wolves, absolutely **no** dogs are allowed on the island. No bikes are allowed on the island either, but this is a backpacker's paradise.

The copper mines of the region prompted the creation of the Michigan Mining School in 1885 for the purpose of training mine engineers. Although still primarily an engineering school, Michigan Technological University has long since expanded to offer a full curriculum. Even though the copper mines have all closed, the historic town of Houghton is still home to two other precious commodities: excellent mountain-bike trails and fresh beer. The riding is minutes from the brewery, and both the Tech Trails and Maasto-Hiihto are easily accessed by bike if town-to-town rides are your sort of thing.

Tech Trails

THE SCOOP: Smooth and rolling cross-country ski trails with miles of developed singletrack winding throughout.

RIDE LENGTH AND TYPE: Variable—with more than 15 miles of rideable trails.

THE BIKE: Actually Michigan Tech's cross-country ski trails, this land of higher learning has been taken under the wing of local mountain bikers and developed into an excellent network of doubletrack, widetrack, and single-track with a smattering of British Columbia–style bridges and stunts thrown in for good measure.

Beginner bikers who stick to the well-mapped and well-marked cross-country ski trails will find this area just per-fect: wide corridors through beautiful northern Michigan pine and hardwood forests with a slice of smooth single-track down the middle. However, the area offers much more if you're willing to do a little exploring. Just keep your eyes peeled for one of the multitude of singletrack trails heading off deeper into the woods to where the real fun begins.

There are dozens of rooty and rocky singletrack spurs twisting among the established ski trails. It'll take a little time to get your bearings, and you may feel like you're a little lost, but never fear because roads and residences border the area. Highway 41 borders the north side and makes a good escape route to assure you'll find your way back to the car if you get turned around during your ride.

The featured attraction of the **Tech Trails** is the stretch of narrow bridges, ramps, and other obstacles the Houghton cyclists have built. Not all of the trail has these features, but you'll know you're on the right track when

119

the singletrack leading up to this area becomes deliberately more difficult before giving way to a half-dozen interesting stunts spread out over a 1½-mile section of trail. From log and stick bridges and ramps to a 30-foot-long log crossing, this section of trail is a great way to experience the famed British Columbia or North Shore style of riding right here in Michigan. Even though the obstacles are elevated and tricky, when dry the rough wood offers great traction for those ready to give them a try. Just be careful and only attempt them if you're willing to suffer the consequences!

DIFFICULTY: Beginner to advanced. As mentioned earlier, the mapped and marked cross-country ski trails make for a great beginner ride. Taking any of the many singletrack spurs ups the difficulty to intermediate, and when you find yourself on the section of stunts you'll know it, as you'll be looking at advanced-level riding right down the middle of the trail.

AEROBIC DIFFICULTY (1–5):
2 (3 on singletrack and stunts)

TECHNICAL DIFFICULTY (1–5):
2 (3 on singletrack and 5 on the stunts)

WARNINGS: Please ride within your ability out here. If the stunts look dangerous to you, it's because they are and you've already thought about it too much. Get off your bike and walk around them.

OTHER TRAILS IN THE AREA: The other must-do rides when in the Houghton area are the **Maasto-Hiihto Cross-Country Ski Trail** and the **Roaring Rapids Trail**. Once again, stick to the Maasto-Hiihto for multiple cross-country loops of novice riding, and check out the nonmotorized Roaring Rapids Trail, which connects to the ski loops, for more advanced singletrack. Roaring Rapids is on private property but has been opened to nonmotorized traffic by the landowner. Please ride responsibly here. North of Houghton in the town of Calumet is another beginner ski trail known as the **Swedetown Cross-Country Trails Area**. There are also endless miles of snowmobile trails throughout the Houghton area. Wide and mostly beginner trails, expect hills and some sandy spots where the sleds (snow-mobiles) have worn through the top layer of black Michigan soil.

CONTACTS: Michigan Technological University, Student Development Complex, Building 24, Houghton, MI 49931; (906) 487-2578. Houghton Chamber of Commerce, 326 Sheldon Avenue, Houghton, MI 49931; (906) 482-5240.

Matt Koss rides the Ramp at Houghton's Tech Trails. Can you?
(Photo by Lori Hauswirth)

MAPS: Michigan Tech has maps of the cross-country ski trails at the front office of the Student Development Complex, which is right on the way to the trail. The main trailhead also has a map post, and the trails themselves are well marked. That is, the cross-country ski trails are well marked; you're on your own when riding the singletrack.

BIKE SHOP: Down Wind Sports, 308 Sheldon Avenue, Houghton, MI 49931; (906) 482-2500. Bike shop by summer, ski shop by winter—and right around the corner from the brewery. Down Wind will make sure you find whatever trails your looking for in the area.

The Library Restaurant, Bar and Brewpub

62 North Isle Royale Street
Houghton, Michigan 49931
(906) 487-5882

THE PUB: Located in downtown Houghton, the modern interior of polished-wood bookshelves and recessed lighting blends nicely with the exposed brick of the original 1898 building. The recent addition of the dining area and brewing facilities offer floor to ceiling views of Portage Lake and the historic mining town of Hancock across the water.

"If you're in the area, then you have to do both."
—Down Wind Sport's employee, Bill Thompson, in answer to the inevitable question of which trail is better, the Maasto-Hiihto or the Tech Trails.

A structural fire back in 1995 completely gutted the Library Restaurant that had been in business since 1967. However, the shell of the historic brick building, which was originally an embalming and cabinet-making business (hey, this was a remote area at one time!), was salvaged. This calamity actually allowed the Library to recreate itself by adding a brew house and to reopen as **The Library Restaurant, Bar and Brewpub** in 1997.

The original building now houses the tavern and bar area. None of the second floor remains, leaving this area a completely open two-story room filled with arched windows, exposed steel support beams, and a collection of random doors and arched windows suspended in the walls high above the wooden floor. Bookshelves filled with encyclopedias, textbooks, law volumes, and other reference books lend credence to the establishment's name. Other books are sandwiched in among the liquor shelves behind the bar and below a sign proclaiming "The Librew'ry."

THE BREW: The Librew'ry keeps eight beers on tap. All are destination beers except the very palatable but uninteresting solution to the Bud drinker, the establishment's best-selling **Keweenaw Golden Ale**. Onto bigger and better: the **Whiteout Wheat** is an unfiltered German-style wheat beer with the clove and banana flavors often associated with true German hefeweizens. The **Copper Town Ale** is an excellent pale ale with a deep copper color and nice bitter finish the way American pales are meant to be. The **Guru IPA** (India pale ale) is a strong, full beer well worth the price of a pint, and the **Pick Axe Porter** is smooth and rich even if it is served a little too cold for a proper porter. The **Java Man Espresso Stout** is a seasonal beer meant for the serious coffee lover, and the **Shafthouse Dry Stout** is the regular stout on tap, smoother and more traditional than the Espresso. Any of these beers could easily be another brewpub's best beer. Order what suits your mood, and you're gonna be pleased.

PRICE OF A PINT: No happy hour so pints are always $2.75, and a 23-ounce stein is a very reasonable $3.50.

OTHER BREWS IN THE AREA: The next closest fresh beer to Houghton is about 2 hours east in the Marquette area. Right on the way to Marquette is Jasper Ridge Brewing Company, 1075 Country Lane, Ishpeming, MI 49849; (906) 485-6017. And, in Marquette itself is the Marquette Harbor Brewery & Vierling Restaurant, 119 South Front Street, Marquette, MI 49855; (906) 228-3533. As Marquette is also a town filled with great riding, please see the entire Marquette description included in this book.

The majestic exterior for an institute of higher learning known as the Library, Restaurant, Bar and Brewpub.

123

Kalamazoo

Smack in the middle between the major metropolitan cities of Detroit and Chicago, Kalamazoo has played a major role in over a dozen industries since it was founded in 1829. Paper, celery, bedding plants, Checker taxi cabs, Gibson guitars, stoves, fishing rods and reels, Roamer automobiles, and maybe most notably, the Upjohn Pill Company (now known as Pharmacia Corporation) still do or have at one time or another called Kalamazoo home. The ensuing and continuing influx of wealth has resulted in the development of many prestigious buildings and neighborhoods. Today many of the town's historic districts feature the changing architectural styles of the past including several Frank Lloyd Wright homes.

In 1959, insightful city leaders closed off Burdick Street, and Kalamazoo became home to the first outdoor pedestrian shopping mall in the United States. Unfortunately, 40 years later, just when the rest of the country had caught on to the idea, two of the four blocks were reopened to accommodate automobile traffic. Still the mall is worth a visit for the shopping and for the Kalamazoo Public Museum anchoring the north end.

Although the city is starting to show its age, Kalamazoo County is still home to over 450 manufacturing firms, many, many museums and theaters, and a relatively new player—beer. Multiple breweries now operate from Kalamazoo, assuring continued prosperity for the town and pleasing beer lovers of southwestern Michigan and Bike & Brew America travelers from beyond.

Kalamazoo

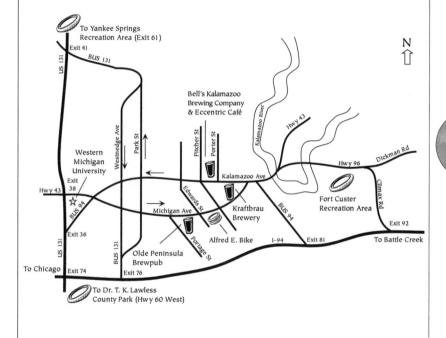

Fort Custer Recreation Area Mountain-Bike Trails

THE SCOOP: Multiple loops each offering a little something for everyone—singletrack, doubletrack, and plenty of fun.

RIDE LENGTH AND TYPE: Four loops of varying difficulty and length can be combined to total over 20 miles.

THE BIKE: Situated right between the Interstate 94 cities of Kalamazoo and Battle Creek, the Cereal Capital of the World, is the **Fort Custer Recreation Area** sporting almost 20 miles of beginner to advanced mountain-bike trails. Formally a military training facility used during the world wars, about 3000 acres were given to the Department of Natural Resources for development as a state recreation area.

Taken under the caring wing of the Michigan Mountain Bike Association's Southwest Chapter, over 20 miles of singletrack and doubletrack have been built, mapped, and excellently maintained. It has become a popular racecourse as well as the location of the annual Dirtstock Mountain Bike Festival every August. Currently there are four loops—labeled Red, Green, Yellow, and Blue—making up the system. The Red and Green loops are rated difficult, the Yellow easy, and the Blue moderate.

By combining the Red and Green loops, you'll keep things interesting and can work a 13-mile challenging ride out of the place. Although rated "difficult," if you have any off-road experience, you should be able to handle everything the Red and Green trails can throw your way. The **Red Loop** and **Yellow Loop** essentially follow the same course with the Red Loop offering more difficult options and then returning to the Yellow Loop. Highlights of the Red Loop include The Trenches, Granny's Garden,

Amusement Park, and Crazy Beaver Loop. Take all of these to get the most out of the trail system.

The Trenches is a fast section of broad turns and quick little hills that were actually dug to train soldiers for World War I. **Granny's Garden** is full of rocks, and the **Amusement Park** has some fun downhills and relatively technical climbs. The **Crazy Beaver Loop** is similar to The Trenches with lots of big turns but slightly longer hills.

The **Green Loop** strikes out around Eagle Lake and offers two creek crossings and some tight, fairly technical singletrack. The trail often goes along the edge of the lake and presents plenty of opportunity for a quick refreshing dip in the summer heat.

The **Blue Loop**, the newest of the bunch and not yet marked, can add an additional 5 miles to your daily total if you take both the **Jackson Hole Loop** and **Whitford Lake Loop**.

DIFFICULTY: Beginner to intermediate. Many Michigan mountain bikers from this side of the state cut their proverbial teeth out here at Fort Custer. Anyone can

Ahhh . . . cruising the singletrack at Yankee Springs State Recreation Area.
(Photo by Kevin Bauman)

127

handle the Yellow Loop, and as your off-road confidence increases, the Blue, Green, and Red won't be far behind.

AEROBIC DIFFICULTY (1–5):

2

TECHNICAL DIFFICULTY (1–5):

3

WARNINGS: You should be aware of hikers, hunters, horses, and the small (3 or 4 inches high) sawed-off trees on the Green Loop. Hit one of those babies and a flat tire would be considered a good-case scenario.

OTHER TRAILS IN THE AREA: About 45 miles north of Kalamazoo is another popular western Michigan biking spot known as **Yankee Springs Recreation Area,** which has a 12.7-mile loop with a couple of shortcuts available to keep the mileage down. Go the whole distance, and the bigger hills and moraines left long ago by glaciers wait near the middle of the trail. A little hillier than Fort Custer, this trail would rank a solid intermediate. About 40 minutes south from Kalamazoo and open spring through November is another popular racecourse known as **Dr. T. K. Lawless County Park,** 10 miles of tight, technical, twisty winding singletrack.

CONTACTS: Fort Custer Recreation Area, 5163 West Fort Custer Drive, Augusta, MI 49012; (616) 731-4200. Southwest Michigan Chapter, MMBA, P.O. Box 19311; www.mmba.org. Kalamazoo Chamber of Commerce, 346 West Michigan Avenue, Kalamazoo, MI 49007; (616) 381-4000.

MAPS: The trails are all very well marked, but to be safe write ahead to Maps, P.O. Box 23, Augusta, MI 49012, and secure a copy of your own for 25 cents and a self-addressed, stamped envelope.

BIKE SHOP: Alfred E. Bike, 320 East Michigan Avenue, Kalamazoo, MI 49007; (616) 349-9423; www.aebike.com. Located a couple of blocks from the Eccentric Café, Alfred will take care of you while in the 'Zoo.

Bell's Kalamazoo Brewing Company and Eccentric Café

355 East Kalamazoo Avenue
Kalamazoo, Michigan 49007
(616) 382-2338
www.bellsbeer.com

THE PUB: Larry Bell's brewing career has come a long way from its humble 1985 beginning of brewing beer out of a 15-gallon soup kettle in a homebrew supply store. Now **Bell's Kalamazoo Brewing Company** produces over 20,000 barrels per year and is one of the most respected regional breweries in the business. Continually pushing the boundaries of what beer can be, the **Bell's Eccentric Café** is definitely a destination for true beer lovers. Situated in a jumbled railyard station off Kalamazoo Avenue and Porter Street, the Eccentric Café is the hub of the surrounding 47-barrel microbrewery (48 counting the sacred soup kettle).

In 1999 the long-popular beer joint added a kitchen to serve gourmet sandwiches and other light fare in what was once the homebrew retail area of the brewery's tasting room. Rumor has it that Bell's long-practiced tradition of cask-conditioning all its kegged ales is being replaced in favor of forced carbonation to keep production costs in line. But the beer is still unfiltered, unpasteurized, and made from some of the best recipes in the Midwest. Fortunately, bottles will still be bottle-conditioned.

Lightly decorated with local art, Larry Bell's son's 55-gallon fish tank, custom stained glass, imported beer posters, and other strange objects, the open and spacious Eccentric Café welcomes you into its sprawling complex. Slate stone floors with a mural of the state of Michigan worked into them and two-story-high walls, which have

BIKE BREW AMERICA

MICHIGAN

been taken back to the building's original brick, complete the airy feel in the pub area. A wooden loft above the kitchen fills a quarter of the room and offers secluded second-story seating with widows overlooking the beer garden and outdoor stage. Two brewing buildings, the General Store, kegs stacked high in every possible niche, and the large wooden deck of the beer garden, complete the outside of the establishment.

THE BREW: Bell's beer consist of five flagships brewed year round, two seasonals that alternate between summer and winter, and a host of specialty brews too numerous to list. And although the café's selection is ever changing and evolving, here's a sampling of what you might find when you visit. Sweet with a fruity flavor, the **Bell's Amber Ale** is the most popular of Bell's beers and a truly unique version of this normally fairly typical ale. If you've never had a Bell's ale before now, this is the one to start with. The **Bell's Porter** is an excellent rendition that becomes extraordinary—like a beer and vanilla ice-cream float—on the rare occasions you find it on hand-pump. The **Bell's Kalamazoo Stout** is, as Assistant Head Brewer Alec Mull so accurately put it, "second to none, a fantastic stout." You'll agree after one sip of this dark, full-bodied, and rich beer.

Of the seasonals, the one you are most likely to encounter after your summertime ride is Bell's interpretation of an American wheat, **Bell's Oberon Ale**. Originally called Solsun (some problems with someone else's trademark resulted in the name change), this may be the one and only American wheat–style beer in the country worth any drive. Not a lightweight, weighing in at 6% alcohol by volume, this unfiltered ale gives a whole new meaning to the world of wheat beers. The beer has a nice copper color and is made with Belgian wheat to give it a spicy, fruity flavor lacking in most beers of this style. Do not leave Kalamazoo without having at least one cup of Oberon Ale while sitting in the beer garden under a sunny sky. Otherwise, it would be criminal.

Other beers to keep an eye out for as they make their

way through the rotation are the **Two Hearted Ale** (an India pale ale), the **Sparkling Ale** (a Belgian tripel pale ale), and, of course, the **Eccentric Ale**, which is brewed once a year for the following year's gala celebration and bit of a freak show that is Eccentric Day. The Eccentric Ale is impossible to describe. Brewed by a different guest brewer each year using whatever ingredients happen to be handy (plus some), be prepared for a monster with lots of hops and lots of alcohol. Aged for a year and costing five bucks a bottle, it's always a huge hit. Eccentric Day is held around the second weekend of each December (whenever the classes at nearby Western Michigan University are out for the semester), and it gives Kalamazoo's populace a chance to dress and express themselves from their inner being. You'll have to just see it to really understand it.

PRICE OF A PINT: No happy hour (all hours are happy according to the bartenders) at the café, but pints are 20-ounce Imperials and still only run between $3.00 and $3.50. And 16-ounce plastic cups for the beer garden are between $2.50 and $3.50 depending on the beer.

OTHER BREWS IN THE AREA: Kalamazoo has no shortage of breweries. Literally right across the street from Bell's is the **Kraftbrau Brewery** at 402 East Kalamazoo Avenue, (616) 384-0288. Kraftbrau doesn't have a kitchen, but you're encouraged to bring your own food with you when you stop in for some of the excellent homemade beer in the taproom. And, if a more traditional brewpub experience is what you're looking for, the **Olde Peninsula Brewpub** is right next door to the Alfred E. Bike at 200 East Michigan Avenue, (616) 343-2739. Now how is that for a beer- and biker-friendly town?

131

Marquette

Located on the south shore of Lake Superior, Marquette was founded in 1849 when its first iron forge was constructed. The town quickly grew into a booming mining community. Still a major iron ore port, Marquette continues this history as the metal to this day plays an important roll in Marquette's growth.

Today, however, Marquette is probably best known for its outdoor recreation, highlighted by the U.S. Olympic Education Center that features the nation's only naturbahn luge track and both 50- and 70-meter ski jumps in

Marquette

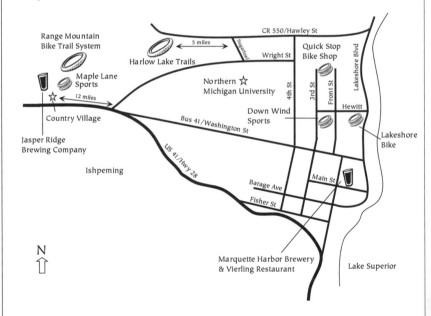

MICHIGAN

A view of downtown Marquette and Lake Superior from atop Sugarloaf Mountain Trail.
(Photo by Kevin Bauman)

addition to premier biathlon and cross-country ski facilities. Tall pine forests, rugged terrain, waterfalls, rivers, and, of course, the largest freshwater lake in the world—Lake Superior—form Marquette's backyard. The region offers a host of activities ranging from simple walks along the beaches and some rather chilly swimming to fishing, boating, and spectacular sea kayaking. Visiting the many lighthouses along Lake Superior's coast and islands is another very popular activity and with two historic lighthouses right in town, Marquette is a great place to start.

Marquette is neighbor to the nearby Hiawatha National Forest and Pictured Rocks National Lakeshore. A dozen waterfalls can be found in Marquette County, and Northern Michigan University, located in Marquette, even has a mountain-bike class on the schedule. Now that's Bike & Brew's idea of higher education! New in 2001 is the inaugural Ore to Shore Point-to-Point Mountain Bike Epic, a 40-mile race from Negaunee (next to Ishpeming) to Marquette. This event is planned to rival even Wisconsin's fabled Chequamegon Fat Tire Festival in length (see the section on Ashland, Wisconsin, for more info on that phatty).

By now it should be obvious. Marquette is a great destination town for many reasons. With excellent riding and fresh beer on tap within minutes of the trails, one of those reasons should be Bike & Brew America.

Harlow Lake Trails

THE SCOOP: Doubletrack and widetrack with expert-level singletrack on Michigan-style slickrock hidden in the mix.
RIDE LENGTH AND TYPE: Variable—at least 15 miles of trails form a network throughout this area.
THE BIKE: Ask anyone from the Upper Peninsula (aka the U.P.), and you'll hear that there is a great deal of riding in the Marquette area. The trouble is finding it. Very little of this so-called "loads of riding" is mapped or marked. Therefore, unless you find a kind local or two to guide you to their personal stash, the closest place that guarantees a solid afternoon in the saddle is the **Harlow Lake Trails.** Miles of old logging roads, cross-country skiing trails, and some deadly singletrack spurs await just 5 miles north of Marquette.

There are many access points for the Harlow Lake Trails with the gravel-pit parking lot being the most central. From the gravel pit, you're on easy doubletrack through deep forests of pine, oak, and maple. An overlook on the western side of the trail system offers a nice rest stop with panoramic views of Lake Superior and the surrounding hills and forests. From this vantage point, look toward the lake, and you'll see Michigan's version of slickrock for the hardy: the bald-rock knolls known as the **Bare Back Trail.**

That's right, slickrock in Michigan, a 1½-mile stretch of steep, ravine-ridden, off-camber rock that will have you off the back of your seat, hike-a-biking with feelings of inferiority, and looking at some of the best scenery Michigan has to offer. As a warning, in order to find the Bare Back Trail from below, you have to keep your eyes open. On your way from the gravel-pit parking lot to Harlow Lake, an unmarked singletrack spur on your right

Adjacent to the Harlow Lake trail network, the Sugarloaf Trail offers rocky terrain and awesome views.
(Photo by Kevin Bauman)

snakes off into the woods about 100 yards past the posted **Overlook Trail** cutoff. It starts off rooty, rocky, and twisting, and just gets gnarlier from there. This is probably a better course for competitive mountain-bike trials than a cross-country mountain-bike trail, but give it a try and don't feel too bad if you find yourself carrying your bike as much as riding it.

However, if you like that beyond-technical type of thing, there is an easier place to find it. Locals have created a railroad tie playground in the gravel pit near where you parked. Only a couple hundred feet long, this elevated course follows railroad ties, 4 by 4 beams, and drainage pipes to test your courage and your balance.

Don't get scared away by these technical routes. The majority of the riding here is casual cross-country ski trails, widetrack, and logging roads that offer enough mild miles to get in a good day on the bike even if there is a little of the ever-present Michigan sand in the picture.

DIFFICULTY: Beginner to advanced. This is another great trail system on which to learn how to ride. In fact this is

where Northern Michigan University's Mountain Bike Class comes to learn the ways of the woods. However, remember, take that Bare Back Trail rock spur to Harlow Lake, and you will be on an advanced ride that is better suited for a trials competition than cross-country mountain biking.

AEROBIC DIFFICULTY (1–5):

2–3 (3 on Bare Back)

TECHNICAL DIFFICULTY (1–5):

2–3 (5 on Bare Back)

WARNINGS: There is some sand out here but nothing too bad. Make sure you pick up a map of the area at the bike shop before coming out because there are a lot of roads and trails crisscrossing the area. Follow the other bike tracks in the sand and you should make it to where you want to go. Also, be aware that some trails in this area don't allow mountain bikes, so watch for postings as you explore.

OTHER TRAILS IN THE AREA: Another great B&B destination only about 12 miles west of Marquette in Ishpeming, Michigan, is known as the **Range Mountain**

Riders descend the spectacular, but challenging, Bare Back Trail.
(Photo by Kevin Bauman)

Bike Trail System. This area has over 25 miles of beginner to advanced trails within riding distance of the Jasper Ridge Brewing Company. For a challenging advanced route through this area, park right at the brewery and follow the **Jasper Ridge Trail** to the Al Quall Recreation Area and the beginning of the technical **Danny's Trail.** Loop back to the brewery from there, or turn your day into an epic by following Michigan Highway 28 to the trails just south of the towns of Ishpeming and Negaunee. These southern trails offer easy to rugged terrain with multiple lakes and scenic views.

CONTACTS: Department of Natural Resources, 110 Ford Road, Marquette, MI 49855; (906) 249-1497. Marquette Chamber of Commerce, 501 South Front Street, Suite 1, Marquette, MI 49855; (906) 226-6591. Interested in the Ore to Shore race? Check out www.oretoshore.com.

MAPS: Lake Superior Press publishes the free *Marquette Region Hike and Bike Trail Guide,* which has both the Harlow Lake Trails and the Range Mountain Trails in it. You can pick it up at any of the bike shops in Marquette and at Maple Lane Sports in Ishpeming.

BIKE SHOP: Marquette has several great shops: Down Wind Sports, 514 North Third Street, Marquette, MI 49855; (906) 226-7112. Lakeshore Bike, 505 Lakeshore Boulevard, Marquette, MI 49855; (906) 228-7547. Quick Stop Bike Shop, 1100 North Third Street, Marquette, MI 49855; (906) 225-1577; www.thequickstop.com. All three of these shops carry free trail guides and will point you in the direction of the trails. Many trails in the area are best traveled when a local acts as a guide, so all three shops have been included so you can check and see if anyone happens to be heading out for a ride. Also, if you plan on making a trip into Ishpeming, check out Maple Lane Sports, Country Village, 1015 Country Lane, Ishpeming, MI 49849; (906) 485-1636. This shop has all the latest maps and details about the Range Mountain Trails.

Marquette Harbor Brewery & Vierling Restaurant

119 South Front Street
Marquette, Michigan 49855
(906) 228-3533

THE PUB: Built in 1883 to house the Vierling Saloon, the historic building on the corner of Front and Main once again serves its original purpose. Renamed after the original owner, the renovated **Marquette Harbor Brewery & Vierling Restaurant** reopened in 1985 as the Vierling Saloon and Sample Room. The "Sample Room" referred to the room in the original "men only" establishment where women were allowed to "sample the wares" while their male escorts drank and socialized in the saloon proper. A lot has changed since those early days! Not the least of these changes are the 1995 addition of a basement brewery and the updated name of the establishment, which was altered and enlarged to reflect that worthy enhancement.

True to the character of the building, a period bar has been restored for the tavern area, and original oil paintings from the Vierling collection hang alongside other period memorabilia from the Marquette area. The brewpub is a block up the bank from the shores of Lake Superior, and the old ore dock in the lower harbor is still visible from the large arched windows in the restaurant's dining room. Add the wooden floors, brick walls, and stained glass, and you feel like you're taking a 100-year step back in time to when the iron ore boom was at its peak and Marquette was a thriving port town in its heyday.

THE BREW: Although the draft beers are no longer "in the wood" as the old Vierling advertisement reads, the brewpub does offer a solid, lineup of eight or nine beers very much true to style guidelines. You won't be disappointed with the **Plank Road Pale, Spear's Tug Stout** (on nitrogen), or the smooth-drinking **Captain's Ripley's Red Ale**. The seasonal **Amos Harlow's Amber** and **Chocolate River Porter** are both excellent and an indication that any of the Marquette Harbor Brewery seasonals will be solid.

The location right on the shores of Lake Superior means that fresh whitefish is the specialty. On the menu are four different varieties with a special of the day thrown in for good measure.

PRICE OF A PINT: No happy hour here but a 15-ounce mug is $2.75 and a 20-ounce pint is a reasonable $3.50. On Thursday nights, mugs drop to $2.50 and a pint drops to $3.00.

OTHER BREWS IN THE AREA: In Ishpeming, 12 miles west of Marquette on Highway 41, is the **Jasper Ridge Brewing Company** at 1075 Country Lane; (906) 485-6017. Jasper Ridge offers a solid line of beers in a modern building behind the Mobil gas station. Not quite the atmosphere of the Vierling establishment, but excellent beers and a prime location right next to the Range Mountain Bike Trail System makes Jasper Ridge a mandatory Bike & Brew stop when you are in the Marquette area.

"I just wish I could go with you."

—Employee at Quick Stop Bike Shop getting a little excited himself after explaining the Harlow Lake and Bare Back Trails.

Traverse City

Even though Traverse City is becoming a very popular place to live in Michigan, the town retains much of its original charm, helped along by the late-nineteenth- and early-twentieth-century buildings and homes that make up the downtown area. Slowly gaining recognition as an excellent wine-making region, Traverse City is much better known as the largest producer of tart red cherries in the

Traverse City

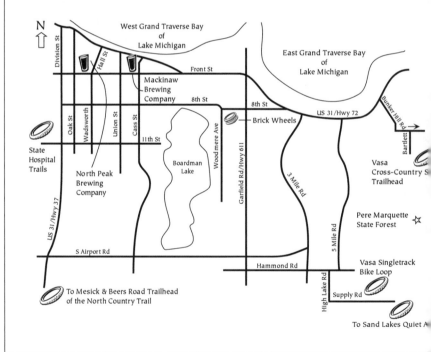

world and for its annual National Cherry Festival to com-memorate that fact.

Located on the crystal-clear waters of the Grand Traverse Bay of Lake Michigan, Traverse City is a great vacation destination for all seasons. In the summer, you have the obvious water activities of sailing, boating, fish-ing, and swimming as well as the not so obvious ones such as kayaking, wind surfing, and scuba diving the per-fectly preserved freshwater shipwrecks in Lake Michigan. On land there is hiking, visiting the nearby Sleeping Bear Dunes National Lakeshore for 64 miles of white sand along the shores of Lake Michigan, golfing on the links of world-class resorts, wine tasting, and picking fresh fruit. Winter activities include cross-country and downhill skiing at nearby Boyne Mountain, Boyne Highlands, and Nubs Knob ski resorts.

With all that going on, don't forget to add mountain biking and beer to the list of things to do in Traverse City. This northwestern Lower Peninsula town is blessed with multiple nearby trails and brewpubs. Mountain biking in and around Traverse City is very popular, and appropriately there are several trails within easy reach of the two downtown brewpubs.

Vasa Singletrack Bike Loop

THE SCOOP: Buffed-out, easygoing singletrack through northern Michigan white pines and deep blue lakes.

RIDE LENGTH AND TYPE: 14-mile singletrack loop with over 100 miles of other singletrack, widetrack, and doubletrack to explore in the surrounding Pere Marquette State Forest.

THE BIKE: The Vasa Trail System is home to the world-famous 50-kilometer (31-mile) cross-country ski race of the same name since 1977 and more recently the Iceman Cometh mountain-bike race, a 2000-person 27-mile point-to-point race that attracts names like Cecilia Potts, Tinker Juarez, and Steve Tilford.

The popularity of the trail, and of mountain biking in general in the Traverse City area, dictated the creation of the **Vasa Singletrack Loop**, a 14-mile mostly beginner-level singletrack loop through the southeast part of the Vasa Trail System.

By sticking to the main singletrack loop, you can enjoy an afternoon of fun switchbacks and fast, hard-packed trails winding around the wooded terrain. There are spots of sand, as in most other places in Michigan, but nothing that makes the trail too technical or stops you from riding. Just remember, this trail is directional (counter-clockwise), and those familiar with it tend to pick up a lot of speed throughout, so don't be surprised to meet some hammer-heads out there or to have a sudden desire to become one yourself.

Looking for more? Then you can venture off the beaten path and explore the multitude of ski trails, snowmobile trails, and "hidden" singletrack that honeycomb the area for a more advanced day of riding. The best way to find some of this hidden stuff is by exploring the day away or tagging along with a local or two who can show you the goods.

DIFFICULTY: Beginner to advanced. By sticking to the Vasa Singletrack Loop, you can keep this ride open to every level of biker. Start exploring the rest of the trail system, and beginners might get in over their heads because of the trail's length and the fact that the deepest, most inner reaches of the Pere Marquette State Forest offers a little bit of everything.

AEROBIC DIFFICULTY (1–5):

2

TECHNICAL DIFFICULTY (1–5):

2

WARNINGS: Be sure to pick up a map of the cross-country ski trails if you plan on exploring off the marked singletrack loop. Although the ski map does not have any of the hidden singletrack marked on it, it does have all the major service roads and landmarks, which will prove very useful for finding your eventual way out.

143

OTHER TRAILS IN THE AREA: The closest trails to downtown are known as **The State Hospital Trails** and traverse about 9 square miles of land full of intermediate to advanced riding for those willing to explore the mass of trails covering the state land behind the abandoned hospital. An easy place to access these trails is right behind the Traverse Bay Area (locals call it TBA) school parking lot. You may get turned around a couple times, but you won't get lost as even here in northern Lower Michigan, urban sprawl will hem you in. It might be better to find a local who can show you the best ways up the hills and the most exciting ways down. Views from the highest points are breathtaking. Almost 400 feet below, the East and West Harbors of Grand Traverse Bay are visible stretching off to the west.

Another intermediate to advanced ride is the **Sand Lakes Quiet Area**—a well-mapped and well-marked system with about 15 miles of rideable trails. Located about 9 miles east of Traverse City, this is also a popular hiking area, so

please ride accordingly and always give way. The best all-day epic riding is a section of **North Country Trail** that comes fairly close to Traverse City. Just out of normal B&B travel distance, the best place to pick up this off-camber, sometimes steep and technical slice of singletrack heaven is just west of the small town of Mesick at the **Beers Road Trailhead**. The problem is you need to buy a special National Forest Service Pass for $15.00 before you're allowed to ride here. Very difficult to come by when you're only in town for the weekend. Contact Huron-Manistee National Forest ahead of time.

CONTACTS: Department of Natural Resources, 970 Emerson Road, Traverse City, MI 49686; (231) 922-5280. TART Trails Inc., P.O. Box 252, Traverse City, MI 49685; (231) 883-8278. Huron-Manistee National Forest, 1755 South Mitchell Street, Cadillac, MI 49601; (231) 775-2421. Traverse City Chamber of Commerce, 202 East Grandview Parkway, Traverse City, MI 49684; (231) 947-5075.

MAPS: You can pick up a free Vasa Singletrack Loop map at Brick Wheels, or just be careful and follow the blue blazes along the well-marked and well-worn trail once you get there.

BIKE SHOP: Brick Wheels, 738 Eighth, Traverse City, MI 49688; (231) 947-4274. Usually ranked in the Top 100 Shops in the country by *Bicycler Retailer and Industry News* and *VeloBusiness*, these folks have everything you'll need for a successful trip to the area including maps, parts, and plenty of advice on where to ride.

Mackinaw Brewing Company

161 East Front Street
Traverse City, Michigan 49684
(231) 933-1100

THE PUB: Both the **Mackinaw Brewing Company** and **North Peak Brewing Company** are outstanding places to go after a ride; it just depends on what you're after. If you're looking for a quiet beer and time to reflect on a day well done, then check out Mackinaw. But if you're looking for a younger crowd and a charged atmosphere, then check under **Other Brews in the Area** as North Peak is where you should be headed.

Located in historic downtown Traverse City in the 1892 Beadle Building, Mackinaw is everything a local tavern should be: friendly, cozy, lots of regulars, great food, happy hour, and a porch out back that offers a beautiful view of Lake Michigan. Brick walls, pressed-tin ceilings, and hardwood floors greet you as you pass by the brew house on your way in from busy Front Street. Grab a seat at the bar with four large suspended TVs or head straight through the narrow restaurant to where a rear deck awaits on warm summer days.

THE BREW: Mackinaw offers a solid lineup of beers with five regulars on tap and a rotating seasonal. The best-selling **Golden Ale** and **Red 8 Ale** are good and offer easy drinking for the masses or session beers for long afternoons on the back deck. The employees' favorite, **Beadles's Best Bitter,** is sweet and malty with just a touch of bitterness to give it its name. The **Peninsula Pale Ale** is great for hopheads, and the **Pig Stout** is served on nitrogen to assure its smooth and creamy nature.

PRICE OF A PINT: An excellent happy hour occurs

Monday through Friday between 4:00 and 6:00 P.M. when pints drop from $3.50 down to $2.00 and free munchies are out in force. Plus, Tuesdays have happy hour from 4:00 P.M. until close with pints only two bucks all night long.

OTHER BREWS IN THE AREA: Traverse City is blessed with two outstanding brewpubs, close in location, just five blocks apart, but different enough in atmosphere that your mood will dictate where you'd like to end up. The **North Peak Brewing Company** at 400 West Front Street, (231) 941-7325, is pretty much the opposite of Mackinaw in everything but the beer, which is excellent at both places. Whereas Mackinaw is narrow and darker, the North Peak is open and airy with light-colored brick and plenty of large windows offering natural light throughout the cavernous building. Fortunately, because of the high ceilings and open floor plan, smoke doesn't linger long here. Outside, a large street-side patio often has live music in the summer.

North Peak offers a fine menu and $2.00 pints Monday through Friday from 3:00 to 6:00 P.M. and always a $2.00 Tap of the Day. This Tap of the Day is rotated through the seven beers with Mondays going to the light and easy-drinking **Northern Light** and Tuesdays devoted to the hop-filled **North Peak Pale Ale**; on Wednesdays the nicely balanced and malty **Steelhead Red** is up to bat, on Thursdays the **Mission Point Porter** does time, Fridays are for **Shirley's Irish Stout**—an excellent stout served on nitrogen—and Saturdays and Sundays go to the two rotating taps. Hence, there is always something on special, even on the weekends. The specials even extend to $4.00 growler refills of the Tap of the Day!

"Mackinaw is meat and potatoes while North Peak is beans and sprouts."
—Mackinaw Brewing Company mug club member astutely compares the two brewpubs in town.

MICHIGAN

BIKE BREW AMERICA

CHAPTER SIX

MINNESOTA

Even though Minnesota is known as the "Land of 10,000 Lakes" (officially it's the North Star State), this spectacular destination is actually home to more than 15,000 lakes. One of these is the mighty Lake Superior, the largest fresh-water lake in the world. Minnesota is also a land of trails and healthy outdoor pursuits such as running, cross-country skiing, and, of course, mountain biking.

From 1860 to about 1900, Minnesota was the leading lumber-producing state in America. And that's saying a lot because at about that same time both Michigan and Wisconsin were busy wiping out their old-growth forests

147

Minnesota

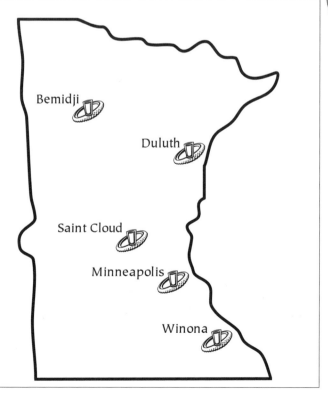

BIKE BREW AMERICA

MINNESOTA

as well. Therefore, though you will be riding in deep forest most of the time during your visit to the Gopher State (because of its overwhelming gopher population), it's gonna be through second- and third-growth forests of oak, maple, elm, aspen, and poplar. Still heavenly, but not the picture-perfect stands of pine from days of old.

The more populated southern region of Minnesota is blessed with an active mountain-bike scene including multiple trails and an energetic race series. The inhabitants also have an appreciation for fine beer with which to properly enjoy such things. The farther north you head, the less defined the mountain-bike trails will be and the more pronounced the cross-country, snowmobile, and motorcycle trails and 4x4 roads become. Mountain bikers are just not as organized an entity up here and are often forced onto these other user groups' trails.

Fortunately, a healthy brewing community does support the biking scene. However, in Minnesota, there is no distribution of beer from a brewpub—no cans, bottles, barrels, or growlers off premises. Just be prepared for this travesty and leave the growler at home.

Bemidji

Bemidji is known as the First City owing to its location virtually on the source of the Mississippi River in nearby Lake Itasca. Up until the town's early Prohibition (which was enacted in 1914 rather than 1920 allegedly because Bemidji was in a geographic "Indian District"), Bemidji was a rowdy and wild town catering to the multitude of lumberjacks who came to town to spend their hard-earned wages at the 264 pubs, taverns, and bars then doing business in the area.

In fact, Bemidji claims to be the birthplace of the most famous of lumberjacks, the mythical Paul Bunyan. Since 1937, the 18-foot statue of Paul Bunyan—the king of the lumberjacks—has stood on the shore of Lake Bemidji, marking his supposed birthplace. A more recent addition, no less massive, is a statue of Babe, Paul Bunyan's famous blue ox.

One of several lakes to be found beneath the blue skies and green trees of Paul Bunyan State Forest.
(Courtesy of Park Rapids Forestry)

149

About 35 miles northeast of Bemidji is what is now known as the Lost Forty Biotic Area. Actually 144 acres, the Lost Forty was accidentally placed inside Coddington Lake in the original Government Land Survey of 1882. This error allowed an old-growth stand of virgin red and white pine to be missed by the loggers at the end of the nineteenth century. Today some of these trees are as old as 350 years and up to 4 feet in diameter! Truly worth a visit if you have time.

Most of the trails around remote Bemidji have been created for purposes other than mountain biking such as logging, hiking, snowmobiling, cross-country skiing, and motorcycle riding. However, there are nearly unlimited miles of these "other" trails. And now that fresh brew is once again pouring inside the city, reminding everyone of Bemidji's proud and colorful past, it's time to get out and explore Minnesota's North Woods.

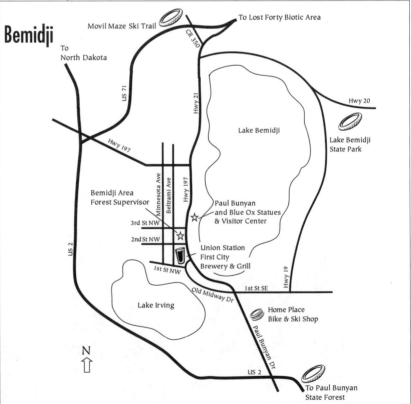

Paul Bunyan State Forest

THE SCOOP: Miles of charted—and uncharted—single-track, doubletrack, and dirt roads.

RIDE LENGTH AND TYPE: Variable—miles of trails with more being built all the time.

THE BIKE: The good news: miles and miles of rideable terrain in this section of Minnesota's **Paul Bunyan State**

Aspen and birch surround you on the trails in Paul Bunyan State Forest.

(Courtesy of Park Rapids Forestry)

Forest. The bad news: these trails intertwine, are constantly changing, and are rarely marked, making getting lost out here a fact of life. A few maps posted at sporadic trail intersections outline the general flow of the trails as they wind through dense forest. Even so, it's still difficult to figure out exactly where you are most of the time, which makes for a very beautiful, but confusing, ride.

With all that said, there is still more than 100 miles of riding through this remote and exquisite section of Minnesota's North Woods. By parking at the **Martineau Trailhead** and riding south, you will discover some of the best singletrack straight away. This singletrack consists of a mix of loamy soil, hard-packed black dirt, sand, and gravel from the motorized travel most common in the area.

Mostly created and maintained by the Norseman Motorcycle Club or "Club Enduro," the singletrack parts of the trail are a little wider than typical mountain-bike–specific singletrack. However, without the club, most of the trails wouldn't be here in the first place. The Enduros have done a good job of following the contours of the terrain, which makes this trail system more mountain bike friendly than most off-road vehicle trails that tend to go straight up and straight back down the hillsides. Another benefit of the motorcyclists' work is the use of colored tape to mark the various loops they use for racing. Careful here! Although these markings are very convenient, tape does fall off and when that happens, it adds to the ease of getting lost out here.

DIFFICULTY: Intermediate to advanced. Because the trails have mostly been created by motorcyclists, with motorcycles in mind, this area is best suited for experienced bikers. Maps are limited and don't even come close to accurately depicting the most current trail information. However, for a group willing to spend some time exploring, this area offers days of enjoyable riding.

AEROBIC DIFFICULTY (1–5):

3–4

TECHNICAL DIFFICULTY (1–5):

3–4

WARNINGS: Get a map and compass and know how to use them before taking on this one. Trails can get overgrown in the summer, which just makes getting lost that much more interesting here in the Paul Bunyan State Forest.

OTHER TRAILS IN THE AREA: The area around Bemidji is loaded with trails, and the farther you go the better. Right in town is **Lake Bemidji State Park,** which offers around 5 miles of easy cross-country ski trails opened to bikes in the summer. Still short on time and looking to get to the brewpub before dark? Check out the **Movil Maze Ski Trail** about 8 miles north of Bemidji. More challenging than Lake Bemidji, Movil offers about 8 miles of beginner cross-country ski trails, plus many miles of additional snowmobile trails intersecting at various points of the ski trail, but no real singletrack. Don't mind a little drive? Then the **Chippewa National Forest** offers 18 easy to difficult mountain-bike trails just north and east of Bemidji. Stop in or call the Cass Lake Forest Headquarters office on Route 3 for free maps and information. The cream of the crop of these trails is the 88-mile section of the **North Country Trail** that begins near the town of Walker, southeast of Bemidji. The section from Minnesota Highway 34 to Minnesota Highway 371 is about 10 miles of wide, fairly easy singletrack—a perfect out-and-back from the parking area on Minnesota 34.

CONTACTS: Department of Natural Resources Forestry, Paul Bunyan State Forest, P.O. Box 113, Park Rapids, MN 56470; (218) 732-3309. Bemidji Area Forest Supervisor, 2220 Bemidji Avenue, Bemidji, MN 56601; (218) 755-2890. U.S. Forest Service, Cass Lake Forest Headquarters Office, Chippewa National Forest, Route 3, Box 244, Cass Lake, MN 56633; (218) 335-8600. Bemidji Chamber of Commerce, 300 Bemidji Avenue North, Bemidji, MN 56601; (218) 751-3541.

MAPS: There is a map kiosk at the Martineau Trailhead, and sometimes map pamphlets are available there as well. To make sure you have one, call the Department of Natural Resources Forestry contact number listed and

"I've been in those woods for 25 years!"

"I've never been THAT lost!!"

—Two forest rangers talk about the possibilities of getting lost in the Paul Bunyan State Forest. An excerpt from Fargo's Island Park Cycles *Ride Guide.*

153

have one sent to you before your visit to the area. If you're on a short schedule, then stop by the Bemidji Area Forest Supervisor in Bemidji and pick a map up.

BIKE SHOP: Home Place Bike and Ski Shop, 431 Paul Bunyan Drive Southeast, Bemidji, MN 56601; (218) 751-3456. This is the place to get the maps of the local cross-country ski trails including Movil Maze.

If you're passing through nearby Fargo, North Dakota, be sure to stop in at Island Park Cycles, 101 South Eighth Street, Fargo, ND 58103; (888) 280-1796; www.ipcycles.com. This shop put its advertising dollars into creating an outstanding free *Ride Guide* to the mountain biking and road riding in the area including the Paul Bunyan State Forest and North Country Trail.

Bemidji

MINNESOTA

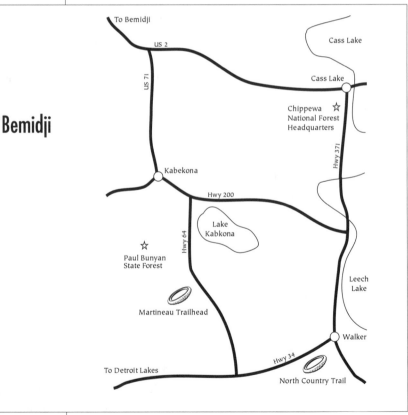

Union Station First City Brewery & Grill

128 First Street, Union Square
Bemidji, Minnesota 55802
(218) 751-9261

THE PUB: A longtime bar and restaurant located in a hundred-year-old Great Northern Railroad Union Station Depot, the welcome addition of a brew house in 1997 made **Union Station First City Brewery & Grill** Bemidji's first brewery in 82 years. Although the classic look of the old depot has been somewhat muddied by a large, modern northern town's touristy façade and the place could use a little restoration to truly bring back the feeling of times gone by, there is no denying the comfortable local pub feel as you walk through the door.

Inside, the classic charm remains and mingles with the dark pub atmosphere. First City's small and cozy bar area is dimly lit and decorated with warm wood panels covered in Captain Morgan Rum mirrors, a three-sided bar with a single TV, a large sociable corner booth, and a few tables. An old sliding loading-dock door adds to the overall train-station atmosphere, and the brew house behind the bar is visible through windows. The separate dining area is stylish in a Victorian sort of way with pressed-tin ceilings, dark wood, and parquet flooring. Even the depot's old ticket window now does time as the drink-order station for the dining room. And, to top it all off, an outdoor patio is open out front on nice days.

THE BREW: First City keeps six beers on tap, including five regulars and one seasonal. Of the regulars, the **Orient Express IPA** (India pale ale) is the best beer brewing and an excellent interpretation of this classic style. The next beer not to miss is the **Coal Trail Porter,** a very good beer that the locals can't get enough of. The list rounds out with **Cannon Ball Red, 1st Street Wheat,** and **Golden Spike Ale.** All decent, but none compares to the IPA and the porter.

PRICE OF A PINT: Ready to take notes? Happy hour is Monday through Friday 4:00 to 7:00 P.M. when pints drop from $2.75 down to $1.75. On Thursday nights from 8:00 P.M. to close is college night, and pints are only a buck. Saturdays the brewpub has a late-night happy hour from 9:00 to 11:00 P.M. when pints are again reduced to $1.75.

OTHER BREWS IN THE AREA: First Street Brewery & Grill is the only brewpub in Bemidji, but another train-station-turned-brewery is 1½ hours away in Fargo, North Dakota.

Located just off Lake Bemidji, the clapboard façade of First City Brewery & Grill houses Bemidji's first brewery in 82 years.

Unfortunately, there is no significant riding within 1 hour or so of Fargo. Too bad because the **Shooting Star Casino's Great Northern Restaurant & Brewery** at 425 Broadway, (701) 293-5257, is nothing less than spectacular. This ex–train station is perfectly restored right down to the mosaic terrazzo floors and tile walls that will make you feel like you're waiting for the next train to Bismarck. A clock tower, which dominates the exterior, was added in 1936 and is still working today. Around back is a brick patio separated from the still-working train tracks by a wrought-iron fence. All the beers here are very good with the **Whistle Stop Stout** (served on nitrogen) and the best-selling **Depot IPA** (India pale ale) taking top honors. The beers are solid and so are the prices; house beers go for $2.00 regularly, and from 5:00 to 7:00 P.M., prices are reduced to a buck. On your way to Paul Bunyan State Forest for the weekend? Then fill up your growler for only $4.00! So while the riding is limited here in Fargo, if you're traveling through this place, it's worth a stop for the beer.

Duluth

Duluth is located on the western tip of Lake Superior only 2342 miles from the Atlantic Ocean via the Saint Lawrence Seaway. As Minnesota's seaport, Duluth deals extensively in iron ore, coal, lumber, and grain, and it is one of the country's largest ports when measured by sheer volume.

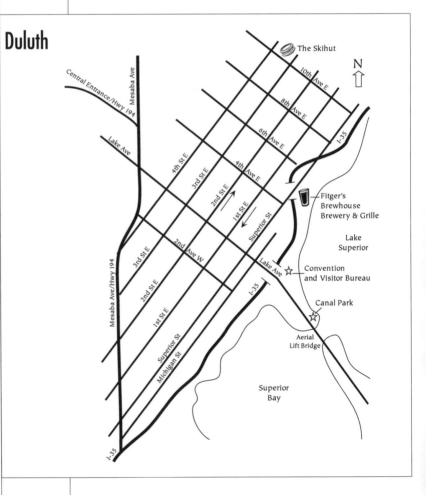

Duluth

Duluth's history as an important port for the lumber and iron industries over the past 150 years gives the city of Duluth the distinguished look of a gracefully aging historic town. Even though the city suffered a depression period throughout the 1970s and 1980s when some of the bigger iron ore mines closed, Duluth has successfully diversified and is once again on the rise, this time as a year-round tourist destination.

An old railroad trestle along the West End Trail bluffs offers a great place to take in Spirit Lake and the state of Wisconsin.

One such attraction is the waterfront area including Canal Park, the Lakewalk along Lake Superior, DeWitt-Seitz Marketplace, Marine Museum, Great Lakes Aquarium, and the Aerial Lift Bridge that dates back to 1905. With more than 50 restaurants within walking distance of this area (including, of course, The Brewhouse at Fitger's Brewhouse Brewery & Grille), Duluth's downtown is once again thriving.

The shoreline of Lake Superior sits at just over 605 feet above sea level but immediately rises another 900 feet to the bluffs high above the lake. This dramatic landscape will remind you of the Pacific Coast with its steep hills and scenic water views and the Victorian houses that cling to these slopes practically scream to mind locations like Seattle or San Francisco. Not only will the scenery impress the eye, it will also provide you with a rare opportunity for extended climbing right here in the middle of the Midwest.

Taking advantage of this terrain is a lot of singletrack. The problem is finding it. Still, if you have patience, or find a local to show you the way, the trouble is worth it as you crisscross the bluffs high above the shore and take in the fantastic views of Lake Superior.

West End Trails

THE SCOOP: Steep, technical singletrack downhill and wide, but loose, doubletrack back up.

RIDE LENGTH AND TYPE: Variable—you can ride out here all day if you don't mind a little exploring.

THE BIKE: On the west side of Duluth, overlooking the Saint Louis River Valley, is what the locals call the **West End Trails.** A huge network of singletrack and widetrack trails traverses the bluff from the downtown Lake Superior Zoo, through Spirit Mountain Recreation Area, and all the way to Jay Cook State Park.

As per usual in northern Minnesota, most of these trails are not marked or mapped. Therefore, although you will be able to find the trails without difficulty, without a local rider to show you the way through this web, you run the risk of getting on some gnarly stuff that will burn you out long before you would normally have to call it a day.

Fortunately, there are some measures you can take to combat this possibility. Traveling through the heart of this trail network is the **Willard Munger State Trail**, the longest paved trail in the nation stretching over 70 miles from Duluth to the town of Hinckley, Minnesota. Also, following the contours of the West End is an old railroad grade now used for motorized all-terrain vehicles. These two moderate low-grade trails offer perfect landmarks and bailouts (not to mention incredible scenic opportunities) when exploring the miles of 4x4 roads and motorbike, hiking, and biking trails that honeycomb this area.

The final measure you can take to assure longevity is by riding any singletrack you find down the mountain and using the multitude of double tracks to climb back up. It's a small thing, but it keeps an already difficult trail from becoming impossible.

DIFFICULTY: Intermediate to advanced. With a local taking you to all the easiest ways up and all the best ways down or, if you're willing to spend some time on the graded trails, you will have a fantastic time out here if you have at least intermediate skills. However, this is a playground for advanced riders, so come expecting to work.

AEROBIC DIFFICULTY (1–5):
4

TECHNICAL DIFFICULTY (1–5):
4

WARNINGS: This is not the place to learn how to ride your bike on singletrack. As there are no maps of the area, only experienced riders with a good sense of direction should ride here.

OTHER TRAILS IN THE AREA: Not quite that adventurous or not interested in exploring your afternoon away? Then try **Jay Cook State Park**, which offers mountain biking on well-established trails. Also, right in town are two popular cross-country ski trails that also make good beginner mountain biking. **Hartley Cross-Country Ski Trail** offers about 3 miles of ski trails as well as the **Guardrail Loop**. Guardrail is 5 miles of advanced tight and twisty single-track hidden on the outskirts of the park—just ride the ski trails until you see the singletrack branching off.

CONTACTS: Although don't expect much help in the way of West End maps, try Duluth Parks and Recreation Department, 12 East Fourth Street, Duluth, MN 55805; (218) 723-3337. Duluth Chamber of Commerce, 118 East Superior Street, Duluth, MN 55802; (218) 722-5501.

MAPS: There really are no maps to the West End Trails. However, stop by at The Skihut Bike Shop, which can supply you with directions to the many access points as well as maps to the many, many cross-country ski trails in the area. This is also a great place to find those kindly locals who will take you under their wing and show you the trails as they are supposed to be ridden.

BIKE SHOP: The Skihut, 1032 East Fourth Street, Duluth, MN 55805; (218) 724-8525; www.theskihut.com. This is the shop when in Duluth. The employees do group rides every Monday night at 6:00 P.M. all summer long that often end up right at the brewpub. Stop in and get the lowdown on the West End Trails from the experts.

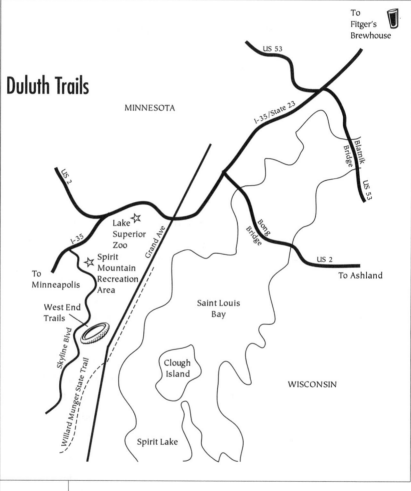

Duluth Trails

Fitger's Brewhouse Brewery & Grille

600 East Superior Street
Duluth, Minnesota
55802
(218) 726-1392
www.brewhouse.net

THE PUB: Once inside the old Fitger Brewery building, now known as the Historic Fitger's Inn & Brewery Complex, you are faced with a daunting collection of restaurants, bars, shops, a first-class hotel, and even a museum. However, all you have to do is follow the prominently displayed wood-clad English storage tanks and brew kettles lining

Hoisting a few pints at Fitger's Brewhouse Brewery & Grille.

the hallway, and you will find the intimate **Fitger's Brewhouse Brewery & Grille.** Once around the corner you will be greeted with the sounds of good conversation and the welcome laughter of the surprisingly quaint and friendly neighborhood pub just inside. Huge ventilation ducts wind up through the bar, filling the two-story room and sheltering the second-floor mezzanine from the noisy bar below.

Rough-hewn stone walls hint at the age of the building, and support posts covered with photos, bumper stickers, and postcards hint at the character of the current tenants. At the end of the nineteenth century, the now-historic Fitger Brewery was what some of the large macrobreweries are today. Surviving Prohibition by becoming a candy and soda maker, Fitger's persevered and was once again able to produce over 100,000 barrels of beer annually after Prohibition was revoked. Not closing its doors for good until 1972, Fitger's old brew kettle still sits in the complex's museum with a single-brewing capacity equal to what Fitger's Brewhouse today puts out in an entire year.

"These weirdos will drink it, I'll drink it, we'll all drink it. Let's go for it!"

—Co-owner Rod Raymond talks about how the brewer has free reign to get "adventurous" if the notion for a new beer should strike.

This is truly the place in Duluth for mountain bikers after a ride. Not only does Fitger's have an outdoor sidewalk patio, live music four to six nights a week, and a smoke-free environment until 10:00 P.M., it also sponsors the local mountain-bike club, the members of which regularly meet at the brewery for beer specials after their Monday night group rides.

THE BREW: Next to the small but busy bar is the dining area and brewery. As the story goes, this room was actually August Fitger's Chemist Room where he developed the very popular and very famous **Fitger's Beer**. During renovation of the brewery, various puzzling mishaps occurred during construction that were blamed on the Ghost of August Fitger. True or not, once the first batch of beer rolled out of the taps, the mysterious happenings stopped. Apparently, the Ghost of August Fitger approved. He has every right to be pleased.

And with no less than three tappers pouring nitrogen brews, you will be pleased too. Of the four regular brews, the best-selling **Lighthouse Golden** is good for what it is but things just get better from there. The **Big Boat Oatmeal Stout** and **Witch Tree ESB** (extra special bitter) are both on nitro and absolutely perfect beers. The **El Nino IPA** (India pale ale) is aged in oak barrels for an authentic IPA that is as close to India in the nineteenth century as you're ever gonna get.

Fitger's Brewhouse also keeps three seasonals on tap that will not disappoint and a couple of guest taps including the locally brewed **Lake Superior Special Ale.**

PRICE OF A PINT: Happy hour is Monday through Friday 3:00 to 6:00 P.M. when pints drop from $3.50 to $2.00 and you get a dollar off appetizers. You'll know you've arrived on time, as the bar will be noisy and packed with regulars. Monday through Thursday, Fitger's has a second happy hour from 8:00 to 9:00 P.M.

OTHER BREWS IN THE AREA: Fitger's Brewhouse is the only brewpub in Duluth, but **Lake Superior Brewing Company** keeps the area stocked with fresh micros that are well worth checking into while shopping the beer shelves in the area.

Author (left) and biker reminisce on Fitger's Brewhouse Brewery & Grille's patio.

Minneapolis

Perhaps more commonly known alongside its counterpart of Saint Paul as one of the Twin Cities, Minneapolis is considered one of the healthiest and most active cities in the country with 1 acre of parkland for every 50 or so residents. Minneapolis was ranked the second-fittest city in America by *Men's Fitness Magazine.* Split down the middle by the Mississippi River with Minneapolis on the west side and Saint Paul on the east, the Twin Cities dominate the economy and culture of Minnesota. *Fortune Magazine* annually ranks the Twin Cities among the top four places in the nation to balance business and family.

The metro area is home to the state's capital, the University of Minnesota, the Mall of America (the largest retail and entertainment complex in the United States), and hundreds of cultural activities including museums, theaters, parks, and zoos. Saint Paul is noted for its European architecture, and Minneapolis is known for its skyline of towering office buildings and the unique Skyway system connecting them all.

Not exactly a warm place in the winter, downtown Minneapolis has 5 miles of glass-enclosed walkways running from building to building above the city streets. The walkways—filled with shops, stores, and restaurants—offer a unique way to get around and give the city a distinctive look in return.

And to top it off, Minneapolis is home to over a dozen breweries and another dozen mountain-bike trails. With those kinds of numbers there is plenty of opportunity to find hard dirt and fresh beer during your visit to Minneapolis.

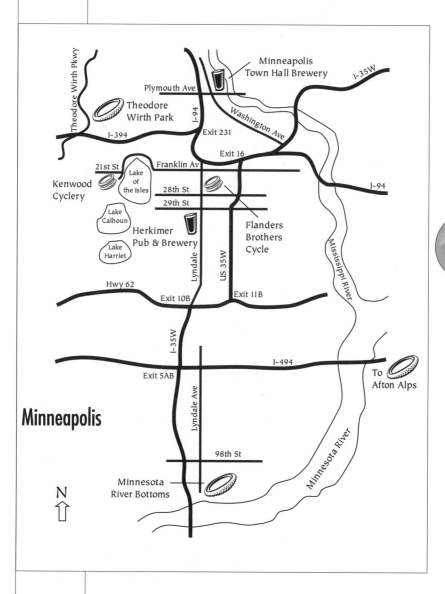

Minneapolis

N ⬆

Minnesota River Bottoms Trail

THE SCOOP: Singletrack along the Minnesota River just minutes south of town.

RIDE LENGTH AND TYPE: More than 10 miles of trail make for more than a 20-mile out-and-back.

THE BIKE: The Minneapolis–Saint Paul metro area is blessed with hundreds of miles of singletrack, paved, and unpaved bike routes. One of the most popular and easiest trails to access is the **Minnesota River Bottoms Trail,** also known as the River Trails. This 10-mile-long trail rolls along the banks and flood plains of the Minnesota River Valley through county parkland, public open space, and certain Minnesota Valley National Wildlife Refuge land that has also been set aside for hiking, biking, and cross-country skiing.

The main trail is usually within sight of the river, flat, and technically easy, but a number of spurs offer more challenging terrain including log piles, tight turns, and sharp dips. By taking the **Mounds Springs Park Route** up onto the bluffs overlooking Long Meadow Lake, the terrain gets prime with climbing singletrack cut right into the hillside. Although this spur may be the most interesting route on the trail, watch for U.S. Fish & Wildlife Service signs proclaiming you are entering a section of the Minnesota Valley National Wildlife Refuge where bikes are forbidden. It's now time to turn back to the tamer lowlands below.

Wildlife refuge aside, this trail gets a lot of use from the local bikers and is a perennial favorite. Although the western side of the trail is very flat with plenty of visibility, making it prime for a little speed, be aware this trail is also a hiking trail, so don't scare any walkers while out getting in your turns. One feature that will slow you down

Bikers take the ferry across Nine Mile Creek at the Minnesota River Bottoms. Good old-fashion Midwest engineering makes this crossing a cinch all year long.

is Nine Mile Creek. Too big to ride or wade across, the local trail crew has built an ingenious ferry system. Ropes anchored to each bank allow the raft, carrying a couple of bikers and their rigs, to be pulled across the creek. This trail is worth the trip just to take part in this engineering feat.

DIFFICULTY: Beginner to intermediate. The trail is mostly wide, smooth, singletrack. Beginners should stick to the main trail and watch their mileage, carefully remembering that there are no shortcuts back to the car as this is an out-and-back ride. The climb to Mounds Springs, various spur trails, and the fact that this is a 20-mile ride if you

do the whole trail make it more than challenging enough for intermediate or advanced riders looking for miles.

AEROBIC DIFFICULTY (1–5):

2 (3 if you do the whole thing)

TECHNICAL DIFFICULTY (1–5):

2

WARNINGS: This is a popular trail in a populated area. Expect other trail users including hikers, joggers, and bikers. Because this is a two-way trail, ride defensively and always give way. The eastern end of the trail enters the Minnesota Valley National Wildlife Refuge and restricts bike travel to trails marked for such use, so be alert while riding in this sensitive area.

OTHER TRAILS IN THE AREA: The Minnesota River Bottoms Trail is the easiest one to find and follow and offers a lot of mileage. If you can find someone from the local biker community to take you for a ride, or don't mind exploring, then do not miss the 20 or so miles of legal riding in **Theodore Wirth Park.** More advanced than the Bottoms and commonly considered the best riding inside the city limits, it's unmapped and extremely difficult to follow without a local leading the way. Willing to travel east? Then check out the 7 miles of trails at **Afton Alps.** It costs $6.00 to ride, but you'll find more climbing and descending here than anywhere else in the Twin Cities area.

CONTACTS: Bloomington Parks and Recreation, 2215 West Old Shakepee Road, Bloomington, MN 55431; (952) 948-8877. Minneapolis Chamber of Commerce, 81 South Ninth Street, Suite 200, Minneapolis, MN 55401; (612) 370-9132.

MAPS: The best source of trail information while in Minneapolis is the *Twin Cities Bike Map* by Little Transport Press. It lists 11 mountain-bike trails as well as road routes, commuter routes, and rail trails and is available at most bike shops. Well worth the $7.95 price tag it carries.

BIKE SHOP: Kenwood Cyclery, 2123 West Twenty-First Street, Minneapolis, MN 55405; (612) 374-4042. This shop is a mountain-biker haven with group rides to Theodore Wirth Park on Monday nights. The employees and friends leave right from the shop and stay off-road the whole way. Closest to the brewpub is Flanders Brothers Cycle, 2707 Lyndale Avenue South, Minneapolis, MN 55408; (612) 872-6994. Flanders caters a little more to the roadie scene than to mountain bikers, but is the closest shop to the brewpub and almost right across the street from Bob's Java Hut, making it a perfect place to pick up a map and study it over a cup of Bob's joe.

The Herkimer Pub & Brewery

2922 Lyndale Avenue South
Minneapolis, MN 55408
(612) 821-0101
www.herkimerpub.citysearch.com

THE PUB: Just south of downtown Minneapolis, the location of "The Herk" is perfect. From here it's a straight shot south to the Minnesota River Bottoms Trails or a local's knowledge to the best riding in the city, the trails in Theodore Wirth Park. Situated three blocks from Bob's Java Hut, a popular biker hangout, and only two blocks from the nearest bike shop, **The Herkimer Pub & Brewery's** locale in Uptown is fat-tire central. Not only is this area the perfect launching point for your explorations of what Minneapolis has to offer, it may also be the best place to find an innocent willing to take you over to Theodore Wirth Park.

The Herk is a trendy pub in a trendy part of Minneapolis's "Uptown" area and caters to a thriving after-work crowd during weekday happy hours. Stressed-concrete floors, colored-tile columns, and a large rectangular bar dominate this recent addition to the area's nightlife. Booth and table seating is arranged around the bar and up front near the street windows. Shuffleboard is the only sport besides excellent dining and, of course, good beer drinking.

THE BREW: Owing to the fact that the owner and brewer, Blake Richardson, schooled with a German brewmaster, all of Herk's beers have a German influence. Featuring four or five beers at any given time, and mostly serving lagers, Blake's lineup includes a refreshing collection of unusual styles. It begins with the smooth and sweet **Herkimer**

Kolsch and the excellent **Dortmunder Pilsner** brewed just like a true German Pils is meant to be and an excellent alternative to your typical yellow Pilsener. On the darker end is the **High Point Dunkel**, an excellent sweet and mild, dark beer reminiscent of an American brown and the best of the bunch. The **Herkimer Schwarzbier**, malty and a touch more crisp than the Dunkel, is solid but very similar to the Dunkel. If you have to choose one, make it a High Point.

PRICE OF A PINT: Happy hour is Monday through Friday from 3:00 to 6:00 P.M. when house beers are 2 for 1! That'll take a little bit from the $3.75 Herkimer normally charges for a glass of beer.

OTHER BREWS IN THE AREA: A horde of brewpubs fill the Minneapolis–Saint Paul metro area, and if you like to take advantage of a downtown location, the **Minneapolis Town Hall Brewery** at 1430 Washington Avenue South, (612) 339-8696, enjoys an early-twentieth-century building with a sidewalk patio in the hustle of downtown Minneapolis.

For what is probably the best overall dining and beer experience in the Minneapolis area, you have to go to the brewpub called **Sherlock's Home**, 11000 Red Circle Drive, (952) 931-0203, in the expensive suburb of Minnetonka. In a modern brick building expertly crafted to mimic an English pub from the nineteenth century, Sherlock's offers an authentic English experience. The brewpub pours four hand-pulled ales and three other handcrafted brews (all of which are cask-conditioned) alongside real darts and gourmet English pub fare. Though you shouldn't exactly wear your bike shorts into this place, it's still a nice suburban brewpub and especially perfect if driving into the city isn't your bag.

173

"Wow, Todd, this sounds way cool. How do I sign up?"

—Pman, aka Tim Bocklund, of Minneapolis-based Salsa Corporation, discovers Bike & Brew America.

Saint Cloud and Milaca

Located on the Mississippi River about 60 miles northwest of Minneapolis–Saint Paul, Saint Cloud is probably best known for its granite production. And thanks to Saint Cloud's long history of granite mining, it is blessed with a historic downtown. Fifth Avenue is complete with a vibrant nightlife, interesting shops, cafés, and several summertime events in the nearby Courthouse Square. Courthouse Square gets its name from the 109-foot-tall domed Stearns County Courthouse. This historic landmark was built in 1922 and completely renovated in 1991; its most recent claim to fame is being the site of the courthouse scene in the movie *The Mighty Ducks*.

The Saint Cloud area is right in the middle of a mountain-bike resurgence spurred by a group known as Bike Blast. A race-promotions and trail-building organization, the Bike Blast folks are up to their helmets building and maintaining three different trails in the area. And, because Saint Cloud plays host to two brewpubs, and both brewers are avid mountain bikers, the Bike & Brew scene in Saint Cloud is one to experience. As both the brewers are mountain-bike brethren, Bike & Brew America is gonna lay out the choices and leave it up to you to decide where to end your day in Saint Cloud.

Combine this active group of beer-drinking cyclists with the cycling- and beer-friendly town of nearby Milaca, and you have a Bike & Brew America destination to remember. Located 30 miles northeast of Saint Cloud, Milaca hosted the First Annual Milaca Bike & Brew Festival on Memorial Day weekend 2001 with the excellent James Page Brewing Company from Minneapolis serving up its fine ales to weary cyclists.

Saint Cloud and Milaca

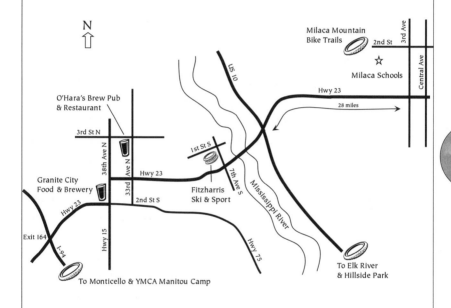

N

Milaca Mountain Bike Trails

3rd Ave

2nd St

Central Ave

Milaca Schools

Hwy 23

US 10

28 miles

O'Hara's Brew Pub & Restaurant

3rd St N

38th Ave N

33rd Ave N

Hwy 23

1st St S

7th Ave S

Mississippi River

Granite City Food & Brewery

Hwy 23

2nd St S

Fitzharris Ski & Sport

Exit 164

Hwy 15

I-94

Hwy 75

To Elk River & Hillside Park

To Monticello & YMCA Manitou Camp

Milaca Mountain-Bike Trails

THE SCOOP: Singletrack, multiuse trail system with more than a little mountain-bike love.

RIDE LENGTH AND TYPE: 14-mile loop following the longest continuous route.

THE BIKE: As already explained, 30 minutes northeast of Saint Cloud is the small friendly town of Milaca. Near Milaca's Rec Park, just across the Rum River, is an excellent trail network built around the area's former waste-disposal ponds and known as the **Milaca Mountain-Bike Trails.** Don't worry, despite the fact that they are now known as the Big Green Lagoon, it's not nearly as bad as it sounds. Nature has reclaimed the area, and healthy wetlands and forest coexist with the miles of singletrack now taking complete advantage of the hills and lands surrounding the holding ponds.

Thanks in part to a mountain-bike-friendly Milaca mayor by the name of Randy Furman, a small cross-country ski and hiking trail along the Rum River has become the focus of the local race-promotions group "Bike Blast" that went to work to dramatically increase the mileage and difficulty of the trail. On the south end of the network lies the group's first project, **Sky Hill.** Not a large hill, by any means, but you won't realize its size limitation as the trail has been expertly designed to use every ounce of terrain this otherwise flat area offers. Uphill switchbacks, sharp downhills that will have you off the back of your saddle, and just barely climbable uphills make up most of Sky Hill.

Direction arrows usefully keep you on track as you make your way around this large trail system. Leaving Sky Hill behind, you make your way to the cross-county trails proper. Better than most, these trails are still singletrack and much easier than Sky Hill with descriptive names like **Dead Man's Run** (the trail travels right behind the local cemetery), **The Meadow, The Pines,** and **Rum River Run.** As you continue away from the river, the entertainment resumes with the fruits of the volunteers' labor evident on the new **North Woods Trails,** the infamous **Bog Monster, Lumber Jack, Back Door, Aspen Maze, Back Door Maze,** and **"D" Hill.**

Next to Sky Hill, the trail's highlight, from a technical point of view, is the 2-mile loop called the Bog Monster on the north side of the trail. Take it! This loop epitomizes what Midwest-style riding can be with tight, twisty trails, log piles, rock piles, roots, and wonderful log boardwalks to get you through the worst of The Bog. An excellent section of trails, so save enough energy for this one; it truly is a blast!

DIFFICULTY: The Milaca Mountain-Bike Trails are great for all levels of riders. Just trying singletrack for the first time? Check out the cross-country ski trails near Rum River. Looking for adventure? Then do the entire loop—you won't go home feeling cheated.

  AEROBIC DIFFICULTY (1–5):
    3 (shorter loops and avoiding Sky Hill
     reduces this rating)
  TECHNICAL DIFFICULTY (1–5):
    3 (sticking to the east-side ski trails
     reduces this rating)

WARNINGS: This trail is where the bikers in the area come to ride, so be prepared to meet other riders on the trail. What are billed as waste-disposal ponds were indeed just that, so don't drink the water and don't go for a dip after the ride. However, the area has made a nice recovery back to natural wetlands with lakes, trees, and plenty of wildlife to make you feel like you're in the woods and not the dump.

OTHER TRAILS IN THE AREA: Closest to Saint Cloud itself is the **Quarry Park and Nature Preserve** at 1802 County Road 137, Waite Park, MN 56387; (320) 255-6172. About

5 miles of moderate mountain-bike trails take you around the 25 granite quarries throughout this 130-acre park. Bike Blast—the folks who brought you the Milaca Mountain-Bike Trails—have been busy with two other trail systems. In Monticello, the **YMCA Manitou Camp** has over 10 miles of singletrack, and in Elk River, the new **Hillside Park** has around 6 miles of wooded singletrack with longer climbs and descents than you'll find at Milaca. The Blast people are hard at work creating trails in this area and can always use more help. If you're interested, contact them at their web address: www.bikeblast.com.

CONTACTS: City of Milaca, 1205 Central Avenue North, Milaca, MN 56353; (320) 983-3141. The Bike Blast race-promotion group has an outstanding web site with full details on trail locations and the race schedule at www.bikeblast.com. Saint Cloud Chamber of Commerce, 30 Sixth Avenue South, Saint Cloud, MN 56301; (320) 251-2940.

MAPS: The city of Milaca recently finished printing and distributing a color map and brochure of the Milaca Mountain-Bike Trails. It's available at all area bike shops including Fitzharris Ski & Sport in Saint Cloud. In addition to these attractive little maps there are metal signs with maps at most intersections on the trail. These are very accurate and keep you on track while exploring this trail. The ponds central to the map give good geographical locators to where you are in relation to where you started.

BIKE SHOP: Fitzharris Ski & Sport, 105 Seventh Avenue South, Saint Cloud, MN 56301; (320) 251-2844. When you visit, be sure to ask for Chris Laumb because when he's not brewing beer over at O'Hara's, he's either riding his mountain bike or working here.

A singletrack of logs welcomes you to the Bog Monster.

O'Hara's Brew Pub & Restaurant

3308 Third Street North
Saint Cloud, Minnesota 56303
(320) 251-9877

THE PUB: O'Hara's has been a family-owned restaurant since 1945. Various remodels and additions over the years have included a basement game room featuring 16 pool tables, a dining and dance room, and, the best of all, in 1996 a fully operational brewery right smack dab in the middle of the sprawling restaurant.

 With drop-ceilings, wall-to-wall carpeting, and televisions in the corners, the front bar and dining area of **O'Hara's Brew Pub & Restaurant** is comfortably low key. Around the brew house is another dining room and second bar that becomes a dance club after 9:00 P.M. Don't worry. If that's not your scene, a third bar downstairs caters to the set preferring a full game room including pool tables, video games, electronic darts, foosball, more TVs, and the fermentation-tank show behind glass.

THE BREW: Find your pastime and take a seat while ordering yourself a pint of O'Hara's beer. Samples are encouraged here, so don't settle for anything less than the perfect pint to please your palette. The entire lineup is solid including the **Golden Honey Wheat**, a light American-style wheat. The **Quarry Rock Red** is a good red full of malty flavor, and the **Pantown Pale Ale** is an English rendition showing moderate hops. Named after one of the founding brothers of O'Hara's, **Sid's Irish Stout** is a smooth, lighter stout that can be enjoyed all day long.

PRICE OF A PINT: Happy hour is Monday through Friday from 4:00 to 7:00 P.M., again from 9:00 P.M. to 1:00 A.M., and yet once more on Sunday from 8:00 P.M. 'til 12:00 A.M.

During these many magical hours, pints drop a quarter to $2.50 and 23-ounce steins are only $3.00. Clearly, the beer is very reasonably priced no matter when you show.

Granite City Food & Brewery

3945 Second Street South
Saint Cloud, Minnesota 56301
(320) 203-9000

THE PUB: Saint Cloud is situated right in the middle of one of the leading granite-producing regions in the county. Appropriately named, **Granite City Food & Brewery** uses this fact, as well as its prime mall location, to draw in customers after a day of battling it out in the stores. The first in a planned line of brewpubs by the owners of the excellent Sherlock's Homes brewpub in Minnetonka (see Minneapolis), Granite City has a couple of things working for it, not the least of which is excellent beer and food. Enough of Sherlock's excellence has rubbed off on this place including serving on nitrogen as well as hand-pumped brews.

Granite City is located in a new building in Saint Cloud's inevitable urban sprawl around the mall. A modern stressed-concrete floor and exposed industrial ceiling complement the large, open, dining area with a center bar. The brewery and kitchen are separated from diners by nothing more than a glass partition.

Regardless of the obvious marketing tactics employed to attract a certain clientele, the place is a huge hit and deserves the business. The beer is top quality and the menu deserves notice. And besides, it's somehow reward-ing to see families coming here after a hard day of buying. This is a place that will put a smile on the most tired shopper or biker after a day on the front.

THE BREW: The required lighter beers are here in the form of **Victory Lager**, **Northern Light**, and the **Pride of Pilsen**. All solid. Working our way to the real goods, **Brother**

Benedic's Mai Bock is nice and dark and strong but not overwhelming. The truly excellent **Duke of Wellington IPA** (India pale ale) is served on both nitrogen and CO_2—the perfect opportunity to compare and determine your favorite serving method.

PRICE OF A PINT: Happy hour is Monday through Thursday from 3:00 to 6:00 P.M. when beers are a buck off, bringing 20-ounce pints down to $2.15 and 12-ounce glasses to just 95 cents. Now that's a deal!

Two pubs deserve two quotes:

"Give me a woman who truly loves beer, and I will conquer the world."

—The German ruler, Kaiser Wilhelm II (1859–1941), quoted on Granite City's menu.

"P.S. I am 52 years old and I love mountain biking and microbrews. I would be one of the first to buy your book."

—Randy Furman, Mayor of Milaca via e-mail to Bike & Brew America.

Winona

Located on an island in the Mississippi River, Winona is surrounded by towering bluffs that stretch along the river valley for miles in both directions. Founded by a steamboat captain named Orrin Smith in 1851, Winona quickly became a prime transportation hub for lumber, wheat, and limestone. This progress in turn created one of the world's wealthiest cities by 1900. The wealth can still be seen in the many historic homes and buildings that make up downtown Winona's Historic Commercial District, which encompasses Minnesota's largest collection of Victorian-era commercial buildings on the Mississippi River.

Even though no longer officially an island as land now attaches Winona to the mainland, the Mississippi River still plays a large part in Winona's daily life. Still a major transportation hub, it's not uncommon to see barges and riverboats making their way to Winona's docks. Also located almost right downtown is Winona State University, another major influence on Winona's personality.

The area around Winona and Red Wing, Minnesota, and La Crosse, Wisconsin, is now rich in other ways as well—brewpubs and mountain-bike trails. And although none of the trails is long enough to keep you occupied all day, they are close enough to each other that you will just have enough time to catch your breath between rides. The brewpubs in Winona and neighboring La Crosse are both rough and unrefined, not what you have come to expect from most brewpubs today. However, the beer is good, their locations impeccable, and if you're in the mood to play, these are both good places for sipping on a fresh pint of ale.

Winona

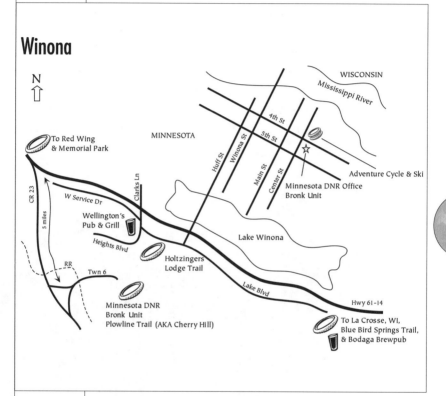

N ⇧

WISCONSIN

Mississippi River

MINNESOTA

4th St

5th St

Winona St

Huff St

Main St

Center St

To Red Wing
& Memorial Park

Adventure Cycle & Ski

Minnesota DNR Office
Bronk Unit

CR 23

5 miles

W Service Dr

Clarks Ln

Wellington's
Pub & Grill

Heights Blvd

Lake Winona

Holtzingers
Lodge Trail

RR

Twn 6

Lake Blvd

Hwy 61-14

Minnesota DNR
Bronk Unit
Plowline Trail (AKA Cherry Hill)

To La Crosse, WI,
Blue Bird Springs Trail,
& Bodaga Brewpub

Holtzingers Lodge Trail

THE SCOOP: Singletrack takes you up 400 feet to the bluffs overlooking the town of Winona and the Mississippi River Valley.

RIDE LENGTH AND TYPE: A 10-mile loop from Backwater Brewing Company's parking lot.

THE BIKE: Although there are not a lot of miles in any one ride in this area, the sheer quantity of good rides put it on

The Mississippi River Valley and all it contains are visible from the bluffs atop Holzingers Lodge Trail.

the Bike & Brew America TO DO list. The most popular
and favorite is known as **Holtzingers Lodge Trail** and just
so happens to be inside Winona's city limits and within 1
mile of the only brewpub in town.

Location aside, this is still a great place to ride. Park in
the shopping mall housing **Backwater Brewing Company**
(in Wellington's Pub & Grill) and ride southeast to the
trailhead via **Lake Boulevard**—just under 1 mile of perfect
warm up.

Once at the lodge and trailhead, you are greeted with a
multiuse trail that begins as an old fire road with directional arrows. These lower roads are known as the **Low
Rollers** and for good reason. They stay to the lower
reaches of the bluffs and undulate with short steep climbs
and plenty of loose rock to keep the doubletrack interesting and challenging. After 2 miles of mostly uphill travel
you will come to a large stone cistern on your right and a
wooden sign proclaiming you have arrived at the
Wildwood Hill Climb. Take this singletrack and begin a
meandering, well-laid-out climb that will take you to the
top of the bluff overlooking Lake Winona and the rest of
the Mississippi River Valley.

Once on top you will enjoy a nice circuit of the hill via a
very entertaining and mildly challenging section of tight
singletrack. By staying to the right at all intersections
except when the trail obviously goes straight downhill,
you will cruise the entire bluff while crossing multiple
bridges, log piles, and other landmarks with names like
Tom's Terrific (a bridge and sharp turn), the **Gall Stones**
(big stones), **Slippery Bastards** (small stones), and the
Four Corners (top of your climb up Wildwood). You
will be rewarded with two nice lookout points offering
incredible bird's-eye views of Winona and the rest of the
valley, including, interestingly enough, the brewpub where
you parked.

After making your way around the upper loop, you will
once again find yourself at Four Corners. Go around the
top again to add a few more miles or take the rightmost
trail and prepare yourself for the real goods. You will be

greeted by a single expert black-diamond sign, just enough so you will know you are now on the **Quarry Trail.** The next 1½ miles has all the tightness, exposure, and off-camber rocked-out trail you could ask for. Enjoy this masterpiece down to where it meets with the Low Rollers trail and a scream of a roller-coaster finish back to the trailhead and waiting brewpub beyond.

DIFFICULTY: Intermediate. The Low Rollers will take some skill, and the total climb is more than 400 feet to the top of the bluffs so a little conditioning is called for. The Quarry Trail is the only truly advanced part of the ride, but you can get around that by carefully going back down Wildwood, making sure to watch for uphill cyclists.

AEROBIC DIFFICULTY (1–5):

3

TECHNICAL DIFFICULTY (1–5):

3

WARNINGS: Signs at the trailhead warn that these trails will be closed to mountain bikers if they are ridden when wet. Respect these warnings, and don't ruin it for the folks in Winona. Also, the Hotzingers Lodge Trail is right above a cemetery. Once again, signs warn bikers not to exit the park via the cemetery or the trail will be closed to off-road bikes. Respect these wishes and turn around if you come to these signs. This is a popular multiuse trail, so be on the lookout for other bikers and hikers and mind the direction arrows when you can.

OTHER TRAILS IN THE AREA: If you really want to make a big day of it, then the other must-do ride in Winona is **Cherry Hill.** Also known as the **Minnesota DNR (Department of Natural Resources) Bronk Unit-Plowline Trail,** it is located just north of Winona on the same ridge of bluffs along the Mississippi River Valley as Holtzingers Lodge. Expect about 8 miles of novice trails up and along the bluffs with another 3 or 4 miles of advanced single-track recently cut in to spice things up a bit. Also a favorite race site for the area, check this trail out at www.cherrybombrace.com.

If you are headed in the La Crosse direction, then **Blue**

Bird Springs is the trail of choice and contains about 7 miles of fire-road climbing and singletrack descents. Built by the La Crosse Velo Club on a private campground, there is a $2.00 fee for use of the trails here. Check out Smith's Cycling & Fitness in La Crosse for the full scoop on this place. And finally, if you are headed in the Red Wing direction, **Memorial Park** is the ride. There you have it. Along the Mississippi River the towns of Red Wing, Winona, and La Crosse have no less than four stellar rides. Enjoy this little lineup of mountain-bike heaven.

CONTACTS: Winona Park Maintenance, 674 Franklin Street, Winona, MN 55987; (507) 457-8205. Minnesota DNR Bronk Unit, 51 East Fourth Street, Suite 411, Winona, MN 55987; (507) 453-2950. Winona Chamber of Commerce, 67 Main Street, Winona, MN 55987; (507) 452-2272.

MAPS: There is a map kiosk at the trailhead, but the best way to get the lowdown on the trail is by stopping by at Adventure Cycle & Ski, which also has a wall map of the trail and plenty of expert advice on how best to ride the area.

BIKE SHOP: Adventure Cycle & Ski, 178 Center Street, Winona, MN 55987; (507) 452-4228; www.advcycle.com. This shop has the pulse of mountain biking in the Winona area, and a stop here is essential if you're new to the area. For the scoop in La Crosse, visit Smith's Cycling & Fitness at 520 South Eighth Street, La Crosse, WI 54601; (608) 784-1175.

Backwater Brewing Company in Wellington's Pub & Grill

Westgate Shopping Center, Highway 14-61
1429 West Service Drive
Winona, Minnesota 55987
(507) 452-2103

THE PUB: This is not your typical Bike & Brew America stopover, and that is exactly why **Backwater Brewing Company in Wellington's Pub & Grill** is so much fun. As it's just 1 mile from the trail, park in the shopping mall's large parking lot, and warm up on Lake Boulevard or the paved bike trail, both of which parallel Highway 14-61 to the Holtzingers Lodge Trailhead. After your ride, come on inside and enjoy some fresh microbrewed beer while bowling a game, shooting some pool, or just kicking back and watching sports while eating a burger.

The long wooden bar down most of one side has windows behind, not offering the traditional views of the brew house you've come to expect, but instead overlooking a 16-lane bowling alley. Saddle up to the bar and watch the pins drop, or order one of Backwater's finest and bowl a few frames yourself. This is definitely a place to come and have some fun. If bowling is not your style, then you'll also find a pool table, foosball, pinball machine, and video games right next to the small brew house. Televisions are everywhere, and you can bet the Vikings will be on the big screen come Sunday afternoon.

Otherwise this place is pretty much what you would expect from a bar inside a bowling alley. Dark interior, TVs, booths, neon beer signs, linoleum tile floor, and a drop ceiling. However, just don't forget about that one big exception—a one-barrel (31-gallon) brewing system behind glass at the far end of the bar.

THE BREW: Backwater has been brewing out of a one-barrel brewing system since 1995, and this brewpub once again proves it's not the quantity but the quality that matters. Although Backwater does experiment around a bit, you will usually find the **Wing Dam Wheat**—an unfiltered American-style wheat—the **Cat Tail Pale Ale**, the **Steamboat Stout**, and the **Rivertown Nut Brown Ale**. Although the Wing Dam Wheat is the best seller here (you are in a bowling alley, after all), the Rivertown Nut Brown is the best. Regardless, all the beers are good, unfiltered, and fresh, and all ring true as far as style goes. Pick the flavor that suits your mood—you won't be disappointed.

PRICE OF A PINT: Happy hour is from 4:30 to 6:30 P.M., and pints drop from $2.75 to $2.00. Interested in bowling? Then it's $2.25 a game and a buck to rent shoes. Just remember you can only get the good beer in the brewery, but the folks there let you bring it with you into the alley.

OTHER BREWS IN THE AREA: The next-nearest fresh beer is 30 miles southeast in La Crosse, Wisconsin. This area is worth the trip for the riding, so plan on stopping at **Bodaga's Brew Pub** at 122 South Fourth Street, (608) 782-0677, for one of the truly excellent **Bodaga India Pale Ales**. Right in downtown La Crosse, it may remind some of the perfect overgrown college dorm room with worn-out couches and tables, video games, electronic darts, and lots of beer. In addition to four house brands and guest taps, Bodaga's stocks more than 400 bottles from around the world. These are kept in a large brass refrigerated lazy susan behind the bar. Right on the busiest intersection in town, the large bank of windows fronting the bar offers excellent views of the busy streets. However, don't plan on eating here; this is a bar in every sense of the word and does not serve food although plans are in the works to add a kitchen.

"If you took one cool section from every trail you've ridden and put it together, you would have Holtzingers."

—Someone named "Borgpet" sums up Holtzinger's Lodge perfectly over the internet.

191

CHAPTER SEVEN

MISSOURI

Bordered on the east by the Mississippi River and bisected by the Missouri River, Missouri has always played a key role in westward expansion. Known as the "Gateway to the West," that sentiment has never been more prominent than it is to the Bike & Brew America traveler heading west to find some dirt. However, just as you shouldn't leave the Midwest out of your mountain-bike vacation plans, DO NOT leave Missouri out of your Midwest plans.

Missouri

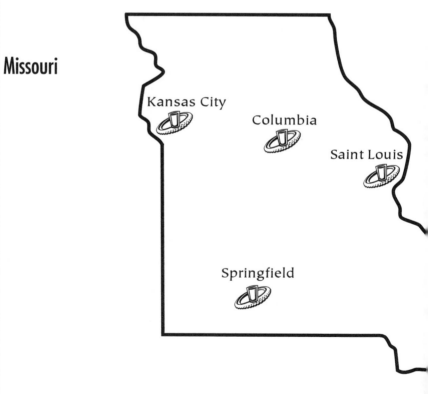

Just south of the Missouri River where the northern and western plains end and the Ozark Mountains begin, things start to get interesting for the Bike & Brew traveler. Although the Ozarks are not tall when compared to the Appalachians or Rocky Mountains, topping out at about 1700 feet above sea level, they more than make up for their lack of stature with sheer ruggedness.

The Ozarks rise 400 to 800 feet above the surrounding lowlands and are cut though by a maze of streams and rivers. The accompanying erosion means a steep and jagged labyrinth of limestone ridges and densely vegetated valleys. Covered in a dense mass of second-growth forest, riding in the Ozarks is about as remote as you can find anywhere in the Midwest.

As you've now guessed, residents of Missouri have a very well kept secret here in the middle of the Show Me State. Even though the Ozarks are vertically challenged, they offer rugged terrain and miles of trails, and the college towns of Columbia and Springfield along with the major metropolises of Saint Louis and Kansas City supply the fresh brews. So the next time you're visiting, or just passing through, grab a local wearing spandex and ask 'em to "Show Me the trails!"

By the way, are you wondering where Missouri got its curious nickname? It's from an 1899 speech from Congressman Willard D. Vandiver where he said a bunch of stuff about not trusting "frothy eloquence" and that if you wanted something from him and his state "You've got to show me." Hmmm, frothy eloquence? That could be brewpub talk, for sure.

Columbia

As you pass through Columbia's downtown business district, you will be struck with the juxtaposed image of a classic late-nineteenth-century main street and a bad *Jetsons* episode. According to local lore, when Columbia was struggling to boost its downtown economy back in the 1970s, it decided to offer covered sidewalks to create an outdoor mall atmosphere and keep rain and sun off the shopping pedestrians. In response to this decision, several huge, poured-concrete arches were built in front of the original brick storefronts. With this one stroke of 1970s genius, the citizens of Columbia were protected from the elements and from the architectural elegance that today can only peek around these ungainly covered structures.

Not to worry, it worked! The entire Columbia downtown is now filled with cafés, restaurants, shops, and people just milling about. Home of the University of Missouri, Columbia is a thriving college town with all the amenities that goes with it, including an outdoor-minded population. Columbia features over 40 city parks plus access to the popular Katy Trail State Park, the longest rails-to-trails conversion in the country, stretching for almost 200 gloriously unmotorized miles across the state.

So as you're traveling from Saint Louis to Kansas City, stop in, go for a ride, and stay for a beer. You'll be impressed with what mid-Missouri has to offer the mountain biker and brew drinker in all of us.

Columbia

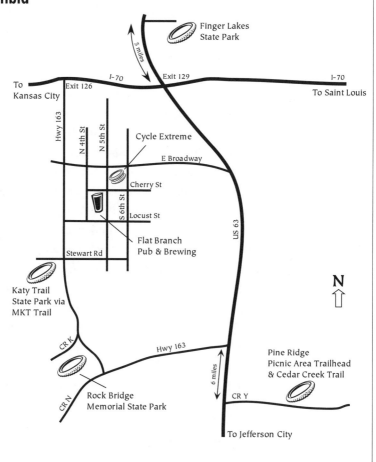

Finger Lakes State Park

I-70

To Kansas City

To Saint Louis

Exit 126

Exit 129

5 miles

Hwy 163

N 4th St

N 5th St

Cycle Extreme

E Broadway

Cherry St

S 6th St

Locust St

Flat Branch Pub & Brewing

Stewart Rd

US 63

Katy Trail State Park via MKT Trail

CR K

Hwy 163

CR N

Rock Bridge Memorial State Park

6 miles

CR Y

Pine Ridge Picnic Area Trailhead & Cedar Creek Trail

To Jefferson City

N

Cedar Creek Ranger District

THE SCOOP: Singletrack switchbacks through pines, pastures, hills, and one huge creek!

RIDE LENGTH AND TYPE: 18-mile out-and-back singletrack or 21.2-mile singletrack and dirt-road loop.

THE BIKE: A short drive southeast of Columbia puts you in the **Cedar Creek Ranger District** of the Mark Twain National Forest without much of a fuss. Here, as the Ozarks begin to raise their limestone heads above the surrounding countryside, mountain bikers and horseback riders make the short drive from Columbia to ride their respective steeds in undisturbed bliss.

The trail can be ridden as an 18-mile out-and-back adventure starting at the **Pine Ridge Picnic Area Trailhead** and turning around at the Cedar Creek crossing or as a 21.2-mile counterclockwise loop known as the **Cedar Creek Trail.** The out-and-back will keep you on singletrack 99% of the time whereas the loop contains about 7 miles of dirt roads. If hours in the saddle are what you're after, there are also two northern loops known as **The Moon** and **Smith Creek**, which will add another 12 miles to your total.

The out-and-back will keep you on the skinny and leave your feet mostly dry with a taste of singletrack in your mouth. However, the true treasures are for those who dare to hoist their bikes over their shoulders and venture across mighty Cedar Creek. This action is not to be considered lightly. Let's just say, come spring, the "Creek" part of "Cedar Creek" is a rather loose term indeed.

Once across the Mighty Cedar, limestone cliffs, small waterfalls, and more singletrack bliss awaits. The north side of the Cedar Creek Trail is also where The Moon and

Smith Creek Loops intersect. Generally speaking, the northwest loop (The Moon) will give you another 7 miles of cow pastures and seldom-traveled gravel roads, and the northeast loop (Smith Creek) will supply 5 miles of technical riding that may leave you hike-a-biking more than once.

DIFFICULTY: Intermediate to advanced. With the exception of the descent into the Cedar Creek valley, there is nothing here to cause any premature aging. However, if you happen to desire the attainment of a more distinguished look, take the Smith Creek Loop as far as you can.

AEROBIC DIFFICULTY (1–5):

4

TECHNICAL DIFFICULTY (1–5):

3 (4 if you take the Smith Creek Loop)

WARNINGS: If you decide to cross Cedar Creek, the trail becomes difficult to follow around the **Devil's Backbone** area as it intersects multiple gravel roads and passes through empty cow pastures. Be sure to bring a compass and pick up a map at the trailhead before venturing forth. A good map of the county roads will also prove useful if you're planning on doing all the loops.

OTHER TRAILS IN THE AREA: Located even closer to Columbia is **Rock Bridge Memorial State Park**. A very popular place to hike, bike, and run the trails, it's a great example of peaceful user coexistence in an urban park. There are multiple small loops that can be combined for over 13 miles of trail. Grab your date and ride the **Devil's Icebox Trail**. Find the cave and have a picnic. The folks here are very particular about not mountain biking on the trails when they're wet, so if there is any question in your mind about trail conditions, call ahead at (573) 442-2249.

About 5 miles north of Columbia is **Finger Lakes State Park** and over 70 miles of motorcycle and all-terrain vehicle trails waiting to be explored. Be warned: these are primarily motorized trails, so you'll be looking at steep, fast, and straight downhills followed by steep and straight uphills. And, although not a singletrack ride by any stretch of the imagination, the **Katy Trail State Park** travels

"National Forest Land: Welcome"

—Sign posted along Cedar Creek Ranger District National Forest boundaries. A welcome sight indeed.

197

MISSOURI

Singletrack lures you into the Cedar Creek Trail system.
(Courtesy of Cedar Creek Ranger District)

almost 200 miles most of the way across the state and can be accessed in downtown Columbia via the **MKT Trail**. Contact the Missouri Department of Natural Resources for more information, P.O. Box 176, Jefferson City, MO 65102; (800) 334-6946.

CONTACTS: Cedar Creek Ranger District, U.S. Department of Agriculture Service Center, 4549 State Road H, Fulton, MO 65251; (573) 592-1400. Columbia Chamber of Commerce, 300 South Providence Road, Columbia, MO 65203; (573) 874-1132.

MAPS: Maps of both Cedar Creek Ranger District and Rock Bridge Memorial State Park are available at the trailheads.

BIKE SHOP: Cycle Extreme, 19 South Sixth Street, Columbia, MO 65201; (573) 874-7044; www.cyclex.com. Located right around the corner from the Flat Branch Brewing Company so that you can drop your rig off to get lubed (after attempting to ride through Cedar Creek); then while you're waiting, you can walk a block over to Fifth Street for a pint of Oil Change Stout at Flat Branch. Not only do the Cycle Extremers give great customer service to out-of-towners, the bike-shop building has the same hanger-shaped roof as the brewpub. How fitting is that?

Flat Branch Pub & Brewing

115 South Fifth Street
Columbia, Missouri 65201
(573) 499-0400
www.flatbranch.com

THE PUB: Located a mere block off Broadway, Columbia's main street, **Flat Branch Pub & Brewing** overlooks the creek of the same name in a beautifully restored industrial warehouse. With a vaulted, hanger-like wooden ceiling, brick walls, and brew house located right between the spacious bar and dining area, Flat Branch more than makes up for the city elders' architectural indiscretions. In fact, sitting on its patio on a summer afternoon sipping a $2.00 happy-hour pint, one can forgive almost anything. Food at the Branch is also worth a second look. Not only is it tasty, but fair pricing and good quantities make this a perfect stop after a hard day in the woods.

THE BREW: The first thing that tells you this is not just another stop at some nameless pub is the beer list. Carrying an impressive array of no less than 11 house beers at any given time, sheer magnitude cries out for a sampler. However, if you don't want to fry your taste buds shopping around, take some advice and get an Oil Change. **Oil Change Stout,** that is. Smooth and creamy, just like stout is meant to be, this nitro-poured dandy will have you lubed up in no time. If you happen by on a Wednesday night, you might get lucky and hit Vintage Night. Once a week Flat Branch rolls out a barrel of one of its past "heavies"—that is, a barleywine, imperial stout, or doppplebock—from a bygone year. Expect to pay top dollar for the privilege, but a properly aged microbrew is a glorious thing indeed. Not Wednesday and stouts aren't your

A view of Cedar Creek from the Rutherford Bridge.
(Courtesy of Cedar Creek Ranger District)

thing? Then you'll have your pick of some 30 or so recipes including the **Katy Trail Pale Ale**, named after those aforementioned 200 glorious biking miles across Missouri. Others you're likely to encounter are the **Flat Branch India Pale Ale, Hudson's ESB** (extra special bitter), **Flat Branch Brown, Honey Wheat, Scottish Ale,** and the **Flat Branch Green Chili Beer** and **Amber Chili Ale**. Not quite so common are multiple Belgian and German ales too numerous to name in addition to another eight seasonals! Overwhelmed with choices? Then make plans to spend a couple of days in Columbia!

PRICE OF A PINT: You're facing the typical $3.50 a pint unless you make it here between 4:00 and 6:00 P.M. or after 10:00 P.M. That's when prices drop to a meager $2.00 and a feeling that all is good in the world is felt by all.

OTHER BREWS IN THE AREA: No other breweries in Columbia, but the **Old Chicago** pizza chain has a restaurant at 1710 I-70 Drive Southwest, (573) 445-0220, that keeps over 30 beers on tap including many regional selections.

Kansas City

"No mountain. No beach. No problem." With that kind of attitude, it's no wonder Kansas City gets a big old phatty from Bike & Brew America. Known as the "City of Fountains," this mid-American city has more fountains than any other city in the world except Rome. Now that's keeping with some pretty respectable company.

As Missouri's largest city, Kansas City has a remarkable skyline featuring several Art Deco–style buildings alongside modern office buildings. Most dramatic of these is the Kansas City Convention Center, unmistakable because of

Kansas City

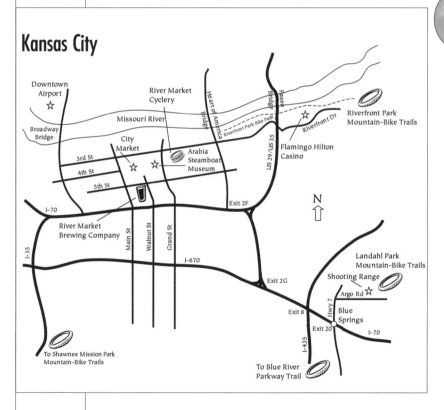

its four 230-foot-tall towers capped with illuminated art deco sculptures, which, at night, can be seen up to 2 miles away. The towers themselves are used to hold up the immense convention center building with a network of suspension cables. The architectural arrangement serves to support 400,000 square feet of column-free space and creates one of the world's largest suspension buildings.

Kansas City is also home to all the cultural and entertainment amenities offered by big cities including the Nelson-Atkins Museum of Art and Kemper Museum of Contemporary Art and Design. Opened in 1999 in the restored Union Station is the Science City at Union Station, a combination of museum, science center, theme park, and theater.

The famous Eighteenth & Vine Historic District is the home of the American Jazz Museum and produced jazz great Charlie "Bird" Parker. Still a jazz and blues hot spot, many jazz and blues clubs can be found throughout the city.

Many areas of town are particularly noteworthy; four of the finest are Westport, Restaurant Row, Country Club Plaza, and the River Market. Historic Westport is a great place to stroll among specialty shops, small eateries, and bars. Thirty-Ninth Street is known as "Restaurant Row" and is the place to go for a full dining experience. Most popular is the Moorish architecture of the upscale shopping and entertainment square known as the Country Club Plaza, which is modeled after Kansas City's sister city of Seville, Spain. And no trip to Kansas City would be complete without visiting the downtown River Market warehouse district, under renovation, for the City Market and for the brewery.

Location, location, location. Conveniently located on Interstate 70 means just about anyone traveling across country will eventually come through here. Don't just point at the big buildings and say, "I didn't know Kansas City was this big!" Stop, go for a ride, and be sure to stay and smell some hops at the local brewery.

Landahl Park Mountain-Bike Trails

THE SCOOP: Smooth, fast singletrack mixed with technical, rocky climbs and descents.

RIDE LENGTH AND TYPE: 10–12-mile loop with many variations possible.

THE BIKE: The **Landahl Park Mountain-Bike Trails** are meticulously maintained by a group of volunteers calling themselves Trail Watchers in cooperation with the Jackson County Parks and Recreation Department. Even in the summer when the Midwest humidity breeds overgrowth, the Trail Watchers keep the place pruned and groomed and the poison ivy to a minimum. Although the trails are only 20 minutes east of Kansas City, they have not become tired and worn out like many urban trails. The active volunteers are one reason and the technical

A racer tackles a tight spot on Dave's Maze at Landahl Park Mountain-Bike Trails.
(Photo by Rob Stitt)

difficulty, which keeps use down to a manageable level, another.

As you are driving to the trailhead on Argo Road, you will get a small teaser of the terrain to come with some amazing hills and valleys that with a little speed feel just like a roller coaster. Once at the trailhead, follow the doubletrack north from the parking lot to the map kiosk. Here the trail splits. To the east lies the beginning of what is known as **Dave's Maze**, and to the west lies the **Turkey Trail.**

Dave's Maze is mostly smooth, fast, and exhilarating but with some log jumps and a few rocky technical sections that will leave the inattentive biker lying next to the rig wondering what just happened. It's not called Dave's Maze for nothing, so expect at least a 2-hour ride exploring the trails out here.

Though Dave's can be tricky, the most notable cause for voluntary and involuntary dismounts at Landahl is known as the **Turkey Trail**. In a *Blair Witch Project* fashion, carefully arranged animal bones welcome riders to their imminent doom on this wickedly designed trail that utilizes every conceivable feature including roots, rocks, trees, ditches, holes, riverbanks, and even a car hood. The Turkey Trail is truly the cherry in the banana split that is Landahl Park.

DIFFICULTY: Intermediate to advanced. Because of the great deal of loose rocks mixed with slickrock shelves, intermediate bikers will have fun but may get in over their heads every once in a while. It's not at all uncommon for a smooth piece of singletrack to suddenly become a steep rock-strewn climb or descent. And then there's the Turkey Trail. Although an interesting test for advanced riders, it is a bit much for the less experienced.

AEROBIC DIFFICULTY (1–5):

3

TECHNICAL DIFFICULTY (1–5):

3 (4 on Turkey Trail)

WARNINGS: This area of the Midwest is known for its poison ivy, and Landahl is no exception, so bring your

"If you make it through the Turkey Trail your first time without putting your foot down, or falling off, you're a mountain-bike god!"
—Craig, one of the builders of Turkey Trail, astutely remarks while giving directions to the infamous trail.

rubbing alcohol and use it after every ride. In addition, Landahl has a unique feature that should be mentioned. The southwest corner of the park is a shooting range. So though the gunfire can be used as an excellent directional aide, when you see a sign warning to STAY OUT SHOOTING RANGE be sure to do just that and STAY OUT! And, if two warnings were not enough, this trail stays wet an amazing amount of time after rains, so be warned: if it's wet, stay off. This careful approach not only protects the trail but your bike as well. The dirt is like Ready-Mix cement, and water will cause it to quickly become a permanent part of your bike's drivetrain.

OTHER TRAILS IN THE AREA: Finished up Landahl and still feel like a couple of miles? Not up for Landahl but still want to go for a ride before settling down in front of a pint? Well the River Market has just the thing. An easy bike ride from the River Market is the **Riverfront Trails**—about 3 miles of wooded singletrack following the Missouri River. Just stop by the River Market Cyclery and ask anyone there for directions. Want more than 3 miles? Then **Shawnee Mission Park** has what you need and is easy to find. About 5–7 miles of moderately technical singletrack await on this popular trail system just over the border in Lenexa, Kansas. The **Blue River Parkway Trail** (also known as **Minor Park**) is a local favorite and offers more than 10 miles of easy to moderate, twisty and turning trails in south Kansas City. It's difficult to find all the trails out here, so be sure and talk to some locals in the know before hitting the trails to get the most bang for your buck on this one.

CONTACTS: Jackson County Parks and Recreation, 22807 East Chapel Road, Blue Springs, MO 64015; (816) 795-8200. Kansas City Chamber of Commerce, 911 Main Street, Suite 2600, Kansas City, MO 64105; (816) 221-2424. A great source of biking information in the Kansas City area for maps, group rides, advocacy, racing, trails, and after-ride trips to the brewpub is the Earth Riders Mountain Bike Club. The best way to get a hold of these riders of the earth is via www.earthriders.org.

MAPS: There is a map kiosk at Landahl's Trailhead outlining most of the trails at Landahl. However, if you'd like to have a map before you show up, check out Earth Riders' excellent web site at www.earthriders.org/Trails/Missouri/LandahlMap.jpg for a copy.

BIKE SHOP: River Market Cyclery, 315 East Third Street, Kansas City, MO 64106; (816) 842-BIKE. Just two blocks northeast of the brewery, this fun little shop will supply you with all you need to get back on the trails and any last-minute info you may need to find the trails. The owner, Jay Williams, built much of the Riverfront Trails, so if you're interested in trying out a moderate ride along the mighty Missouri stop in and ask for directions. Later in the day you can raise a pint in his honor!

River Market Brewing Company

500 Walnut Street
Kansas City, Missouri 64106
(816) 471-6300
www.rivermarketbrews.com

THE PUB: Located in the regenerated factory and warehouse district just north of Kansas City's business area is the historic River Market. Centered around the popular City Market, this area is now considered hot real estate and is filling up each year with more and more restaurants and bars. The **River Market Brewing Company** is considered one of the area's urban pioneers and has been located in the old Opera House since the market area's rebirth began back in 1994. This fairly upscale brewpub features a friendly, long wooden bar where the regulars can be found drinking from personalized ceramic mugs. It's perfect for quiet conversation.

THE BREW: Located mere blocks from Kansas City's downtown office buildings, River Market caters to the lunch crowd and after-work nine-to-fivers. For this reason, head-brewer Brian Reinecke strives for consistent, if not terribly risky, beer recipes when it comes to the brewpub's four staple beers. The staff members considers it their job to convert as many domestic drinkers to the finer things in life, namely drinking fresh beer. Correspondingly, their lightest beer—the **Bomber's Blond**—is an easy step up from Bud or Miller. From there, the **River Market Red** is an easy session drinker—light on the hops with a nice malt emphasis. A little more hop heavy is the English-style **River Market Pale Ale**. Chances are you've already been converted, so go straight to the **River Market Porter,** and you should be happy for the evening.

River Market's real secrets lie in its ever-changing monthly offerings of specialty beers that are continually worked into the lineup. The **Spanish Fly Rye, Der Leifserfallen Bock, Blue Oyster Alt, Eighty Shilling Scottish Ale,** and the award-winning **Eight Ball Cream Stout** are just a few making the rotation. A word of caution here. Brian's favorite style of beer is Belgian so when he has the **Saint Arnold's Trappist-Style Tipel** on tap, watch out! Be sure to take advantage of it, but be careful. It's 12% alcohol, and it shows! However, it is an excellent brew so be sure and have a sample even if a full pint sounds like a bit much.

PRICE OF A PINT: Happy hour is Monday through Thursday between 4:30 and 6:30 P.M. and knocks a buck off the $3.25 cost of a pint. Happen to be driving through? The best deal in town is their 64-ounce growler of beer to go. Two bucks gets you the half-gallon brown-glass jug (perfect for keeping beer dark and happy) and eight more dollars fills it up. Since growlers are a must on any Bike & Brew vacation, may as well get a brown one that will keep the beer fresh longer—plus, even with the growler's cost, that's only $2.50 a pint.

OTHER BREWS IN THE AREA: Deep in the restaurant and entertainment district of Westport is the **McCoy's Public House and Brewkitchen** at 4057 Pennsylvania Avenue, Kansas City, MO 64111, (816) 960-0866. Westport is a great area to go carousing, so after checking out the oldest bar in Kansas City (O'Kelly's Irish Pub right across the street from McCoy's), you may as well stop in for a fresh beer. Sort of out in the 'burbs is Kansas City's first brewpub, the always-excellent 75th **Street Brewery**, 520 West Seventy-Fifth Street, Kansas City, MO 64114; (816) 523-4677.

Saint Louis

Even before Lewis and Clark set out from Saint Louis in 1804 on their historic journey to explore the West, the city has been an important port on the Mississippi and Missouri Rivers. Today this history can still be discovered along the cobblestone streets of Laclede's Landing. Now a nine-block entertainment district of restored red-brick warehouses along the Mississippi River, Laclede's was once filled with cotton, tobacco, and other steamboat cargo on its way west to the developing nation.

Synonymous with Saint Louis is the image of the Gateway Arch. The real thing, completed in 1965, towers 630 feet above the Mississippi River near Laclede's Landing. The arch is spectacular from its base by the Great River if you happen by on a moonlit night. Or, you can still take an interior elevator car up to the top of this magnificent structure for views of the surrounding cityscape.

Maybe the only thing more synonymous with Saint Louis than the Gateway Arch is beer. Ever since Adolphus Busch and Eberhard Anheuser immigrated here in the nineteenth century, Saint Louis has been on the map as a beer town. This otherwise glorious stature comes with the dubious honor of being home to the largest brewery in the world—The Anheuser Busch Companies—and one of the reasons America fell into the Dark Ages of the pasteurized American Pilsener for the past 30 years. It's under this beer Goliath's shadow that microbrewing has not only revived itself but has thrived even in the face of an adversary as large as Anheuser-Busch. The town of Saint Louis was ready for a change, and the microbrew revolution of the past 20 years has delivered.

The metropolitan area is also a remarkable bike destination. For a "nooner," you have great riding right in the metro area. With just a little more time and effort, the Mark Twain National Forest offers the best ride in Missouri, if not the entire Midwest. It's remote, challenging, technical (without being destructive), and incredibly scenic. And, if the extra time spent driving back to Saint Louis only wets your appetite even more for some fresh local beer, all the better.

Saint Louis

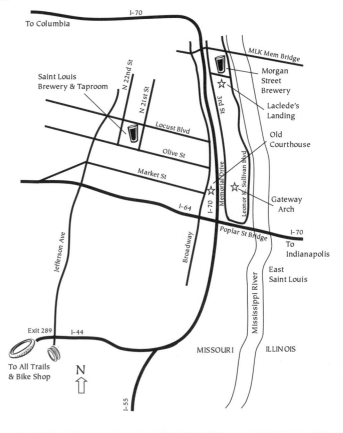

Berryman Trail

THE SCOOP: If you're not riding singletrack, you're not riding Berryman Trail!

RIDE LENGTH AND TYPE: 25-mile singletrack loop.

THE BIKE: Okay, you're gonna have to break a few Bike & Brew ground rules with this one but you won't regret it. About 80 miles southwest of Saint Louis (breaking the 30-minute rule by more than a bit), **Berryman Trail** is worth every single mile (and minute) of the trip. Written up by those glossy bike-magazine types as "the best singletrack between the Smokies and the Rockies," Bike & Brew would be doing you, the B&B readership, a disservice if this trail was not included here.

Located deep in national forest land, the Berryman is 100% USDA Grade A Singletrack! Fairly low usage, well-marked and well-maintained—and not a two-track, road, or rubber mat to worry about the entire way. It was mostly created by the Civilian Conservation Corps during the 1930s, and modern-day trail makers could stand to learn a thing or two from those old timers.

Leaving clockwise from the **Brazil Creek Trailhead**, you're immediately engulfed in singletrack switchbacking paradise. Never does the trail take you straight up or down a hill. It meanders along the contour lines gracefully and seductively, pulling you into the midst of over 25 gloriously executed singletrack miles.

Lush pine forests cover the tops of the ridges; hardwoods accompany you as you sink into valleys. The partial gravel and sometimes rocky trail is actually carved right into the hillsides forcing the trail to remain singletrack over the years of constant use. It also provides great drainage in a state whose trails are otherwise renowned

"The Berryman Trail is like George Foreman. It doesn't knock you out with a single punch, it just keeps jabbing you, round after round, mile after mile. By the time it's over, you don't even know what hit you. That is, if you're even standing at all."

—Nicholas Ranson, local Renaissance man: doctor, mountain biker, triathlete, and homebrewer extraordinaire.

MISSOURI

for slow drying times. Never does Berryman throw anything too technical at you, but at no time does it let up either. Always flowing, always giving more, it challenges you to push one more higher gear, to give a little more effort, promising—and delivering—a little more fat-tire euphoria.

Saint Louis Trails

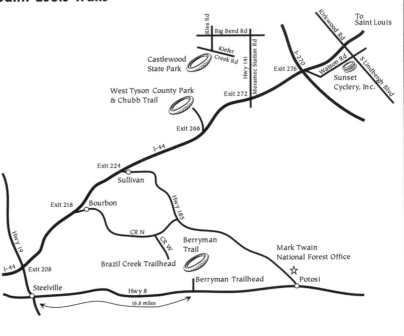

DIFFICULTY: Intermediate to advanced. No one section is more than an intermediate rider or even an ambitious beginner can handle. The problem is this baby is a loop with no real bailout options, so when you pile up all 25 miles, things start becoming advanced. Be prepared for a very long day in the saddle if you aren't used to more than a couple of hours of physical activity.

AEROBIC DIFFICULTY (1–5):

4

TECHNICAL DIFFICULTY (1–5):

3

WARNINGS: Be prepared mentally and physically for a ride of more than 3 hours. Even though it's only 25 miles, Berryman just doesn't back down, and even if you bail out on one of the local roads, you still have some major pedaling to do to get back to your car.

OTHER TRAILS IN THE AREA: You don't have to go all the way to Berryman to find fantastic riding in the Saint Louis area. Located a mere 25 miles south of downtown are two great parks with miles of mountain-bike trails waiting to be explored. Taking Interstate 44 west to exit 266 lands you at West Tyson County Park and the **Chubb Trail**. From the **Chubb Trailhead**, the first 3½-mile stretch is hilly, rocky, technical singletrack that will leave you begging for more or just plain begging. After those first few miles, things mellow considerably down to the Meramec River bottoms for another 3½ miles of easy river-levee riding before you must turn around and head back the way you came for a 14-mile out-and-back total.

Even closer to town is **Castlewood State Park** again off Interstate 44 at exit 272, which is actually directly across the Meramec River from the Chubb Trail. Castlewood has terrain similar to Chubb's only less technical and with a more "park-like" atmosphere because you continually circle back to the main parking areas and cross multiple roads while riding the abundance of trail loops. However, given the proximity to Saint Louis and over 10 miles of trails, a little "park-like" atmosphere is a small price to pay for this much great riding.

Quinn Kirkpatrick cleans the sheer limestone steps of the Chubb Trail.
(Courtesy of Quinn Kirkpatrick)

CONTACTS: Mark Twain National Forest, Potosi-Fredericktown District, P.O. Box 188, Potosi, MO 63664; (573) 438-5427. Chubb Trail, Saint Louis County Parks, 41 South Central, Clayton, MO 63105; (314) 889-2863. Castlewood State Park, 1401 Kiefer Creek Road, Ballwin, MO 63021; (636) 527-6481. Saint Louis Chamber of Commerce, 211 North Broadway, Saint Louis, MO 63102; (314) 444-1150.

MAPS: Either give the above contacts a call to get an official trail map or check out the Granada Cyclery & Fitness web site at www.granadacyclery.com for maps and directions to all three of the trails mentioned here. This shop is a little out of Bike & Brew America's path; still it's an excellent shop in Saint Charles, Missouri.

BIKE SHOP: Sunset Cyclery Inc., 10746 Sunset Hills Plaza, Saint Louis, MO 63127; (314) 966-5505. This shop is right off Interstate 44 barely 5 miles east of the Castlewood State Park exit. Not only is this shop centrally located for all your mountain-biking needs, the Saint Louis Brewery sponsors their race team! Now how cool is that?

Saint Louis Brewery and Tap Room

2100 Locust Street
Saint Louis, Missouri 63103
(314) 241-BEER(2337)
www.schlafly.com

THE PUB: Located outside traditional Saint Louis hot spots, known as the Loop and Landing areas, some might say the location of Saint Louis' first brewpub was a bit off. Add the fact that they wanted to serve up microbrews right in beer Goliath Anheuser-Busch's backyard and some might say Saint Louis Brewery's president, Tom Schlafly, is a bit more than off. That is, until you walk up to the impressive exterior. Built for the John S. Swift Printing Company between 1902 and 1904, and on the National Registry of Historic Buildings, this place pretty much calls out, "I'm a brewpub and proud of it! Bud be damned!"

Opened December 26, 1991, the **Saint Louis Brewery and Tap Room** was quickly voted best new restaurant in Saint Louis by the local populace. So come for the food but stay for the beer 'cause Schlafly's has plenty brewing, with over 30 different varieties given time in the tank over the course of a year.

As you walk through the entry courtyard with balcony patio overhead and impressive brick walls all around, you have a choice to make. Beer and food to the left in the Tap Room's pub-like atmosphere or beer and games to the right in the Den's casual bar and game-room atmosphere. Either way, you'll be surrounded by brew kettles and face a daunting selection of beers.

THE BREW: Here's where the real fun begins. With no less than eight (or so) recipes competing for tap time on any

given day, you're not gonna go home thirsty.

   With so many to choose from, you should start your adventure by heading straight to the seasonal beers. The "regulars" (**Schlafly Pale Ale**, **Schlafly Hefeweizen**, and **Schlafly Oatmeal Stout**) are all solid, but they're also distributed on a fairly wide basis throughout Missouri, so you can have one of them when slumming at a regular restaurant. What you're really here for is the specialty and seasonal beers like the **Schlafly Nitro Irish Stout** come Saint Patty's day or **Schlafly Oktoberfest** in the fall. There are way too many to list 'em all. Just suffice it to say that anything that comes around only once a year has got to be good. The seasonal not your style? The Tap Room side of the brewery always carries some of the ales caskconditioned including the Schlafly Pale Ale, another great place to begin your Schlafly adventure. Regardless of the style you happen to choose, be it nitro, cask-conditioned, seasonal, bottled, or draft, there is no better way to wash the dirt from your throat after a day in the saddle than with a Schlafly's.

PRICE OF A PINT: Typical big-city brewpub prices abound at $3.50 a pint with no happy hour in sight. If you happen to be here in October, be sure to check out Oktoberfest when Schlafly's blocks off the south parking lot for a good old-fashioned brew-fest party.

OTHER BREWS IN THE AREA: Morgan Street Brewery, 721 North Second Street, Saint Louis, MO 63102; (314) 231-9970. Located in the oldest building in the popular Laclede's Landing historic area, Morgan Street Brewery offers a great festive atmosphere and microbrewed beers if you're into a large party-bar scene. A place for a quiet beer this is not, but if you have the gang together looking for action, this whole area is the place to go. If the scene there is not what you're after, take the elevators to the top of the nearby 630-foot Gateway Arch and have a look around.

Springfield

Tucked into the western foothills of the Ozark Plateau,
Springfield serves as a perfect launching point for any
Ozark-bound adventure. In addition to the biking opportunities this prime location offers, Springfield is host to some
higher pursuits including no less than eight universities
and colleges.

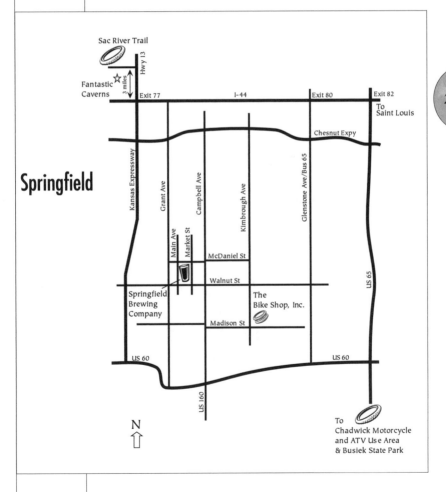

Once you tire of all the biking, canoeing, and hiking this area has to offer, just 40 miles south of Springfield is the strange but ever-popular Branson, Missouri—a bizarre mix of Las Vegas show meeting the Ozark's version of Nashville. Country-music lovers make annual pilgrimages to what is quite frankly a tourist trap. However, if that's your bag, then knock yourself out.

A little closer to home and maybe not quite so loud is the popular pastime of spelunking. Thousands of years of surface and underground water erosion have left the Ozarks riddled with caves, springs, and sinkholes. One of the most popular such caves is the nearby Fantastic Caverns, just east of Springfield. Again, don't expect a

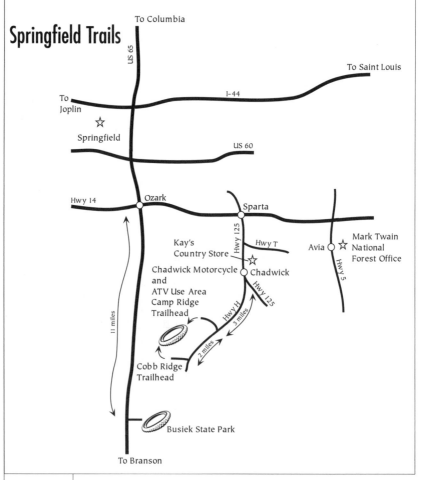

Springfield Trails

To Columbia

US 65

To Saint Louis

To Joplin

I-44

☆
Springfield

US 60

Hwy 14   Ozark   Sparta

Kay's Country Store   Hwy 125   Hwy T   Avia   Mark Twain National Forest Office

Chadwick Motorcycle and ATV Use Area   Chadwick   Hwy 125   Hwy 5

Camp Ridge Trailhead

11 miles

Hwy H   2 miles   3 miles

Cobb Ridge Trailhead

Busiek State Park

To Branson

private adventure as these caves are big enough to drive jeeps into. And some do.

And, of course, the Chadwick Motorcycle and ATV (all-terrain vehicle for you city folk) area is there to welcome you with open arms and open trails when you tire of making excuses not to be riding your bike. With close to 100 miles of trails to explore, you'll wonder why you ever went to Branson in the first place.

Springfield Brewing Company's open warehouse interior offers a community bar downstairs, pool tables, and another bar upstairs.

Chadwick Motorcycle and ATV Use Area

THE SCOOP: Almost 100 miles of ATV, motorcycle, and mountain-bike doubletrack and singletrack trails.

RIDE LENGTH AND TYPE: Variable—with a 12-mile loop of the prime stuff to get you started.

THE BIKE: Looking for a day or entire weekend of riding? Then the **Chadwick Motorcycle and ATV Use Area** is where you're gonna want to head. Twelve square miles of steep ridges and deep hollows riddled with singletrack and doubletrack trails means you won't go home feeling empty from this magical Ozark land of mountain-bike gluttony.

Designed and created by motorcycles and four wheelers, the majority of the trails are staggeringly steep, eroded, and strewn with jagged rocks suitable for advanced riders only. However, with nearly 100 miles of open trails, plenty of options present themselves for more intermediate-level mountain-biking terrain, so you just have to be careful how you go about your ride. The trails wind through ridges and hollows ranging between 1000 and 1350 feet in elevation, making the trick here to find the most exciting way down and then the most manageable way back up. Even though 350 feet does not sound like a lot of elevation if you're from a more endowed landscape, when it's steep and technical with loose rock and limestone ledges— which look more like the Jolly Green Giant's porch steps than a trail—it's no Sunday picnic.

If you're visiting for the first time and you don't have a Chadwick veteran along to guide you through this maze of trails, the best thing to do is get a map and park at Camp Ridge Campground. From Camp Ridge, jump on **Trail 113** and head south from the campground to the much her-alded must-do **Trail 108**. Take Trail 108 west and prepare for what can only be described as a B&B Hotmile. This plush mile of smooth, fast, wide-open downhill is what *Bike Magazine* has called "phat air friendly" with plenty of opportunities to launch yourself into space as you blast your way down this sweetie of a doubletrack. Trail 108 eventually ends back at Trail 113. From there, take Trail 113 left (west) to **Trail 105** heading due south. This is kind of where the fun ends for a while as the climbing begins and you make your way up Trail 105 to **Trail 171**—a full-blown dirt road and probably the easiest way to regain lost altitude at Chadwick (Trail 171 can also be reached from Trail 113 via Trails 171B and 171A for a slightly easier, but less interesting, climb than Trail 105 offers). Trail 171 intersects **Trail 101** near the top of the ridge at **Cobb Ridge Campground,** which makes for a nice resting point and a convenient bailout via nearby Highway H if the trail so far has not been your style or the siren song of the brewpub is calling you.

Once you're ready, take Trail 101 west for an excellent scenic loop, which rolls through Flyblow Hollow and Peckout Hollow and eventually returning to Cobb Ridge Campground. The ride so far will tally in right around 10 miles. If that's all you have in your tank, jump back on **Trail 171** and out to **Highway H** and head north to where your car is parked at Camp Ridge Campground about 2 miles away. Not finished yet? Get creative and find your own way back via trails or retrace your earlier route down Trails 171, 105, 113, 108, and 113 and back to your car for a 14-mile balloon-on-a-string ride. As an alternate finish, take Trail 110 instead of Trail 108 back up Camp Ridge.

Other highlights throughout the trail system that you may want to make time for are **Trails 104, 115,** and **124B (Dairy Queen Hill)**—all excellent, gnarled-up downhills when approached from the proper directions (the top) or just plain impossible from the wrong direction (the bottom). **DIFFICULTY:** Advanced. Although it is possible to keep the riding on an even intermediate level by closely following the directions above, most of the trails are just plain savage and should be attempted only by accomplished cyclists.

AEROBIC DIFFICULTY (1–5):

4

TECHNICAL DIFFICULTY (1–5):

4

WARNINGS: There is a $5 per day or $35 annual use fee for Chadwick. You can pick up a pass at the Ava Ranger Station or Kay's Country Store in Chadwick. This is primarily a motorized trail. Not only does that mean many of the ups and downs will be straight shots through some big terrain, it also means you need to be wary of running into a couple hundred pounds of machinery around each corner. Fortunately, you can hear them coming a long way off. And, although this kinda ruins the feeling of remote wilderness, it does warn you to get out of the way. Also, there is a good chance of really getting lost out here. Make sure you have a map, plenty of food and water, and lots of tools as things have a way of breaking on ATV trails. And, just to make things stay real interesting, when you're fixing those flats, don't wander off into the woods too much. This area is also known for its rattlesnakes and ticks. The DEET you were told to pack will help with the ticks, but check every inch of your body after a ride anyway. If you find any, pull them out slowly and firmly, trying to get the whole thing. If you develop any unusual symptoms like a rash or flu within the next 2–3 weeks, see a doctor immediately and report that you were in a tick-infested area.

OTHER TRAILS IN THE AREA: For a sampling of Chadwick, but not nearly as remote or dangerous, check out **Busiek State Park** about 25 miles south of Springfield right off US 65. With about 20 miles of moderate to advanced non-motorized multiuse singletrack and doubletrack, this is a nice close getaway that's perfect for less intense outings than Chadwick. Closer to home and not nearly as technical or epic as either Busiek or Chadwick is the **Sac River Trail.** Only 3 miles north of Springfield, this network of trails has about 10 miles of intertwined fast and fun singletrack. The best way to get familiar with the area is by doing the 3-mile outer loop of the park. That way, when you get turned around on the interior trails, you will have some idea of where you are in relation to the trailhead. Even though you stand a good chance of getting turned around on these trails, you will never really be LOST as the park is bordered by Highway 13 on the east side, a barbed wire fence on the north side, the Sac River on the west, and the park's access road on the south. Keep riding and eventually you will come to one of these landmarks and find your way back to the parking lot.

CONTACTS: U.S. Forest Service, Ava–Cassville–Willow Springs Ranger District, Business Route 5 South, P.O. Box 188, Ava, MO 65608; (417) 683-4428. Springfield Chamber of Commerce, 202 South John Q. Hammons Parkway, Springfield, MO 65806; (417) 862-5567.

MAPS: The Forest Service prints a free map of the area, and the trailheads are usually stocked with them. Just to make sure you get one and know where you're going, you should secure a copy of the map from The Bike Shop, Inc. in Springfield and highlight the route outlined above before you even hit the trails.

BIKE SHOP: The Bike Shop, Inc., 607 East Madison, Springfield, MO 65806; (417) 831-4594. This enterprise is couple of blocks from the brewery. The owner, Shawn Kraft, keeps Chadwick maps at his shop free for the asking. Plus, his girlfriend works over at the brewery, and what can be a better recommendation than that?

Springfield Brewing Company

305 South Market Street
Springfield, Missouri 65806
(417) 832-TAPS(8277)
www.springfieldbrewingco.com

THE PUB: The **Springfield Brewing Company** is located in a large brick warehouse that was gutted and rebuilt as a brewpub, which opened in 1997. A classy place with just the right amount of rehabilitated old and shiny new. The original brick walls have been retained along with the exposed ceiling beams and ventilation pipes running throughout the restaurant. That's the old. The highlight of the new is the impressive 15-barrel, computerized, stainless-steel brewery sitting behind glass so polished it's like a trophy display case. And in some aspects it is. Built by the Paul Mueller Company, also located in Springfield, this is their demo brewery where they bring prospective clients interested in purchasing a brewing system. Keep that in mind if you happen to be in the market for a home brewing system upgrade. . . .

"So you're working right now? Right on!"
—A bartender at Springfield Brewing Company figures out Bike & Brew America.

Not just a pretty face, the Springfield Brewing Company has plenty of utilitarian features as well. Downstairs, a large, oval, community bar lovingly protects the state-of-the-art brew house. Deck seating out back and patio seating up front on Market Street offer pleasant outdoor options, and upstairs a second bar caters to a full pool hall complete with a separately ventilated cigar lounge with leather couches and arm chairs. Also upstairs is a separate banquet hall that opens up for live music and additional elbow room when things really start happening.

THE BREW: Enough about character. Can this place actually put that fancy, bigger than life, brewing system to

The grain silo flags in weary bikers to the fresh beer and the plentiful deck and patio seating at Springfield Brewing Company.
(Courtesy of Springfield Brewing Company)

good use? The answer is a resounding YES! Four regulars make the yearly taps, plus a seasonal specialty and rotating specialty round out the six house brews. You'll find more than a few lagers here as the ability to lager is one of the benefits of having such a large brewery. Of the regulars, the **Springfield Unfiltered Wheat** is a typical American-style wheat beer; it's the pub's most popular brew and a very drinkable introduction to the finer things in life. The **Springfield Munich Lager** is next—a very nice beer and very much in style. Things get more interesting with the liberal use of Cascade hops in the employees' favorite **Springfield Pale Ale** and darn right perfect with the nitrogen-mixed **Springfield Porter**, a rich creamy affair perfect for the drinking.

225

The brews here at Springfield have a definite German flare to them partially owing to the fact that one of the brewers, Craig Heisner, studied in Weihenstephan, Germany. Owing to this good fortune, a German seasonal specialty rotates through every three months; a **kolsch** in the spring, a **hefeweizen** in the summer, a **märzen** in the fall (for Oktoberfest), and a **doppelbock** in the winter. A perfect beer for every season.

PRICE OF A PINT: Monday through Friday from 4:00 to 7:00 P.M. and again at 11:00 P.M. to closing time, pints drop from $2.75 to $2.00. Plus, upstairs there are a variety of daily drink and food specials on the chalkboard that are worth looking into.

OTHER BREWS IN THE AREA: All the other brewpubs have closed in Springfield, but if you're headed west to Joplin, be sure to check out the **Iron Horse Restaurant & Brewpub** at 2850 South Rangeline Road; (417) 624-7900. It's a friendly place with good beer and good food.

CHAPTER EIGHT

NEBRASKA

Even though early explorers described Nebraska as the "Great American Desert," it turned out they were very wrong. Now known as the Cornhusker State, 96% of Nebraska's 77,407 square miles is used for all types of agriculture ranging from veggies to world-famous Nebraska beef cattle.

A large territory right in the middle of westward expansion without much threatening terrain means that no less than 10 important westward-expansion trails crossed through its borders including the Oregon, Mormon, and Lewis and Clark Trails. The special geographic features at both Chimney Rock National Historic Site and Scotts Bluff

Nebraska

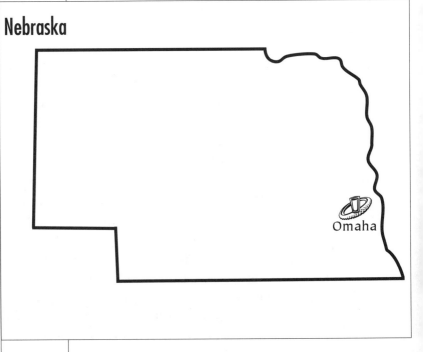

Omaha

National Monument served as valuable landmarks for pioneers using the Oregon Trail. And both segments of the Missouri River that are now designated as a National Recreation River flow along Nebraska's northern border and are still in much the same state as when used by Lewis and Clark on their trek to the Pacific Ocean.

Eastern Nebraska has its share of brewpubs with Omaha, Lincoln, Hastings, and Columbus all serving up fresh suds. However, as one bike shop proprietor near Hastings so eloquently put it, "There ain't no mountains here. We see the sun come up in the corn fields, and we see the sun set in the corn fields." A great quote to be sure, but it won't exactly inspire you to pack up the bike and hit the road.

Nebraska's saving grace comes in and around the Missouri and Platte River Valleys where there is significant terrain and plenty of trail systems taking advantage of it. As these are within reach of Omaha and some utterly fantastic beer, that's where you should set up shop when visiting the area.

Views from the Missouri River Bluffs at Indian Cave State Park in southeastern Nebraska.
(Photo by Rob Stitt)

Omaha

Ever since President Lincoln decided to locate the eastern terminus of the First Continental Railroad in Omaha on the banks of the Missouri River, transportation has played an important roll in the city's future. Even today, as the largest city in Nebraska and located close to the geographic center of the country, rail, truck, and air all keep Omaha a major transportation hub. Also known as the "800-number capital of the nation," Omaha's telecommunication and telemarketing industry plays an important function employing more than 20,000 people.

Consistently ranked as one of the top places to live in the country, these industries are part of what makes Omaha a metropolitan city with symphony, opera, ballet, 11 colleges and universities, and fine dining (including, of course, a selection of excellent brewpubs). The Henry Doorly Zoo has the world's largest indoor rain forest and the second largest free-flight aviary. The Bemis Center for Contemporary Arts attracts artists from all over the world and is America's only major international urban artist colony.

Smack dab between Omaha and the college town of Lincoln, Platte River State Park offers a great biking escape with miles of rugged biking that is commonly considered the best Nebraska has to offer. Just down Interstate 80, and not far from the trail, the historic Old Market and Wholesale District of downtown Omaha offers a top-quality brewpub setting. So, the next time Interstate 80 takes you through the Cornhusker State, bring your bike and your thirst and see the best of both that Nebraska has to offer right here in the Heartland of America.

Omaha

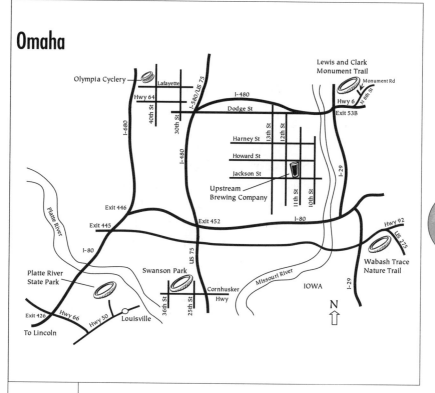

Olympia Cyclery

Lewis and Clark
Monument Trail

Lafayette

Monument Rd

Hwy 64

Hwy 6

40th St

30th St

I-580/US 75

I-480

Dodge St

Exit 53B

I-680

I-480

Harney St

13th St

12th St

Howard St

Jackson St

Upstream
Brewing Company

11th St

10th St

I-29

Platte River

Exit 446

Exit 452

I-80

Hwy 92

US 275

229

Exit 445

I-80

US 75

Wabash Trace
Nature Trail

Platte River
State Park

Swanson Park

Missouri River

IOWA

I-29

Cornhusker
Hwy

36th St

25th St

Exit 426

Hwy 66

Hwy 50

Louisville

To Lincoln

N

Platte River State Park

THE SCOOP: Singletrack through the forested bluffs overlooking the Platte River Valley.

RIDE LENGTH AND TYPE: Variable—over 16 miles of trails to explore.

THE BIKE: Located on the bluffs above the Platte River, **Platte River State Park** offers what is probably the best mountain biking in Nebraska. The terrain is challenging with frequent climbs and descents into steep ravines, sharp blind corners, and enough fallen trees to keep the speed in check throughout most of the trail.

Using the 85-foot-tall Lincoln Journal Observation Tower as your starting point, the trails to the west of the tower are for hiking and biking whereas the trails to the east are primarily for horse use and are off limits to mountain bikers during the "horse months" of May through October between the "horse times" of 9:00 A.M. and 4:00 P.M. As luck would have it, these eastern trails lead to some of the better riding in the park, so it's worth your while to plan your visit for the early morning or late afternoon.

If you plan an afternoon ride, arrive a little early and begin your ride to the west of the tower where you will find 10 miles of tight, rocky, and steep hiking terrain that includes a small waterfall on the forested Stone Creek ravine. Warm your legs up on these trails in anticipation of the sounding of the four o'clock dinner bell.

Once the bell tolls, follow the trail as it rolls along above the Platte River and then cross over Decker Creek to the other trail system winding through the **Sjogren Wilderness Tract**. Although this area is off-limits during "horse hours," it is more remote than the main hiking trails and offers the longest climbs and best descents in the park.

Once you've uncovered all the trails in the park, it's time to climb the tower and catch the setting sun before heading into Omaha's Old Market District for fresh brew at the unsurpassed Upstream Brewing Company.

DIFFICULTY: Intermediate to advanced. This trail will really knock it to beginners and not-quite-intermediate riders, but the various park roads offer plenty of bailout opportunities just when you need them most.

AEROBIC DIFFICULTY (1–5):
3

TECHNICAL DIFFICULTY (1–5):
3

WARNINGS: Platte River is a popular state park with campers, horseback riders, and bikers. The equestrians own the trails to the east of the Lincoln Journal Tower from 9:00 A.M. to 4:00 P.M. every day from Memorial Day until the end of October. Early May also sees some horse tour duty, so call in advance just to make sure. Otherwise, you just have to wait until after 4:00 P.M. to experience the really good stuff.

OTHER TRAILS IN THE AREA: Swanson Park offers another 5 miles of in-town riding just south of Omaha in Bellevue. Just on the other side of the Missouri River in Iowa is the **Lewis & Clark Monument Trail**, which offers 5 miles of tight, twisty, switchbacking singletrack leading to fantastic views of the river from the bluffs above. And also across the river, starting in Council Bluffs, Iowa, and traveling 63 miles to the Missouri border is the popular **Wabash Trace Nature Trail**, a crushed-limestone path. Used by hikers and horse riders in addition to bikers, this trail has several horse trails branching from it if you want to spice up the ride a bit.

CONTACTS: Platte River State Park, 14421 346th Street, Louisville, NE 68037; (402) 234-2217. Greater Omaha Chamber of Commerce, 1301 Harney Street, Omaha, NE 68102; (402) 346-5000.

MAPS: A trail map is available at the park office when you pay your $2.50 park admission fee (or $14.00 annual Nebraska State Park fee).

BIKE BREW AMERICA

NEBRASKA

BIKE SHOP: Olympia Cyclery, 1324 North Fortieth Street, Omaha, NE 68131; (402) 554-1940. Or Bike Rack Inc., 2528 South 130th Avenue, Omaha, NE 68144; (402) 333-1031.

Upstream Brewing Company

514 South Eleventh Street
Omaha, Nebraska 68102
(402) 344-0200
www.upstreambrewing.com

THE PUB: Situated in the revitalized Old Market Area of downtown Omaha, you know you're in for something good as soon as you walk off the brick streets into the restored, early-twentieth-century firehouse that now houses **Upstream Brewing Company.** Shiny bright tanks offer a showroom-quality brewery nicely offset by the industrial warehouse look of worn brick walls, large windows, and ventilation ductwork with the added whimsy of random playing cards stuck to the ceiling.

Walking past the street-side patio, which offers a nice place to enjoy a beer and up-close views of the Old Market, you are greeted with a large copper-topped four-sided community bar and a couple of TVs to catch the news or game. A large dining area under an open ceiling with views of the spotless brewery completes the first-level picture.

Upstairs in Upstream you'll find an antique bar from the mid-nineteenth century serving up your favorite Upstream ales and a beer-parlor area with casual balcony seating overlooking the dining room below. The other half of the large upstairs is equipped with 13 full-sized pool tables and a couple of foosball tables. A second deck off to one side overlooks the Old Market and offers a taste of Midwestern hospitality with heat lamps to keep you warm on cool spring and fall evenings.

THE BREW: Upstream keeps seven regulars on tap and a rotating seasonal. Of the regulars, the best sellers are the

"Don't filter the beer— that's why God gave me a liver!"

—Steve, brewer at Crane River Brewpub and Café in Lincoln, Nebraska, discussing the theory of evolution—of man AND beer.

smooth and easy-drinking **Gold Coast Blonde** and the more flavorful **Railyard Ale**, an English-style pale ale with a malty body and low hop finish. Upstream keeps on tap the excellent **Heartland Hefeweizen** with the requisite banana and clove flavors and then ups it a notch with the brewpub's next three big beers. The employees' favorite, and probably the best beer in the house, is the **Dundee 90 Shilling Scotch Ale**, a smooth, malty beer with a slightly smoky flavor. Next on the love chart is the **Firehouse ESB** (extra special bitter) with just the proper amount of hops in this medium-bodied ale. And Upstream rounds things out with the nicely brewed **Blackstone Stout**, a nice cream stout just begging to be placed under the nitro.

PRICE OF A PINT: Happy hour is daily from 4:00 to 6:00 P.M. when pints drop a buck from $3.00 to $2.00.

OTHER BREWS IN THE AREA: If you're headed to Lincoln, the capitol city of Nebraska and home of the University of Nebraska, after your ride at Platte River State Park be sure to check out the **Crane River Brewpub and Café**, 200 North Eleventh Street, (402) 476-7766. At Crane River, the **Sod House Altbier** is the employees' favorite, so it always goes the fastest, but it's the **Carhenge Ale** that is the customers' favorite. Named after Nebraska's version of Stonehenge—built by a farmer out of old cars—this beer isn't always on tap but worth a try when it is.

CHAPTER NINE

NORTH DAKOTA

Now mostly flat and covered in prairie farms and pastures, North Dakota was once under a large inland sea. About 200 million years ago, dinosaurs thrived along the shores of this sea near the area of what is now known as the North Dakota Badlands, a stretch of bizarre rock formations, bleak buttes rising independently from the surrounding plains, and crazily colored hills stretching along the southwestern edge of the state. This area, the rocks of which include the Hell Creek Formation, has produced many famous dinosaur discoveries including one of only 12 Tyrannosaurus rex fossils ever found.

235

North Dakota

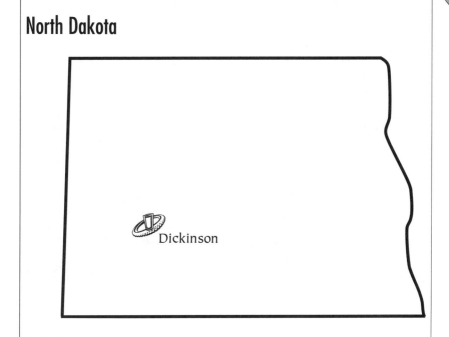

Dickinson

A more recent attraction, just north of North Dakota's capital city, Bismarck, is the Fort Mandan State Historic Site where Lewis and Clark weathered their first winter west of the Mississippi in 1804–1805 and recruited the French-Canadian fur trapper Toussaint Charbonneau and his Shoshone Indian wife Sacagawea as guides and interpreters.

With just over 700,000 residents in the entire state, North Dakota also has the good fortune of having more national wildlife refuges than any other state, which in turn, leads to wildlife-viewing opportunities matched by few states. Bighorn sheep, bison, wild horses, elk, moose, deer, antelope, coyote, prairie dogs, and resident and migratory birds are some of what you can see while visiting these areas scattered around the state.

The downside of a state this sparsely populated is it just doesn't have enough people to support many brewpubs. North Dakota's Bike & Brew saving grace comes in the form of fresh beer in Dickinson and the exceptional nearby trails in the historic frontier town of Medora. And fortunately, this one Bike & Brew America destination is worth the trip to North Dakota all by itself.

A short spur near the south end of the Maah Daah Hey Trail offers great singletrack and better views of the Little Missouri River.
(Photo by Dave Pryor)

NORTH DAKOTA

Dickinson

Dickinson, once known as the "Queen of the Prairie" because her lights could be seen for many miles by early pioneers, is Bike & Brew America's North Dakota oasis. Less than 40 miles from Medora and the 120-mile-long Maah Daah Hey Trail, Dickinson supplies the beer and Medora supplies the riding.

From the prairie grasslands and farms of Dickinson, you travel west to the fancifully colored and wildly sculpted hills of the Badlands of North Dakota. Here you'll find a land of low river washes and distant wind-swept buttes

Dickinson

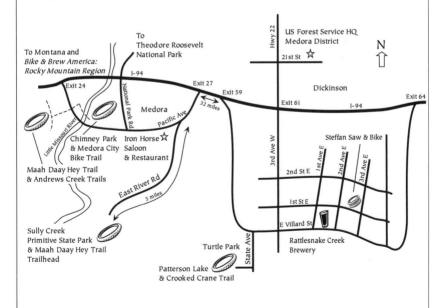

Leroy and
Jacob ride the
Rattlesnake
Revenge Race
Course near
the south end
of the Maah
Daah Hey
Trail.

Leroy and Jacob ride the Rattlesnake Revenge Race Course near the south end of the Maah Daah Hey Trail.

with names like White, Camelback, Sentinel, and Square. Although you're not gonna find much lush, green, shady forest out here, what you'll miss in shade you'll more than make up for in incredibly scenery.

Founded in 1883 by the Frenchman Marquis De Mores with money from his rich father-in-law, the old western town of Medora is now the gateway to North Dakota's number one tourist attraction, Theodore Roosevelt National Park. The park was established in 1978 as much to protect the beauty of the surrounding Badlands as to honor the Twenty-Sixth President of the United States who, during his presidency, founded the National Forest Service and five national parks. Theodore Roosevelt himself loved this area and spent 13 years ranching here. In fact, he is often quoted as saying that his Badland experiences are what enabled him to become president.

It's here, stretching between both Theodore Roosevelt National Park Units, that the Maah Daah Hey travels 120 miles through the Badlands. And it's here that Dickinson is once again known as the "Queen of the Prairie" because her lights can still be seen for miles and they serve as a beacon for those thirsting for fresh beer! So set your sights on the Badlands of North Dakota for your next Bike & Brew Adventure, and who knows, it might just be the reason you become president some day.

The Maah Daah Hey Trail & Andrews Creek Trails

THE SCOOP: Over 100 miles of North Dakota Badland riding at its finest.

RIDE LENGTH AND TYPE: Variable—options for a 120-mile point-to-point multiday adventure to a very manageable 13-mile balloon-on-a-string ride.

The crossing of the mighty Little Missouri River near Sullys Creek State Primitive Park begins (or ends) your Maah Daah Hey adventure.
(Photo by Dave Pryor)

THE BIKE: If you ride only one trail in North Dakota, make it some, or all, of the **Maah Daah Hey Trail**. The name comes from the Mandan Indians and means "an area that has been or will be around for a long time." We mountain bikers can only hope. Completed in 1999, the Maah Daah Hey extends south 120 miles from essentially the North Unit of the Theodore Roosevelt National Park to the historic town of Medora. Campsites are situated every 15 miles

along the trail as it crosses through the Little Missouri National Grasslands, over the Little Missouri River, and through both units of Theodore National Park. Even though mountain bikes are not allowed in these two national park units, and alternative routes are required, the Maah Daah Hey makes an excellent multi-day epic equal to the famed Kokopelli's Trail of Colorado and Utah.

Not quite up for the whole nine yards? No problem. The area around the Maah Daah Hey's southern terminus is the

239

NORTH
DAKOTA

most traveled part of the trail and offers various spur trails to explore. The best place to begin your journey into the Maah Daah Hey and surrounding badlands is by parking at Chimney Park on the west side of Medora.

From **Chimney Park**, ride the paved **Medora City Bike Trail** 2 miles west to a small bridge. Once over the bridge, carefully cross Pacific Avenue and look for singletrack on the other side of the road. Take the singletrack, and you will soon see the brown-turtle trail markers indicating that you are on the **Maah Daah Hey Trail** proper. Known for its firm determination, steadfastness, patience, long life, and fortitude, the turtle is an appropriate symbol. You'll agree after a day or two on these trails.

Once on the singletrack across Pacific Avenue, you'll have three options. (1) Follow the Maah Daah Hey Trail for a well-traveled 5 miles to Sully Creek Primitive State Park for a 14-mile out-and-back total, including the 2-mile paved path from Chimney Park. (2) Follow the Maah Daah Hey Trail to Sully Creek Primitive State Park as before, but follow the **East River Road** leading from the campground back to Medora for an 11-mile loop. Or (3) follow the turtles almost exactly 1 mile, keeping an eye out for a less-traveled singletrack spur off to your right. This spur takes you to the network of singletrack and doubletrack trails known locally as the **Andrews Creek Trails**.

If you plan on this third option, the best route to take is the **Rattlesnake Revenge Race Course**. A 7-mile loop plotted for the annual Rattlesnake Revenge Race, this loop offers an excellent array of badland terrain. From the Maah Daah Hey Trail, you follow a singletrack path that takes you down through cottonwood trees in the Little Missouri Wash and up to the "Why Not" intersection and the race loop proper. A mix of singletrack and rough doubletrack takes you on extended climbs and descents through an arid terrain of shrub land, junipers, cow bones, and absolutely incredible views of the surrounding badlands of North Dakota.

Your best bet to find your way around this loop is by first visiting Steffan Saw & Bike in Dickinson. A map was created for the race and getting a good look at it before you attempt this trail is important. Once you complete the loop, and the "Why Not" intersection is behind you, it's a short ride through the wash and back to the Maah Daah Hey Trail. From there, either head back into Medora or farther south all the way to Scully Creek Primitive State Park, depending on how many miles are in you.

Riding Maah Daah Hey singletrack through the Badlands of North Dakota.

DIFFICULTY: Intermediate. The southern section of the Maah Daah Hey Trail is the most traveled section of the entire trail and also the easiest. If you find your way into Andrews Creek Trails, expect more of the same terrain only a little choppier and with some technical spots scattered throughout. Only advanced riders who have prepared properly should attempt the whole 120-mile trail.

AEROBIC DIFFICULTY (1–5):

3

TECHNICAL DIFFICULTY (1–5):

3

WARNINGS: Tread lightly. Try to stay on established trails, yield to everyone you see including hikers, equestrians, cattle, wild horses, bighorn sheep, horned toads, and rattlesnakes. It was named Rattlesnake Revenge for a reason! Also, be prepared to carry all of your water and have plenty of extra tubes. Chances are good you will flat out here.

OTHER TRAILS IN THE AREA: Right in Dickinson and not nearly the investment in time and energy the Maah Daah Hey requires is the beginner-level 17-mile **Crooked Crane Trail** circling Patterson Lake. Mostly widetrack and mown fields, this is a relaxing alternative to the Maah Daah Hey. Speaking of which, other segments of the Maah Daah Hey perhaps worth dabbling in go from the border of Theodore Roosevelt National Park North Unit and head south. Note: the trail passes through the national park just north of this area, and the owner of the private land surrounding the park charges an INCREDIBLE twenty bucks ($20!!) to ride through his land in order to continue the trail. It's best just to avoid this nonsense and start the trail south of his land. Also, the **Devil Pass Area** of the trail is commonly considered the best riding and best scenery of the whole trail.

CONTACTS: U.S. Forest Service, Medora District, 161 Twenty-First Street West, Dickinson, ND 58601; (701) 225-5151. The North Dakota Tourism Department keeps a Maah Daah Hey web site at www.maahdaahhey.com. Dickinson Parks & Recreation, 615 West Broadway Street, Dickinson, ND 58601; (701) 225-2074. Dickinson Chamber of Commerce, 314 Third Avenue West, Dickinson, ND 58601; (701) 225-5115.

MAPS: Topographic maps of the entire Maah Daah Hey Trail are available at Steffan Saw & Bike and at the Medora District Ranger's office. The Rattlesnake Revenge map board and maps of the Crooked Crane Trail are also available at Steffan's.

BIKE SHOP: Steffan Saw & Bike, 121 Third Avenue East, Dickinson, ND 58601; (701) 225-5075. Yes, you've been reading it correctly: Saw & Bike. Not only can you get your Stihl power saw serviced by the experts here, you can pick up maps for both the Maah Daah Hey and Crooked Crane Trails.

Rattlesnake Creek Brewery & Grill

2 West Villard
Dickinson, North Dakota 58601
(701) 483-9518

THE PUB: In the center of Dickinson's old downtown is an early-twentieth-century long brick building that has done time as a barbershop, bakery, bowling alley, and most recently a pharmacy until finally opening as the **Rattlesnake Creek Brewery & Grill** in December of 1995. Now that the old pharmacy's dark paneling has been stripped off the original brick walls, the green carpet pulled up to reveal hardwood floors beneath, and the drop ceilings thrown out to uncover the original tin ceilings, the old building once again shows off its simple, but ideal, interior.

Dining is downstairs near the historic bar, the rear hutch of which was made from Missouri cherry and salvaged from Brockway, Montana. The actual bar came from nearby Medora (where, if you're lucky, you rode earlier today), and both sections are over 100 years old. Upstairs recently underwent a facelift and now hosts a pool table, dart machine, and another bar area.

THE BREW: When the current owner, Dale Tuhy, took over in 1998, the first thing he did was tone down the hop content of the beers to better appeal to a town that may not quite be ready for the real thing. Not to worry! Business is good and Dale's beers are still excellent even though you probably won't find an India pale ale in the lineup anytime soon. Given the reduction in hops, the lighter beers such as the **White Butte Wheat** and **Bluehawk EPA** (extra pale ale) are both light, smooth, and very drinkable after a summer's day or week on the Maah Daah Hey Trail.

The Maah Daah Hey works its way through the Badlands of North Dakota.

(Photo by Dave Pryor)

Things start getting fashionable with the **Rattlesnake Red**, a nice malty beer with a splash of Cascade hops aroma thrown in. And the **Chipper's Brown Ale**, one of the Rattlesnake's most popular, is very balanced between the malt and hops. The best beer in the house is the **Lodgepole Porter**, an excellent porter with a hint of chocolate and toffee at the finish. Served via a mixed nitrogen and CO_2 tap, it is slightly less carbonated than usual and very, very smooth.

PRICE OF A PINT: Happy hour is Monday through Thursday from 8:00 to 10:00 P.M. and Friday from 3:00 to 6:00 P.M. when all pints are only $2.00. The rest of the time the standard cost is $2.75.

OTHER BREWS IN THE AREA: If all you're looking for is something cold, hoppy, and close to the Maah Daah Hey, then give the **Iron Horse Saloon & Restaurant** a try at 123 Robert Vesco Way, Medora, ND 58645; (701) 623-9894.

CHAPTER TEN

OHIO

Ohio is a diverse combination of agriculture and forest, cities and industry. You can find everything from the world's largest population of Amish people to the industrial metropolitan cities of Cincinnati, Cleveland, Columbus, and Toledo.

Considering that the Buckeye State—named for the buckeye trees common in its forests—is the seventh most populated state in the country but only the thirty-fifth largest, Ohio is still home to a healthy dose of national and state forest land and parks. However, for the most part, mountain bikes have been lumped into the "motor-

245

Ohio

Akron

Ohio River Valley

OHIO

ized vehicle" category and are not allowed on public trails, making quality legal trails a real challenge to find. This banishment, as much as anything else, has created a trend in Ohio to foster private trails open to the public for a nominal trail-use fee. The best of these trails, Vulture's Knob, is also the best legal trail central and northern Ohio has to offer and probably Ohioan's favorite fat-tire destination.

Southern Ohio is in much better shape. The Ohio River Valley is an almost mountainous region of the Appalachian Foothills stretching across the southern border of Ohio along, you guessed it, the Ohio River. The region is also home to the Wayne National Forest and numerous state parks and forests. Filled with history, the river towns support a nice community of brewpubs and microbreweries. Even though the area has not progressed on trail-access issues as fast as most of the country, a recent shift in some land managers' acceptance of mountain bikes has opened the door a crack. Thus a few areas of note are emerging.

Akron

Currently known as the "Rubber Capitol of the World," Akron was not always the home of Goodrich, Firestone, Goodyear, and General Tire. Cereal, cigars, sewer pipes, dirigibles (rigid blimps), and marbles were all made in Akron at one time or another. However, it was the discovery of vulcanization (the forming of rubber into solid shapes) by Mr. Goodrich and Dr. Goodyear that "solidified" Akron's claim to fame.

Today, in addition to the corporate offices for many major tire companies, Akron is home to the largest dirigible hanger in the world. This building is so large that it has its own atmosphere. Also, the Inventor's Hall of Fame

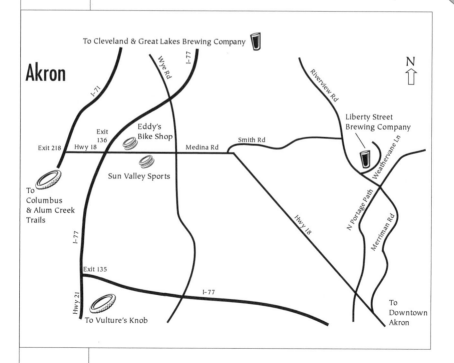

is located in Akron, and not far away is both the Football Hall of Fame in Canton and the Rock & Roll Hall of Fame and Museum in nearby Cleveland.

Reaching the privately owned and maintained mountain-bike trails at Vulture's Knob is a bit of a drive, but the creative trails are worth it. Catch the Lizard Lounge on a sunny afternoon or race day and soak up some of the local bike scene. Ohio mountain bikers come from all over the state to ride this trail, and there is a reason—actually a lot of reasons: bridges, logs, rocks, ramps, hairpin turns, winding singletrack, steep climbs, and descents, to name a few. All of them are exceedingly challenging, and each one of them is begging for you to give it a try, or fall off your bike in the attempt. The Liberty Street Brewing Company is four stars across the board and well worth the drive back into Akron.

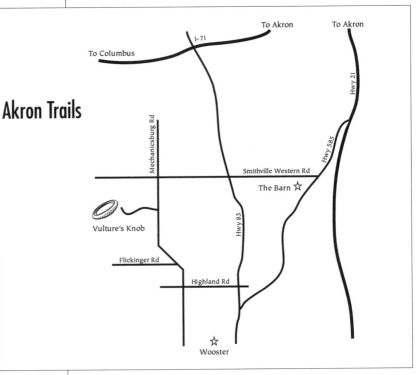

Akron Trails

Vulture's Knob

THE SCOOP: Twisty, winding, off-camber, and technical with short sharp hills; this privately owned trail is worth the drive.

RIDE LENGTH AND TYPE: 9-mile loop.

THE BIKE: Legal biking on public land is a scarce commodity anywhere in Ohio, and the northeast region has the least. Drastic times call for drastic measures, so back in 1996 along came Dr. Knob and his creation: **Vulture's**

The Lizard Lounge welcomes you to your impeding doom at The Knob.

Knob, a privately owned and maintained trail system about 30 miles west of Akron.

Driving through the flat and tame farm fields just outside Wooster, you'll wonder what could possibly be worth the drive to this remote locale. A painted sign of a smirking vulture on Mechanicsburg Road directs you down a dirt road as flat and unassuming as the rest of the land in this region of Ohio. However, you'll know you're in the right place as you round the last stand of trees and spy the rough-sawn log cabin known as the Lizard Lounge.

Hosting a full mountain-bike race schedule including night races, a 24-Hour Race, and even an Adventure Race, "The Knob" is commonly considered the best legal single-track riding in northeast Ohio if not the entire state. This little piece of land in pretty much the middle of nowhere has gained quite a following and has developed into the premier mountain-bike scene in Ohio.

The trail itself starts out innocently enough as a single-track path through what is obviously the race-marshalling

area, and that's about where the innocence ends. By using every ounce of terrain like only someone who grew up playing, hunting, and living on this land ever could, Dr. Knob (aka Mark Condry) and plenty of friends have created a trail that rivals anything the North Shore has to offer—except maybe the hills. . . .

Small painted signs give some indication about what to expect around the next turn with names like **Rock Tunnel, Fern Gully, Oh Sh—!, Friar Bryan's Forest, Ant City**, and **Todd De Tour**, . . . well you get the idea. Creative and fun. That is until you fall down. And you will fall down. It may be over one of a dozen log bridges like the one stretching over **Gold Fish Pond**. (No goldfish here, but you may find a missing person or two.) Or, maybe it will be on your way down **The Gorge** or over the **Suspension Bridge**. Wherever it may be, it will happen. Just a matter of time.

If you're holding up well by the time you hit McAfee Road, take this dirt road about a quarter mile south to the new section of trail called **Killbuck Run**. Here you will find a section of elevated trail known as **The Serpent**. One false move on this quarter-mile-long suspended log and bridge trail, and you will go down. The only break here (if you can call it that) is you will probably fall into a swamp. Although messy, you will probably survive the tumble of more than 4 feet. Proceed with confidence or do not proceed at all.

DIFFICULTY: Intermediate to advanced. You have to keep in mind that this trail was deliberately created to be difficult. Do not come here as a beginner unless you don't mind walking half or more of the course. Intermediate riders should use their judgment before attempting the multitude of trail obstacles, and all riders should attempt The Serpent with either extreme confidence or stupidity.

AEROBIC DIFFICULTY (1–5):

3

TECHNICAL DIFFICULTY (1–5):

4 (5 if you do everything)

WARNINGS: Besides the summertime mosquitoes, your biggest concern will be the trail. Assuming that the trail is why you're here in the first place, plan on a $3.00 trail fee at the Lizard Lounge. New in 2000 is limited riding dates. From November 1 to March 31, the Killbuck Run section is completely closed, and the rest of the course (about 6 miles) is open to the public on Sunday only.

OTHER TRAILS IN THE AREA: Unfortunately, this is Ohio, and there just aren't a lot of legal trails to choose from. Talk to the folks at Sun Valley Sports or Eddy's Bike Shop, and maybe they will take you for a ride on some of their local trails. Otherwise, **Alum Creek** offers about 7 miles of overused and undermaintained singletrack right outside Columbus, Ohio, about a 2-hour drive from Akron.

CONTACTS: The most complete and up-to-date source of information about the trail and various races is at www.vulturesknob.com. For specifics, you can call Dr. Knob (Mark Condry) at (330) 264-7636 or Todd Caldwell at (330) 345-1159. Fairlawn Area Chamber of Commerce, P.O. Box 13388, Akron, OH 44334; (330) 849-0402.

MAPS: Racecourse maps are available at Sun Valley Sports and Eddy's Bike Shop in Akron or on the web at www.vulturesknob.com. The landscape of Vulture's Knob is constantly changing as new trails are built and old ones are redirected. At last count there was about 9 miles of trails (including the new Killbuck Run section), but that total will surely change before you get a chance to visit. The good news is this is such an active racecourse that the trails are usually marked and perfectly maintained. Usually. Be prepared for a couple of downed signs and barriers, but if you just follow the tracks you should be fine.

BIKE SHOP: Eddy's Bike Shop, 3991 Medina Road, Akron, OH 44333; (330) 666-2453; www.eddysbikeshop.com. Or across the street at Sun Valley Sports, 3900 Medina Road, Suite U, Akron, OH 44333; (330) 666-9000. These shops are pretty much across the street from one another, and both sponsor and ride the races over at The Knob.

A popular race course throughout the summer, don't let Vulture's Knob's benign trailhead fool you.

Liberty Street Brewing Company

1238 Weathervane Lane
Akron, Ohio 44313
(330) 869-BEER(2337)

THE PUB: It's here in this city that owes its wavering wealth to the fortunes of the auto industry that the **Liberty Street Brewing Company** makes its home in the lower level of a large brick building meant to look as if it hails from Colonial America when in actuality, it hails from modern Akron.

This dark and friendly English-style pub has a century-old oak bar from Durham, England, taking up most of the pub area with a few discrete booths filling in the rest. The dining area is open to views of the brew house and access to the brilliantly decorated banquet halls reminiscent of an English manor's dark, paneled interior. Don't leave without trying the incredible food—and try not to track the remains of Vulture's Knob's "Tastes Like Chicken Trail" on the nice carpet! Even though the beer and food here are some of the best you will find anywhere, you won't be kicked out for wearing your bike shorts. Nevertheless, you may feel more comfortable in street clothes and after a wash behind the ears—especially after falling into the Gold Fish Pond back at Vultures.

Not just a brewpub, Liberty claims to be the only micro-brewery in the world to earn *Wine Spectator Magazine's* Award of Excellence. The kitchen is also what you would expect from a first-class restaurant. All food is locally produced or flown in for freshness, and every sauce, dip, soup, appetizer, meal, dessert, hunk of bread, and even the mayonnaise is made from scratch.

THE BREW: The house favorite, **Dragonslayer Scottish**

"Just leave me the menu condom."

—Ever conscious of their rubber heritage, Liberty Bar Manager and Beer Goddess, Michele, offers up a souvenir copy of the beer menu while keeping its plastic cover for the bar.

OHIO

BIKE BREW AMERICA

Export Style Ale is the only beer that you'll always find on tap here and the one you should have if you're here for the first time. Liberty has brewed 41 recipes since opening in 1994, and many of those beers have garnered awards. Some of the beers that make appearances throughout the year include the **Hellcat Lager**, a Great American Beer Festival Gold Medalist; the **Mad Cow Stout**, a creamy full-bodied, vanilla treat; the **Blue Babe Ale**, a strong malty

beer with a hop bite at the end; and the **Cascade Locks Pale Ale**, the perfect American-style pale ale. Each of these beers is superb, and each yields a perfect pint of happiness. Basically, you truly cannot go wrong when saddling up to the old English bar here. Enjoy!

PRICE OF A PINT: Not open on Mondays, Liberty's hours begin at 4:00 P.M. Tuesday through Friday, noon on Saturday, and 1:00 P.M. (until only 8:00 P.M.) Sunday. On the days the brewpub is open, happy hour is from 4:30 until 6:30 P.M., and all

Liberty Street Brewing Company is worth the drive back to Akron after your experience at Vulture's Knob and the Lizard Lounge.

pints drop from $3.25 to $2.50. Pitchers of beer are reduced $2.00.

OTHER BREWS IN THE AREA: The Liberty is the best you'll find in Akron, but if you're headed to Cleveland for the evening, don't even think about missing **Great Lakes Brewing Company** located in the West Side Market area at 2516 Market Street, (216) 771-4404. Great Lakes is arguably the best brewpub in the state and one of the country's finest. Well worth the trip even though you won't find any legal riding closer than Vulture's Knob.

Ohio River Valley

Any Bike & Brew America trip to southeastern Ohio should begin in the town of Athens. Athens is charged with an eclectic atmosphere combining the historic winding brick streets and grand old university buildings with a hip, student-influenced, progressive culture. Incorporated as a city in 1912, Athens is home to the venerable Ohio University, which was founded in 1804, predating the town by over 100 years!

Bordering on the Monday Creek area of the Wayne National Forest and just 30 miles from Lake Hope State Park's 14 legal miles of newly minted singletrack, Athens could be the most mountain-bike-friendly town in all of southern Ohio. However, the brewpub there doesn't yet serve food on a regular basis, and this deficit disqualifies Athens as a stand-alone Bike & Brew America destination.

Therefore your next stop in southern Ohio is about 45 minutes away from Athens in the even more historic town of Marietta. Named as a tribute to Queen Marie Antoinette for French assistance in the American Revolution, Marietta, dating back all the way to 1788, is the oldest permanent settlement in Ohio. Today, owing to two separate oil booms in the late-nineteenth and early-twentieth centuries, Marietta is a charming river town of large Victorian houses with a downtown lined with ornate brick buildings.

And fortunately, Marietta's brewpub is the real deal, serving a full menu alongside plenty of fresh beer. Plus, the hiking trails in the Marietta Unit of the Wayne National Forest have recently been opened to mountain biking and, although challenging and remote, are just waiting to be explored.

Sounds perfect! Unfortunately, Marietta has thus far done nothing to publicize or foster the use of this amazing asset. So, once again, America has moved past Marietta. First it was when the railroad went through Parkersburg, West Virginia, to the south. Then the National Road (today better known as Interstate 70) went through Zanesville to the north. Now most mountain bikers forego Marietta by heading across the Ohio River to Parkersburg for their riding needs and information. Don't you make that same mistake.

255

After battling it out on Lake Hope State Park's single-track, be sure to save time for a quick dip in refreshing Lake Hope.
(Courtesy of Lake Hope State Park)

Athens Area and Lake Hope State Park

THE SCOOP: Singletrack, multiuse trail system with more than a little mountain-bike love.

RIDE LENGTH AND TYPE: 20-mile out-and-back total with shorter routes and an option to make a loop by using various park and forest roads.

THE BIKE: By no means the closest trail system to Athens, as the Dorr Run Trail in the Monday Creek area of the Wayne National Forest earns that distinction, **Lake Hope State Park** is the best and one of Ohio's most ambitious state park mountain-bike projects ever. Located about 30 miles from Athens in the heavily forested and rugged heart of Ohio's iron district, Lake Hope State Park is filled with

Athens

remnants of the iron-smelting industry that once flourished in southern Ohio. The most dramatic sign of this past is the Hope Furnace, which was built over 100 years ago and now serves as an excellent trailhead for the Lake Hope mountain-bike trails.

By the end of 2000, Lake Hope was home to over 14 miles of narrow, well-constructed, succulent singletrack with more miles under construction. The best way to access this southern Ohio phenomenon is the **Hope Furnace Trail,** which begins next to the Hope Furnace itself. The Hope Furnace Trail follows Lake Hope's northwestern shoreline for 3 singletrack miles to the lake's dam and beach area where the 2½-mile, aptly named **Sidewinder Trail** picks up on just the other side of Cabin Ridge Road. After Sidewinder, you can loop back around to the Hope Furnace Trail via the **Little Sandy Trail** (for a 10½-mile balloon-on-a-string ride) or continue onto the newer 3½-mile **Copperhead Trail** to extend the ride even farther. Things get a little difficult to follow here as the trail intersects Cabin Ridge Road and Long Ridge Road multiple times—make sure you have a map so you know where to find the next section of Copperhead. Copperhead eventually intersects Lake Ridge Road and **Wildcat Trail—** a 1-mile dead-end extension—and the new, as-this-book-goes-to-press "under construction" trail that, when complete, will take you almost the whole way to Furnace Ridge Road and back to your waiting vehicle next to Hope Furnace. Currently, the end of Wildcat Trail is the turn-around point for the full 20-mile out-and-back, unless you want to follow Lake Ridge Road northwest to Long Ridge Road, which will also take you to Furnace Ridge Road and back to your starting point via a loop.

DIFFICULTY: Lake Hope is an intermediate trail with a number of possible bailouts to accommodate all levels of riders.

    AEROBIC DIFFICULTY (1–5):

        3

    TECHNICAL DIFFICULTY (1–5):

        3

WARNINGS: Make sure you pick up a copy of the trail map at the park office or print yourself a copy of the map off of Cycle Path's web site. The trail crosses many roads, which is convenient if you want to bail but can be a pain if you don't know where (or if) the trail picks up on the other side.

OTHER TRAILS IN THE AREA: Closest to Athens and the place to go if you'd rather spend your time riding than driving is the **Monday Creek Off-Road Vehicle Trails** in nearby Wayne National Forest. From the **Dorr Run Trailhead** located just off Highway 33, you have access to over 70 miles of 4x4 widetrack just waiting to be explored. However, be prepared to meet those 4x4s and motorcycles as this is primarily a motorized trail. And be prepared not to find any singletrack. Remember, any riding in Wayne National Forest requires you to obtain a national forest daily or yearly pass available from Cycle Path bike shop or the Athens Ranger station. A day pass is $5.00 or an annual pass is $25.00—or you're looking at a $35.00 fine.

CONTACTS: Lake Hope State Park, 27331 State Route 278, McArthur, OH 45651; (740) 596-4938; www.users.ohi-olinks.com/~lakehope. U.S. Forest Service, Athens Ranger District, 219 Columbus Road, Athens, OH 45701; (740) 592-0200; www.fs.fed.us/r9/wayne. Athens Chamber of Commerce, 5 North Court Street, Athens, OH 45701; (740) 594-2251.

MAPS: Maps of Lake Hope are available at the Cycle Path bike shop, on-line at both Cycle Path and Lake Hope's web sites, and even at the Ranger's office. With that kind of availability, you have no excuse whatsoever not to have one! Monday Creek maps are available at Cycle Path and the Athens Ranger District.

BIKE SHOP: Cycle Path, 104 West Union, Athens, OH 45701; (740) 593-8482; www.athenscyclepath.com. A cool little shop just down the street from O'Hooley's Pub & Brewery, Cycle Path can supply you with the maps or the passes to enjoy the nearby national forest.

O'Hooley's Pub & Brewery

24 West Union Street
Athens, Ohio 45701
(740) 594-BREW(2739)
www.frognet.net/~ohooleys

THE PUB: Located in the "Uptown" area of Athens and hidden away on Union Street almost directly across from Ohio University's Student Union, **O'Hooley's Pub & Brewery** is the epitome of a student hangout right down to the stained linoleum tiles and well-worn furniture.

Not to fear, opening at 4:00 P.M., O'Hooley's has a casual and relaxed setting until the sun goes down. Then it's live music a couple nights a week (Celtic music on Mondays), real dartboards, and an outdoor patio to round out the entertainment. Even though O'Hooley's does not yet serve food and is in dire need of an interior face lift, this Athens staple has been serving fine brews from a full-fledged, state-of-the-art brew house since 1996.

THE BREW: The **O'Hooley's Golden Ale** is the self-admitted introductory beer, but things get more interesting with the award-winning **Ohio Pale Ale**, an American-style IPA (India pale ale). Even without the bitterness or alcohol content usually associated with the real thing, this is a nice beer and a continual best seller. The other top-shelf seller is **O'Hooley's Porter**; it's robust with lots of chocolate, served on nitrogen, and the second-best beer in the place behind the genuine **O'Hooley's IPA** (India pale ale). Loaded with malt and hopped to the gills, this is the beer of choice when visiting Athens.

PRICE OF A PINT: Owing to its prime college locale, Power Hour is Sunday through Thursday from 8:00 to 9:00 P.M.

259

OHIO

when pints drop down to a buck from the $2.50 to $2.75 they normally cost.

OTHER BREWS IN THE AREA: If you're looking for food to go with fresh beer, then you have to head over to Marietta, Ohio, and the **Marietta Brewing Company** for that luxury until O'Hooley's finishes the job and puts in that long-promised kitchen.

"Cool! Someone is covering the scene down here!"
—A Cycle Path employee sells Bike & Brew America on Athens.

Marietta Area and Wayne National Forest

THE SCOOP: Almost unlimited singletrack miles form this remote backcountry adventure.

RIDE LENGTH AND TYPE: Variable with over 70 miles of singletrack making up the eight interconnecting trail systems in this national forest unit.

THE BIKE: Not exactly a discovered biking phenomenon yet, the **Marietta Unit of the Wayne National Forest** is the only national forest unit that allows bikes to use the hiking trails in this U.S. Forest Service district. Remote and designed for hikers who disdain switchbacks, these trails are not for the inexperienced. With trails going straight up and down, the rough terrain of the Ohio River Valley, a lot of deadfall that needs to be crossed, and very limited places for food, water, or help, cyclists who attempt this area must be self-sufficient and ready for an adventure.

Marietta

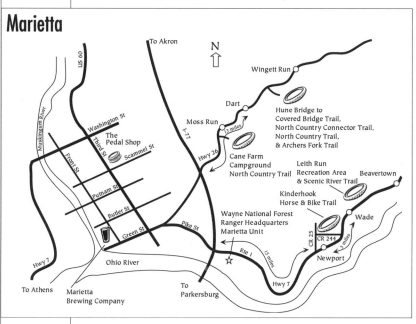

However, if a true backcountry experience is what you consider mountain biking at its finest, then this is the place for you. Various loops, spurs, and connectors equal over 35 singletrack miles! And that's not including the 41 additional miles the bike-friendly **North Country Trail** adds as it passes through the forest unit and connects to the unit's trails.

The historic covered Hune Bridge is the southern end of the Covered Bridge Trail in the Wayne National Forest near Marietta.
(Courtesy of Wayne National Forest)

OHIO

Only about 5 miles from Marietta is Lane Farm Campground and the closest access point to the beckoning North Country Trail. The next closest access to this mega-trail from Marietta is either the **Covered Bridge Trail** or the **North Country Connector Trail**. The Covered Bridge Trail is a 4-mile point-to-point trail with a rare and historic wooden covered bridge at each end—both over 100 years old. The North Country Connector Trail is an additional 3½ miles and links up the Covered Bridge Trail to the North Country Trail and **Archers Fork Trail**, a 9½-mile loop that crosses a 51-foot-long natural arch.

Maybe the best epic singletrack loop in Ohio begins at the **Leith Run Recreation Area** and uses the 3½-mile **Scenic River Trail** to connect to a 4-mile section of the **North Country Trail**, which then hits the east side of the Archers Fork Trail for about 3 miles before intersecting the

3½-mile **Ohio View Connector Trail**. Are you dizzy yet? The Connector Trail finally allows access to the killer climbs and killer views of the Ohio River and the 7-mile point-to-point **Ohio View Trail**. The Ohio View Trail eventually drops you out on **Highway 7**, a short (relative to what you just went through) 6-mile road ride back to your waiting vehicle, almost 30 miles after you began your day. In a word: epic! As you can see, no matter what trail you pick, your adventure will just be beginning.

DIFFICULTY: Virtually undiscovered, the Marietta Unit of the Wayne National Forest is not for the inexperienced or timid. You'll be on your own in some pretty rough territory, so prepare accordingly.

AEROBIC DIFFICULTY (1–5):

4

TECHNICAL DIFFICULTY (1–5):

4

WARNINGS: Besides the remoteness of the ride and the self-sufficiency required, any riding you plan to do in Wayne National Forest requires you to obtain a national forest daily or yearly pass, available at any ranger station or at The Pedal Shop bike shop in town for $5.00 and $25.00, respectively.

OTHER TRAILS IN THE AREA: The least remote of the trails in the Marietta Unit of the Wayne National Forest is **Kinderhook**, a 16-mile self-contained trail system. Kinderhook does not connect to the other Marietta trails, and it does allow horses. Still, it is a little closer to town and offers plenty of riding if you're not quite ready to spend the whole day out in the boonies. After you have exhausted all these options, be sure to head the short distance over to Athens for more Ohio River Valley action at **Lake Hope State Park**.

CONTACTS: U.S. Forest Service, Wayne National Forest, Marietta Unit, Route 1, Box 132, Marietta, OH 45750; (740) 373-9055. Marietta Chamber of Commerce, 316 Third Street, Marietta, OH 45750; (740) 373-5176.

MAPS: Marietta's ranger station has excellent maps of all the forest unit's biking trails available for only $1.00. The

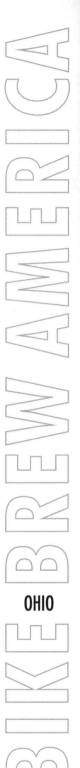

The Archers Fork Trail takes you across Irish Run Natural Bridge—39 feet in the air! (Courtesy of Wayne National Forest)

rangers also have North Country Pathway maps available for 50 cents. Working out to just over 2 cents per mapped mile, that's a bargain! Please remember these maps are an absolute must if you plan on tackling any of the Wayne National Forest Trails mentioned herein. If you don't think you'll be able to make the ranger station during the week to pick them up, call ahead and have them sent to you.

BIKE SHOP: The Pedal Shop, 404 Third Street, Marietta, OH 45750; (740) 374-8584. It's the only shop in town and don't be surprised if the owner tries to talk you out of riding around Marietta. He will warn you that the trails are too hard and too far away and it's too difficult to obtain national forest passes, even though he does sell them in his shop. And with those cautions in mind, please do be warned this area is not for the faint of heart. However, with more legal singletrack within 30 miles than any other bike shop in Ohio can claim, Marietta should not be ignored! And remember, The Pedal Shop is the only place actually in town where you can buy the necessary national forest passes if the ranger station is closed, so plan ahead!

Although Athens is loaded down with bike shops, the next closest shop to Marietta is actually in Parkersburg, West Virginia. So, if The Pedal Shop's service area is backed up on the day you need a fix, check out Bob's Bicycle Shop, 159A Nicolette Road, Parkersburg, WV 26101; (304) 424-6317.

Marietta Brewing Company

167 Front Street
Marietta, Ohio 45750
(740) 373-BREW(2739)

THE PUB: Almost on the Ohio River itself, the **Marietta Brewing Company** delivers more of what you've come to expect in a brewpub with a full menu, nicely restored brick interior, hardwood floors, tin ceilings, and skylights. Replicas of early-twentieth-century French advertisement posters are painted on the walls and add a nice smartness to this pub in Marietta's historic downtown.

The brew house dominates the pub entrance. The fermentation vessels are actually built up over the brew house on metal catwalks, and the whole setup is visible through the large windows facing the street. The dining area is primarily in the back of the restaurant, but still feels connected to the comfortable and friendly front bar area with its high ceilings, skylights, and open floor plan.

THE BREW: Besides a full menu, which includes a build-your-own pasta special, Marietta offers an interesting array of beer. Marietta brews three lagers including **George's First**, an American Pilsener ready for the masses, and the **True Meridian**, this one an amber lager with more body and crisp Saaz hops. The unfiltered **Marietta Weizenbock** is also a lager, but it is made from 50% wheat and 50% dark Munich malt for a pleasant variation. The award-winning **McLaren's Scotch Ale** is rich and smoky flavored and uses a whiskey malt in the mash. The **Marietta Oatmeal Stout** rounds out the beer bill with a robust and full flavor.

PRICE OF A PINT: No happy hour and a 14-ounce glass of beer will cost you $2.50.

OHIO

"Mountain-bike trails? You have to go to Colorado or someplace like that for mountain-bike trails."

—The owner of The Pedal Shop obviously has a different definition of "mountain-bike trails" than we Bike & Brewers do.

OTHER BREWS IN THE AREA: If you have more time to spend in the Marietta area, check out Athens, Ohio, and **O'Hooley's Pub & Brewery.** It doesn't serve food, but it does have some unique ales on tap.

CHAPTER ELEVEN

SOUTH DAKOTA

Loaded with colorful characters and history, the Black Hills region in the southwest corner of the state is your South Dakota Bike & Brew America destination.

Rising out of the fertile, flat to rolling plains of eastern South Dakota, the Black Hills are a mountainous region of ponderosa pine–covered hills stretching into the distance as far as the eye can see.

South Dakota

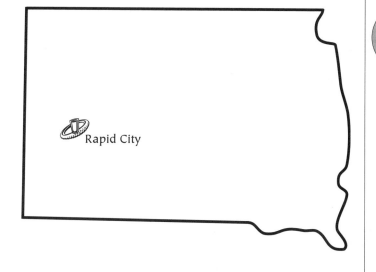

Rapid City

267

The Black Hills were once a Sioux Indian reservation, but that all changed when gold was discovered at the Homestake Gold Mine near the town of Lead. Still one of the richest mining regions in the country, since 1980 the Sioux have refused a Supreme Court settlement for $122 million in compensation for land illegally taken from them, instead wanting the return of their land.

BIKE BREW AMERICA

SOUTH
DAKOTA

On a lighter note, the Black Hills region is now home to several national parks and monuments including the most famous of them all, the Mount Rushmore National Memorial. Built between 1927 and 1941, this massive sculpture features the 60-foot-high faces of four of America's greatest presidents: George Washington, Thomas Jefferson, Abraham Lincoln, and Theodore Roosevelt.

Much like its northern counterpart, North Dakota, there's just not a lot of fresh beer brewing in South Dakota. However, all it takes is one good brewer, and fortunately the western side of the state has one. Rapid City is the gateway to exploring the Black Hills, its national parks and monuments, casinos, caves, and, of course, the mountain-bike trails in the surrounding 1.2 million acres of the Black Hills National Forest.

Rapid City

Located on the edge of the Black Hills in southwestern South Dakota, Rapid City is the perfect base from which to explore the region. Founded in 1876 after gold was discovered in the nearby hills, Rapid City is now the second-largest city in the state. It caters to Black Hills tourism as

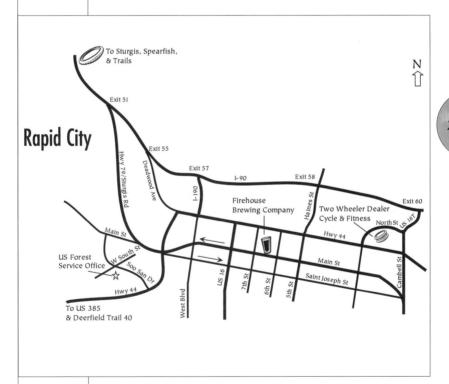

much as anything else. Included in the many attractions are five national parks and monuments within a couple hours' drive from town: Mount Rushmore National Memorial, Wind Cave National Park, Devils Tower National Park, Badlands National Park, and Jewel Cave National Monument.

Only slightly less popular than Mount Rushmore is the Harley-Davidson Motorcycle rally held in nearby Sturgis each August. Since 1940, thousands of Harley-Davidson bikers from all over the country have been making the annual pilgrimage to the small town of Sturgis just west of Rapid City.

Averaging around 4000 feet, and maxing out at 7242 feet on top of Harney Peak, the Black Hills will be the highest-elevation biking you will do in the Midwest region of the country. Featuring the 111-mile Centennial Trail as its crowning jewel, the Black Hills National Forest has more than 300 miles of trails, most of which are open to mountain biking.

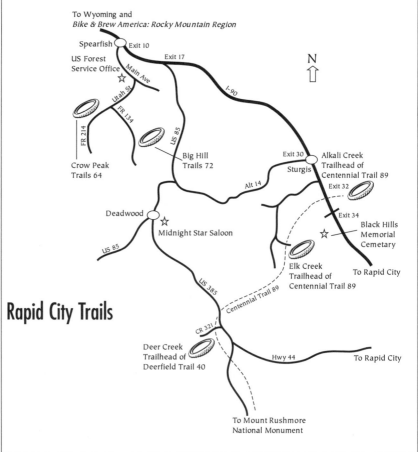

To Wyoming and
Bike & Brew America: Rocky Mountain Region

Spearfish — Exit 10

US Forest Service Office

Exit 17

Main Ave

Utah St

I-90

N

FR 134

FR 214

US 85

Big Hill Trails 72

Crow Peak Trails 64

Exit 30 — Alkali Creek Trailhead of Centennial Trail 89

Sturgis

Exit 32

Alt 14

Exit 34

Deadwood

Midnight Star Saloon

Black Hills Memorial Cemetary

US 85

Elk Creek Trailhead of Centennial Trail 89

To Rapid City

SOUTH DAKOTA

US 385

Rapid City Trails

Centennial Trail 89

CR 321

Deer Creek Trailhead of Deerfield Trail 40

Hwy 44

To Rapid City

To Mount Rushmore National Monument

BIKE BREW AMERICA

Centennial Trail (Trail 89): Alkali Creek Section

THE SCOOP: III miles of singletrack traveling through the Black Hills of South Dakota.

RIDE LENGTH AND TYPE: 22½-mile out-and-back total to the **Elk Creek Trailhead** with unlimited options for longer, or shorter, rides.

THE BIKE: South Dakota honored its centennial in 1989 with the dedication of the III-mile **Centennial Trail**, also known as **Trail 89**. It's all singletrack, and most of it is open to mountain bikes. Now that's a fitting anniversary celebration! The longest trail in the Black Hills, Centennial travels from Bear Butte State Park south all the way to Elk Mountain Campground and encompasses every type of terrain the Black Hills has to offer.

The best place to begin this smorgasbord of Black Hills singletrack is at the **Alkali Creek Trailhead**. Located right off Interstate 90, it's the easiest to find and as one of the most trodden sections, it's also the easiest to follow. Brown trail markers labeled with the unmistakable "89" denote the Centennial Trail so well it's hard to get lost even without a map. Just head south across the Alkali Creek Trailhead's dirt parking lot, pick up the singletrack and ride toward the interstate, and start following the signs. You'll soon cross under the expressway through a huge drainpipe—even though the periodic presence of cattle makes this a somewhat smelly proposition, it is still a very effective method of avoiding the expressway. Barely 1 mile after this slightly noxious crossing, you enter the fresh pine forest and leave the cow pastures and sounds of Interstate 90 far behind.

Now you're climbing at a mellow grade though a nice stand of pines, following the contours of the valley on a slightly rocky but still very rideable trail. You'll encounter a little bit of sand from the countless hooves that have passed by, but nothing impassable. Soon your valley riding will change to ridge riding, and you will briefly break free from the surrounding pine cover for a view of your surroundings. After this brief glimpse of the Black Hills, the trail begins to traverse a gentle hill by switchbacking across the face on a pine-needle–covered singletrack trail dappled with sunlight breaking through the boughs.

After you reach the summit of this gradual hill (you've climbed 400 feet over the past 2 miles), prepare for a

Tall pines follow you through much of your single-track journey south from the Alkali Creek Trail-head of the Centennial Trail (no. 89).

steep and loose-rock descent that'll drop you out onto a fast and smooth B&B Hotmile before putting you into a dry creek bed and the start of your second major climb. Another 400 feet over the next 2 miles. Starting to get the picture of what this trail is like?

This kind of "torture" can go on for as long as you're interested and able, but at some point you're gonna have to make one of the toughest decisions you'll face all day—when to turn around. Well, not to fear. Remember all that gradual climbing? By turning around at the top of the second major climb (around the 6½-mile point), you'll be in for a mostly downhill trip all the way back down the mountain, through the cow pastures, under Interstate 90, and back to reality. Want more mileage? Then keep heading all the way to **Elk Creek Trailhead** for a 22½-mile out-and-back total.

DIFFICULTY: When broken down into manageable sections, the Centennial Trail is a picture perfect intermediate ride. If you start thinking about knocking off the whole thing in an afternoon, then advanced is the only way to describe it.

AEROBIC DIFFICULTY (1–5):

3

TECHNICAL DIFFICULTY (1–5):

3

WARNINGS: The trail starts out traveling through cow pastures. Most of the fences have rideable ramps for hikers and bikers, but if you find some gates that must be opened and closed manually, make sure you leave them the way you found them. Even though well traveled, this is still a remote area. Please prepare accordingly. Also remember that mountain bikes are not allowed on the trails in Wind Cave National Park and the Black Elk Wilderness. Bypass routes are signed to detour around these areas.

OTHER TRAILS IN THE AREA: Obviously any other Centennial trailhead will offer more singletrack terrain than you can cover in a single day. The next trailhead southwest of Alkali is **Elk Creek,** and the Centennial Trail

there is a little less traveled and correspondingly more difficult. Finished off the Centennial before noon and looking for more? **The Deerfield Trail (Trail 40)** offers another 28 miles of trail, including the **Deerfield Lake Loop Trail (Trail 40L).** It's the balloon-on-a-string type of trail, only the string is 18 miles long and the balloon has a 10-mile circumference. Looking for something a little milder? Then near Spearfish is the beginner **Big Hill Trails (Trail 72)**, a cross-country ski trail that offers over 16 miles of beginner to intermediate trails. Short and very advanced, the **Crow Peak Trails (Trail 64)** offers a 1600-foot climb in the 3½ miles that make up this difficult out-and-back trail to the top of Crows Peak and spectacular views of Wyoming, Montana, and South Dakota.

CONTACTS: U.S. Forest Service, Pactola-Harney Ranger District, 803 Soo San Drive, Rapid City, SD 57702; (605) 343-1567. U.S. Forest Service, Spearfish Ranger District, 2014 North Main, Spearfish, SD 57783; (605) 642-4622. Rapid City Chamber of Commerce, 444 Mount Rushmore Road, Rapid City, SD 57701; (605) 343-1744.

MAPS: A map kiosk at the Alkali Creek Trailhead offers a map board and glossy "to go" maps of the Centennial Trail. Maps of the other trails mentioned here are available at the ranger station in Rapid City or Spearfish. The U.S. Forest Service also publishes a free glossy trail guide graphically showing the locations of all trails in the Black Hills and whether they are open to mountain bikes—an excellent resource to get your bearings straight when first visiting the area.

BIKE SHOP: Two Wheeler Dealer Cycle & Fitness, 100 East Boulevard North, Rapid City, SD 57701; (605) 343-0524.

Firehouse Brewing Company

610 Main Street
Rapid City, South Dakota 57701
(605) 348-1915
www.firehousebrewing.com

A 1915 original, the Rapid City Fire Department is now home to the Firehouse Brewing Company in downtown Rapid City.

THE PUB: Outside, the original fire-engine-red garage doors of the 1915 Rapid City Fire Department building still make up the face of the **Firehouse Brewing Company**. Inside, raised tables allow a look through the windows of these giant doors out onto Main Street. Several fire-hydrant tap handles behind the square community bar take center stage with, you guessed it, a usable pole descending from the pub's second floor.

Turned into a sort of fireman hall of fame, the entire restaurant is decorated in fire fighting–related memorabilia. An antique fire trolley hangs from the tin ceiling, and the whole place is decorated in fireman badges, antique hose nozzles, fire-department photos, helmets, fire extinguishers, and fire-jumper uniforms.

The bar area is downstairs with additional dining upstairs around the

BIKE BREW AMERICA

SOUTH DAKOTA

large banistered opening in the first floor ceiling. An outdoor brick patio is adjacent to the bar and offers live music on summer weekends.

THE BREW: Since 1992, Firehouse has been pumping fresh beer for the Black Hills of South Dakota. Usually, three standard brews and two specials will be tapped at any time. The **Firehouse Extra Pale Ale** is the lightest but still quite good with a surprising amount of malt flavor for this style of beer. Next up on the depth chart is the **Chukkar Ale**—an English-style pale ale with a higher alcohol content and surprisingly nice hoppy bite. The **Smoke Jumper Stout** rounds out the regulars with a smooth body and bitter coffee finish. Expect two other seasonals chosen from the 12 recipes usually brewed, including the **Buffalo Bitter**, **Firehouse Red**, **Firehouse IPA** (India pale ale), and **Strong Arm Porter**.

PRICE OF A PINT: Happy hour is daily from 3:00 to 6:00 P.M. with pints down to $2.00 from the regular price of $3.00.

OTHER BREWS IN THE AREA: On the third floor of the Firehouse is the **Fat Boys Beach Club**, a dance club that opens at 7:00 P.M. with pool, foosball, multiple TVs, and Firehouse brews. Got wheels? Then head to the restored historic gambling town of Deadwood about 35 miles northwest of Rapid City. Here you'll find Kevin Costner's **Midnight Star Saloon**. Although not a brewpub, it does serve some fine ales including the Great American Beer Festival gold medal–winning **Midnight Star Ale**, brewed exclusively for Kevin by the Sioux Falls Brewing Company in Sioux Falls, South Dakota.

CHAPTER TWELVE

WISCONSIN

Known as the Badger State because of the lead rush of 1827 when the miners would build their homes into the hillsides like badgers, Wisconsin actually is friendlier than its nickname implies. Today, the familiar cheesehead hats of the Green Bay Packers remind American football fans that Wisconsin produces over 30% of the cheese consumed in this country.

Wisconsin

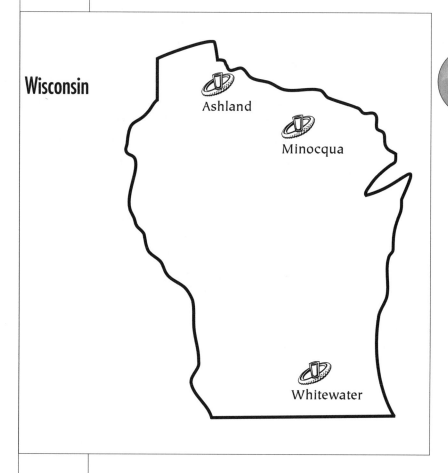

Ashland

Minocqua

Whitewater

BIKE BREW AMERICA

WISCONSIN

Dominated by second-growth forests, lakes, and glaciated terrain, northern Wisconsin is very similar in geography to both northern Michigan and northern Minnesota. However, in stark contrast with the northern regions of these neighboring states, Wisconsin's trails are organized, mapped, marked, and maintained beyond belief. Although most of these trails are cross-country ski trails or 4x4 and firebreak roads, the sheer quantity of the possibilities makes northern Wisconsin a mountain biker's vacation destination.

Two large and important clubs are responsible for this mountain-bike-friendly region of Wisconsin. The most well known of these is the Chequamegon Area Mountain Bike Association or CAMBA. Based in Hayward, Wisconsin, their reach includes most of northwest Wisconsin's Chequamegon National Forest—in which over 300 miles of trails have been designated and marked for mountain-bike use. The Hayward area was made famous by the annual Chequamegon Fat Tire Festival held there each September since 1983. This race attracts 2500 bikers from all over the nation and is commonly considered one of the premier fat-tire events. Smaller and less known, but just as effective, the Vilas Area Mountain Bike and Ski Association (VAMBASA) does much the same in northeast Wisconsin.

Southern Wisconsin may be better known for the brewing industry in Milwaukee than mountain-bike trails. Nevertheless, the very popular Kettle Moraine State Forest Trails near Whitewater, Wisconsin, attract riders by the thousands from Milwaukee, Madison, and Chicago each year.

Ashland

Located on the Chequamegon Bay on the south shore of Lake Superior, Ashland offers a blissful summertime getaway for vacationers to Wisconsin's north woods. An important port for the Midwest, the large coal dock stretches out over the water and can be easily seen from downtown Ashland.

In addition to checking out the ample mountain-biking opportunities offered in this remote locale, be sure and save some time to visit the nearby Apostle Islands National Lakeshore. Home to 21 islands, 12 miles of mainland shoreline, lighthouses, sea caves, and old-growth

Ashland

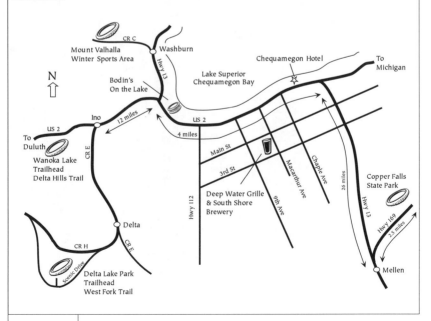

forest, this area may be one of the few reasons in Ashland not to be on the trail or in the pub.

The mountain-bike riding in the area is virtually unlimited with six nearby CAMBA clusters and a multitude of cross-country ski trails. The closest brewery to this biking paradise is Ashland's Deep Water Grille and South Shore Brewing Company, only 20 miles from the nearest Chequamegon Trailhead.

CAMBA assurance markers keep you on track through the birch, maple and oak along the West Fork Trail.

West Fork Trail: Delta Cluster of the Chequamegon Area Mountain Bike Association (CAMBA)

THE SCOOP: One of many loops the CAMBA has mapped and marked in the Chequamegon National Forest.

RIDE LENGTH AND TYPE: 11.3-mile loop.

THE BIKE: The Chequamegon National Forest in northern Wisconsin has been taken under the wing of CAMBA (Chequamegon Area Mountain Bike Association). Divided up into six "clusters," the forest offers over 300 miles of mapped routes of singletrack, doubletrack, dirt, and paved roads. From the famous **Chequamegon Fat Tire Festival Trail** in the **Cable Cluster** to a mix of singletrack and road riding in the **Delta Cluster**, each area offers a slightly different terrain and type of trail to explore.

The easiest cluster to access from the beer haven of Ashland (it's the only brewpub even close to this CAMBA mountain-bike heaven) is the Delta Cluster. From the **Wanoka Lake Trailhead**, take the **Delta Hills Trail**, or from the **Delta Lake Park Trailhead**, take the **West Fork Trail**. The Wanoka Lake Trailhead and the Delta Hills Trail may be easier to find, but the Delta Lake Park Trailhead and the West Fork Trail have the most singletrack.

A loop (as most CAMBA rides are), this trail will take you past lakes and streams, into fern-covered valleys, and through open forests of pine, aspen, maple, and oak. Although it's certainly possible, you'll have a hard time getting lost with the comforting presence of CAMBA's "reassurance" markers and frequent numbered signs matching up with CAMBA's trail maps known as "landmarks."

Mostly a beginner ride, the singletrack has enough roots and glaciated rocks to slip you up, and thus singletrack is categorized as intermediate. It's well worth the effort as

the low underbrush in most places allows nice views into the forest. If you're looking for more miles, the southwest corner of the West Fork Trail intersects with the intermediate **Tall Pines Trail Loop**, which can be added for another 10.8 miles of adventure.

DIFFICULTY: Beginner to intermediate. The singletrack part of this ride is intermediate, but the rest is beginner material. If you're looking for a more advanced ride, then add the Tall Pines Trail Loop for a 22-mile total.

AEROBIC DIFFICULTY (1–5):

2

TECHNICAL DIFFICULTY (1–5):

3

WARNINGS: Even though CAMBA offers one of the best-marked national forest trail systems in the country, trails change and the reassurance markers can be knocked down or vandalized. Make sure you have the most current map available, and keep track of where you are on it even though it is sometimes tempting just to follow the blue reassurance signs with the cool little bikers on them.

OTHER TRAILS IN THE AREA: As mentioned already, easier to find and located just a bit farther west on U.S. Highway 2 is the **Wanoka Lake Trailhead** and the starting point for the 15.8-mile intermediate to advanced **Delta Hills Trail**, not much singletrack but still a worthy northern Wisconsin ride. Once you purchase the CAMBA mountain-bike maps, you've pretty much tapped into an unlimited resource for epic riding. Just check out the descriptions and pick the ride that suits you. However, if you exhaust all 300 CAMBA miles or just want something a little closer to the brewery, the **Mount Valhalla Winter-Sports Area** offers almost 20 miles of rideable ski trails even if they do tend to be somewhat sandy. If you go, the **Teuton Trails** have less sand and are on the best side of the park for riding. **Copper Falls State Park** offers ancient lava flows, deep gorges, and spectacular waterfalls, rivers, and lakes throughout the 8 miles of intermediate mountain-bike trails available.

CONTACTS: CAMBA, P.O. Box 280, Cable, WI 54821; (800) 234-6635; www.cambatrails.org. Chequamegon Fat

Tire Festival; www.cheqfattire.com. Cable Area Chamber of Commerce, P.O. Box 141, Cable, WI 54821; (800) 533-7454; www.cable4fun.com. Ashland Chamber of Commerce, 320 Fourth Street West, Ashland, WI 54806; (715) 682-2500.

MAPS: "Wow!" is what you'll say when you pick up a package of CAMBA maps at Bodin's On The Lake bike shop. For only $5.00 you get seven huge maps with detailed trail directions of all six CAMBA trail clusters—some 300 miles of mapped trails covering over 1600 square miles! If five bucks is too much, Bodin's usually has individual cluster maps for sale, so there should be no excuses about not having a map and getting lost.

BIKE SHOP: Bodin's On The Lake, Lake Shore Drive, U.S. Highway 2 West, Ashland, WI 54806; (715) 682-6441. Located on your way out of Ashland toward the Delta Cluster, this is the place to get CAMBA maps, directions, and last-minute equipment. Bodin's also has free maps of the many ski trails available in Wisconsin for mountain biking including Mount Valhalla Winter-Sports Area and Copper Falls State Park.

The Delta Hills trail passes by the remote beauty of Patsy Lake.
(Photo by Quinn Kirkpatrick)

Deep Water Grille & South Shore Brewery

808 West Main Street
Ashland, Wisconsin 54806
(715) 682-9199
www.southshorebrewery.com

*The Bike &
Brew
America
truck arrives
just as
construction
begins on the
Deep Water
Grille &
South Shore
Brewery's
new brew-
house.*

THE PUB: Disaster struck the former Railyard Pub & South Shore Brewery on April Fools Day 2000. Stopping by the restaurant for a last-minute errand before heading to Superior, Wisconsin, for a brewfest, the owner noticed smoke rising from the roof. Four hours later, the Railyard Pub was all but destroyed with only the shell of the historic brownstone building still standing majestically at the end of Third Street overlooking downtown Ashland and Lake Superior.

THE BREW: Not to despair! The owners are well on their way to a 2001 opening in another historic downtown building. The new pub, renamed **Deep Water Grille & South Shore Brewery**, will sit in a 6000-square-foot building with a twenty-barrel brewery cranking out their flagship **South Shore Nut Brown Ale** in addition to the other 23 styles South Shore used to produce on their former three-barrel system inside the old Railyard Pub.

With the new and improved brewery, the owners hope to begin large-scale distribution of their ales and eventually rebuild the old depot building. In the meantime, their new location in the historic Wilmarth Building, still within sight of Lake Superior's south shore, will be pouring South Shore ales right on the edge of the world's largest freshwater lake.

PRICE OF A PINT: The Deep Water Grille is scheduled to open in the spring of 2001 with pints of beer ringing in at $3.00 but no happy hour in sight.

OTHER BREWS IN THE AREA: Sorry—this is the extreme edge of northern Wisconsin, and we're lucky for the dedication to good beer South Shore supplies. Many of the bars along Main Street carry South Shore's Nut Brown, but that's about as close as you're gonna get to variety here in the upper north woods of Wisconsin.

285

"Not right now. I have a barrel in the back, but we have to finish up the Leine's here first."
—Bartender at Hotel Chequamegon when asked if South Shore Brown was on tap.

"Well, we better get started then!"
—Stranger, and Leinenkugel beer lover, at end of the bar.

Minocqua

One of several logging towns that sprang up throughout this region of Wisconsin at the turn of the twentieth
century, Minocqua is now centrally located among a
unique array of abandoned railroad rights-of-way and
old logging roads. Although lumberjacks had completely
cut the original forest by 1910, second-growth tall pine
and hardwood trees have once again reclaimed the north
woods of Wisconsin.

Known as the "The Island City," and once completely
surrounded by Lake Minocqua, the name still fits the bill,
as this part of northern Wisconsin is home to one of the
largest concentrations of freshwater in America. Thanks
to the over 3200 lakes and streams in the area, Minocqua
was voted "one of the 10 best places to live and waterski in America" by *Waterski Magazine* in 1996.

Not just a water wonderland, the public land surrounding Minocqua is simply loaded with riding possibilities.
The logging roads and now-railless right-of-ways from
those early logging days make an extensive network of
trails that sees all types of users. From snowmobiles and
cross-country skiers in the winter to hikers and mountain
bikers in the summer, these trails fill the Northern
Highland–American Legion State Forest. And what makes
this area better than most is not just that there are miles
of trails, but that the Vilas Area Mountain Bike and Ski
Association (VAMBASA) has done a fantastic job of mapping, marking, and maintaining these trails so locals and
vacationers alike may enjoy them.

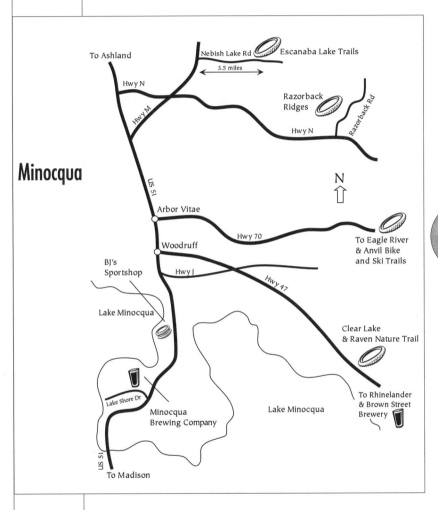

Minocqua

To Ashland

Hwy N

Hwy M

Nebish Lake Rd — Escanaba Lake Trails

3.5 miles

Razorback Ridges

Razorback Rd

Hwy N

US 51

Arbor Vitae

Woodruff

BJ's Sportshop

Hwy 70

Hwy J

Hwy 47

To Eagle River & Anvil Bike and Ski Trails

N

Lake Minocqua

Clear Lake & Raven Nature Trail

Lake Shore Dr

Minocqua Brewing Company

Lake Minocqua

To Rhinelander & Brown Street Brewery

US 51

To Madison

Razorback Ridges

THE SCOOP: Cross-country ski-trail system with miles of developed singletrack winding throughout lakes and forests.

RIDE LENGTH AND TYPE: Variable—with over 30 miles of singletrack, widetrack, and doubletrack available.

THE BIKE: Razorback Ridges is the place to begin your exploration of this land of plenty. It offers riding for all ability levels and actually encourages biking on its multitude of ski and singletrack trails. Home to the popular "Ride the Ridges" mountain-bike race each year, numerous singletrack loops have been cut around the existing widetrack ski trails to offer additional singletrack fun for intermediate and advanced riders.

The ski trails are great for beginners and those interested in keeping it peaceful, but after intersection 6, things will start getting interesting for the rest of you. The **Expert Loop** tightens things up with singletrack, sharp turns, short climbs, and plenty of roots and rocks to get in the way. The towering trees and dense underbrush assure you stay on the trail, and well-marked intersections assure you won't get lost. In fact, by just sticking to the singletrack and using the ski trails as connectors, you can easily put together over 10 miles of singletrack trails winding through the wooded forest and numerous lakes.

On a hot day, an excursion to Blueberry Lake offers excellent singletrack and refreshingly cool, clear, and deep water. Of course, the ski trails offer lots of flat-out fun—you can really let it out because the 15-foot-wide lanes give great visibility while the blaze of smooth singletrack down the middle gives great traction.

DIFFICULTY: Beginner to intermediate. The ski trails are all about beginner mountain biking. The singletrack is tougher but still nothing that a determined intermediate rider won't be able to handle.

> **AEROBIC DIFFICULTY (1–5):**
> 2 (3 on singletrack)
> **TECHNICAL DIFFICULTY (1–5):**
> 2 (3 on singletrack)

WARNINGS: All the trails are directional at Razorback Ridge so be sure to watch the postings and travel in the correct direction.

OTHER TRAILS IN THE AREA: Not to sound like a broken record (maybe it's from going around all those loops!), but the Minocqua area is filled with riding. The closest is the **Raven Nature Trail,** a mostly beginner trail if you stick to the inside loop. Things get more difficult if you wander to the outer loop. The **Escanaba Lake Trails** are a local favorite with about 7 miles of rolling-fun singletrack. For a different look to your riding, check out the 12 or so miles at **Anvil Bike and Ski Trails** where the forest is big and dark and some say resembles the Black Forest in Germany.

CONTACTS: VAMBASA, P.O. Box 189, Arbor Vitae, WI 54568; (715) 479-6074; www.vambasa.com. Minocqua Chamber of Commerce, 8216 U.S. Highway 51 South, Minocqua, WI 54548; (715) 356-5266.

MAPS: Razorback Ridge has its own trail map, which is available free at BJ's Sportshop in Minocqua and in the warming hut at Razorback Ridge's Trailhead. Also at BJ's, for a $1.00 donation, you can get the VAMBASA's Bicycle Map that details a dozen Vilas-area biking trails.

BIKE SHOP: BJ's Sportshop; 917 U.S. Highway 51 North, Minocqua, WI 54548; (715) 356-3900. Right on the shore of Lake Minocqua and right off of U.S. Highway 51, you can't miss the shop on your way through the small island town. BJ's has the Razorback Ridge and VAMBASA Bicycle Maps, plus the advice to go with it.

Minocqua Brewing Company

238 Lake Shore Drive
Minocqua, WI 54548
(715) 358-3040
www.minocquabrewingco.com

THE PUB: A solid dark brick building originally built by the Masons in 1927 and then renovated and reopened as **Minocqua Brewing Company**, the restaurant now offers lakeview dining downstairs in the restaurant and pub area and upstairs fun and games in the sports bar.

Located right on the shores of Lake Minocqua in the old Mason's Lodge, Local 330 is now an ideal Bike & Brew America layover. Minocqua Brewing Company (MBC) is just minutes from the Northern Highland–American Legion State Forest, its 3200 lakes, streams, and ponds and hundreds of miles of trails. It's only fitting that in a land of such plenty, this bastion of fresh beer now resides perfectly situated "On the Island" ready to replenish weary vacationers from Milwaukee, Madison, Chicago, and beyond.

THE BREW: Since opening in 1997, it has taken MBC a couple of years to earn the locals' acceptance in an area where folks want very little to do with anything other than an inexpensive American-style lager. Eventually quality overcomes all adversity and things are starting to change. The coup came when MBC hit gold at the 1999 Great American Beer Festival in the specialty beers category with the **Island City Wild Rice Lager,** all but insuring Minocqua's continued success.

Since the gold, the Wild Rice Lager is the best-selling beer but by no means the only good beer here. In fact, after the obligatory **Island City Northern Wheat Ale,** a

> *"I like to bike and swim so I plan most of my rides accordingly."*
> —Rich Robertson of BJ's Sportshop talks about how he picks his rides. With over 3200 lakes, streams, and ponds in the area, that's not a bad idea. So how about a little bike, swim, and brew?

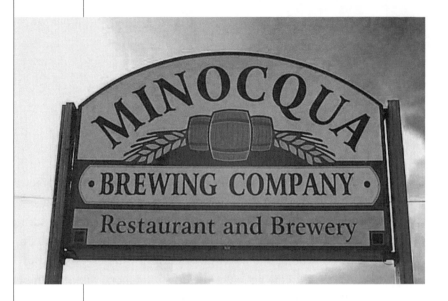

Minocqua Brewing Company is home to the fine array of Island City beers including the Great American Beer Festival winner, Island City Wild Rice Lager.
(Courtesy of Minocqua Brewing Company)

typical American-style wheat, things are four star across the board. The **Island City Pale Ale** is a bold rendition with lots of malt flavors and even more hops. The **Island City Red Ale** is a smooth caramel delight using light German hops to assure that the caramel stays ahead of the hops.

And things just get better from there with the **Island City Rye Porter**. What may be the only porter out there brewed with rye, it's an absolute treat, starting off smooth and light and finishing with a mellow licorice flavor. A definite must.

PRICE OF A PINT: No happy hour in the summer so pints are a steep $3.50 unless you order the beer of the day. You don't get to pick the flavor, but it's a much more reasonable $2.50 all day long.

OTHER BREWS IN THE AREA: There are no other breweries in Minocqua, but the **Thirsty Whale Restaurant** offers a deck right on the lake and within view of the boat ramp, which can provide some pretty entertaining stuff even if the beer isn't as fresh as over at the brewing company. The town of Rhinelander about 26 miles southeast of Minocqua has the **Brown Street Brewery** at 16 North Brown Street, (715) 362-6232, if you are headed in that direction after your day in the woods.

Whitewater

Whitewater, an active college town with a campus of the University of Wisconsin, Whitewater is also a bike town with one of Trek Bicycle Corporation's manufacturing and distribution plants just down the road. This influx of the young and adventurous brings with it a nice mix of extreme activities including mountain biking, hang gliding, paragliding, a rock-climbing gym, multiple bike shops, bike clubs, and, of course, a taste for microbrewed beer.

Whitewater

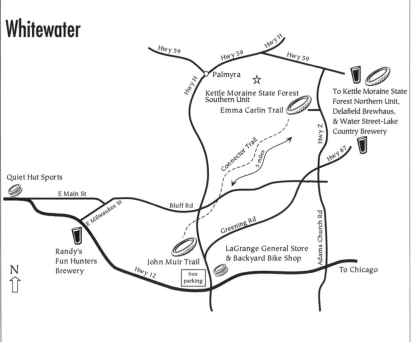

As the town closest and most accessible to the incredibly popular Kettle Moraine State Forest, Whitewater is the perfect place to top off your trip to southern Wisconsin.

Kettle Moraine is the geologic name for the unusual glacially formed landscape that makes up the majority of the Kettle Moraine State Forest. Deposits left by the last glacier to reach this part of southeastern Wisconsin, appropriately named the Wisconsin Glacier, created an interesting landscape of hills, ridges, bluffs, open prairie, lakes, and marshes stretching almost 100 miles in length and ranging between 100 and 320 feet in height. What does this geohistory lesson have to do with Bike & Brew America? It just so happens that this timely geologic event, which occurred over 10,000 years ago, now makes for perfect fat-tire fodder, some of the best of which is located a mere 10 miles from downtown Whitewater. So enjoy your stay!

Kettle Moraine State Forest

THE SCOOP: Over 20 miles of well-buffed singletrack located between Milwaukee and Chicago.

RIDE LENGTH AND TYPE: 24 miles—however, a ride of any length can be mixed and matched from the various loops making up the trail system.

THE BIKE: Right smack in the middle of the 20,500-acre **Kettle Moraine State Forest Southern Unit** lie two biking trail systems that, when connected, create an epic 24-mile adventure of gradually sloping trails mixed with ripping-fast open sections and steep (but short) thigh-burning hills. It's not the technical difficulty that will get you here; it's the sheer quantity of singletrack miles that will have you returning again and again to this Midwest biking para-dise. These trails are smooth and fast affairs that will beg you to put it in the big ring and crank it up.

The entire trail system forms a slightly lopsided barbell shape. The more than 10 miles of the **John Muir Trail** are on one end, and the more than 4 miles of the slightly more challenging **Emma Carlin Trail** are on the other with a 5-mile connector trail between the two. Start from the John Muir Trail, do the outer 10-mile loop, and then take the 5-mile **Connector Trail** over to the 4-mile Emma Carlin Trail and back again for a total right around 24 miles. And, because you will be tempted to hug the big ring for most of the ride, by the end you will be both deliriously happy and completely exhausted.

If there is any fault at all about Kettle Moraine, it's the fact that the trails may be too perfect and too well main-tained. What a terrible problem to have, right? This area is a destination for bikers from both Wisconsin and Illinois, and constant use by thousands of bikes have buffed the trail to a near-perfect hardpack condition where even the rocks and roots are polished to a glistening sheen from countless rubber nobbies passing over them. To combat the effects of so much traffic, what might be challenging steep hill climbs have actually been paved to prevent erosion. Although this works remarkably well (and does remind one of Moab slickrock if you stretch your imagination a bit), it turns what would otherwise be a technically challenging climb into little more than a downshift to a slightly easier gear and physical grunt as you blast by it in search of the next downhill.

With that whine out of the way, I definitely want you to know that these trails are directional, smooth, fast, and fun. The best way to tackle the trails is from the southern John Muir end as the LaGrange General Store & Backyard Bike Shop is located less than 1 mile from the trailhead and has plenty of free parking for bikers. By parking in bike-friendly LaGrange's spare lot and riding to the trailhead, you'll save the $7.00 out-of-state Wisconsin State Park's parking fee. Use it later at the brewpub. Still, be prepared for the $3.00 Wisconsin State Trail Pass use fee (or $10.00 for a season pass), but that money is well spent as it goes directly to trail maintenance, maps, and

Riders use the Connector Trail to combine the John Muir Trails with the Emma Carlin Trails in the Kettle Moraine State Forest. (Photo by Quinn Kirkpatrick)

signs. Without this fee, this magnificent trail system wouldn't be here for your use, so pay up with a smile as you hit the dirt.

DIFFICULTY: Beginner to intermediate. These trails are all perfectly manicured and marked. The John Muir Trail is laid out in such a way as to allow riders to do loops of 1.5 miles, 4 miles, 5.3 miles, 6.8 miles, 10 miles, 20 miles, or the 24-mile Kettle Moraine Grand Daddy.

AEROBIC DIFFICULTY (1–5):

2–3 (depending on length)

TECHNICAL DIFFICULTY (1–5):

2–3 (with the Emma Carlin Trail getting the 3)

WARNINGS: These trails are for mountain bikers and hikers. They are directional, so just follow the markers, keep your eyes open, and you should be fine. No motorized vehicles or horses are allowed although you may encounter some hikers and hunters. The real concern for you here is the weather. The trail will be closed when it's muddy, and if you ride anyway, you're looking at a $75 dollar fine! Hey, there's a reason the trail is in such good condition. The best way to avoid an unnecessary trip to the trail is by calling the Trail Conditions Hotline at (262) 594-6200. Also, be aware that the trail is completely closed between February 15 and March 31. After that date, call and check if the trails have officially been opened yet.

OTHER TRAILS IN THE AREA: Riders come from Chicago, Milwaukee, and Madison to ride the Kettle Moraine State Forest Southern Unit, and the trails there have something for everyone. If you still gotta have more, then the Northern Unit of the Kettle Moraine State Forest has the **Greenbush Trail,** another 11 miles of easy cross-country ski trails open to mountain bikes, and the **New Fane Trail,** 8 miles of intermediate trails open to bikes. In addition, the Northern Unit of the park also has a multitude of dirt roads that are open to bikes. The **Whitewater Ice Age Bicycle Trail** begins at the Whitewater Lake Ranger Station and offers 48.7 miles of bicycle touring to the town of Evansville, Wisconsin.

CONTACTS: Kettle Moraine State Forest, Southern Unit, S91 W39091 Highway 59, Eagle, WI 53119; (262) 594-6200. Whitewater Chamber of Commerce, 402 West Main Street, Whitewater, WI 53190; (262) 473-4005.

MAPS: Maps are at both trailheads, and map signposts are at all trail intersections. By using the maps and trail descriptions, you shouldn't have any problems planning and executing the perfect ride for yourself. The Backyard Bike Shop in the LaGrange General Store also has trail maps if you like to plan in advance. Pick one up when you stop in for a java before the ride.

BIKE SHOP: LaGrange General Store & Backyard Bike Shop, W6098 Highway 12, Whitewater, WI 53190; (262) 495-3327; www.backyardbikes.com. This funky little shop and restaurant caters especially to bikers and is the biking scene in the Whitewater area. With bike shop, deli, coffee, and ice cream, this place has it all including a nice selection of local micros for after the ride. Another well-equipped shop if you're already in Whitewater proper is Quiet Hut Sports, 186 West Main Street, Whitewater, WI 53190, (262) 473-2950.

Randy's Fun Hunters Brewery

841 East Milwaukee Street (U.S. Highway 12)
Whitewater, Wisconsin 53190
(262) 473-8000
www.funhunters.com

"Just Hunter Brau Oatmeal Stout. We don't have any fancy names like Butthead Porter or Wild Ride Red. Our names say it all."
—Bike & Brew America asks about a couple of beer names.

THE PUB: Randy's Fun Hunters Brewery is in a newer building on the outskirts of Whitewater. A restaurant since the 1970s, the owners added a brewery in 1994 and now offer a nice selection of fresh beer within 10 minutes of the trails. Although the building itself is a large modern lodge-type structure, inside you'll find plenty of old photos of historic Whitewater. Most interesting of these are the old black and white pictures of the Fun Hunters Club, which the restaurant takes part of its name from. The Fun Hunters were a nineteenth-century club from Whitewater; the members would load up on beer, provisions, more beer, boats, yet more beer, and tents before heading out to nearby Lake Koshkonong to sing, dance, and drink all that beer. If only they had bikes back then. . . .

Also, be sure to find the framed citation on the wall concerning one of the most famous students of the illustrious University of Wisconsin–Whitewater, none other than John Belushi. He was picked up for hitchhiking back in 1967 while he was a student, and his city paperwork hangs on Randy's walls like a diploma.

THE BREW: Once you're done browsing the walls, settle into the dark and comfortable bar area, the nicely appointed dining room, or outside on the small stone patio and order yourself one of Randy's finest. Randy, the owner and other half of the brewpub's namesake, actually looked into adding a microbrewery back in the early 1980s, but the lack of a scientific background kept him out

299

The LaGrange General store offers free parking for the trails, a fully outfitted bike shop, and a nice selection of microbrews for when the riding is done.

of the evolving industry. However, with the huge growth of the microbrewery industry came easier access to state-of-the-art brewing systems, so in 1994 Randy took the proverbial plunge, adding the brewery and graduating from the Siebel Institute of Brewing Technology.

Randy now keeps four regular "Hunter Braus" and a seasonal on tap. Of the regulars, the two lighter brews, **Hunter Brau Wheat Ale** and **Amber Lager**, are both clean, smooth, easy-drinking American-style beers. **Hunter Brau Pale Ale** is a step up the adventure ladder with a bit more bitterness. **Hunter Brau Oatmeal Stout** served on nitrogen is the house's crowning jewel—creamy, full bodied, and a complete joy to drink.

PRICE OF A PINT: No happy hour except during Packer games when pints drop a buck, which brings the regular $3.00 pint down to $2.00. Also, keep in mind that the place is closed on Mondays.

OTHER BREWS IN THE AREA: The **LaGrange General Store & Backyard Bike Shop** sits almost at the **John Muir Trailhead** and sells micros that can be consumed on premises or taken back to camp. For another brewpub you have to travel 18 miles northeast to the small town of Delafield, which hosts no less than two brewpubs in a town of a little more than 5000 people. The **Delafield Brewhaus** is at 3832 Hillside Road, (262) 646-7821, and serves a mean barleywine, but probably the better of the two is **Water Street–Lake Country Brewery**, (262) 646-7878.

APPENDIX

WELCOME TO THE CONCRETE JUNGLE

(Various forms of this article previously appeared in *Michigan Cyclist* and *Playground* magazines as "How to Conquer the Concrete Jungle" by Todd Mercer)

No time to pack up the gear, load the bike onto the car, and head for your favorite trail? Short winter days cutting into your riding time? Rain forcing you off the trails? Your pals already left and you can't find the keys to the car? Don't have a car? Well, don't worry. There is a whole world of mountain biking to explore right outside your front door.

That's right, you heard correctly, your home is surrounded by a mecca of technical trails, grueling uphill climbs, heart-pounding jumps, and life-threatening descents. Your town has everything a good mountain-bike trail has and more. So when you can't get to the woods, head for the jungle. The concrete jungle, that is.

Doesn't sound appealing to you? School kids and working stiffs ride their bikes through town, not *real* mountain bikers. Right? Wrong. There's no question about the excitement and challenges of riding through the wilderness. Now ride this thought through that singletrack mind of yours: Trees in the wilderness are stationary and made of wood, trees in the urban jungle travel around 35 miles per hour and are made of steel. Given a choice, which game of chicken sounds more exciting to you?

The following will share the secrets of riding your mountain bike on the streets of your town in order to improve fitness, hone riding skills, show off for the city dwellers, and still have time for a stop at your favorite brewpub on the way home. Starting to sound a little more interesting, isn't it?

Let's talk preparation. There is simply nothing that beats city riding for convenience. You walk your bike out the front door and ride away. No removing your front wheel and squeezing your rig in the back seat or strapping it to the roof. No driving through rush-hour traffic just to get to the highway that leads to the road that will take you to the trail. The urban trail starts and ends with your sidewalk.

Another amenity the city provides is, well, civilization. So, just like any good scout, be prepared to use your surroundings and pack some cash. Water bottle run dry before you're ready to call it quits? Feel that bonk coming on? Need some food? Stop at the corner store and pick up what you need.

Of course, still pack all the same tools you do for the trail. A 5-mile walk back to the trailhead is as much fun as a 5-mile walk back to your house. Which is to say, none at all. Much better to ride, so pack those patches. Got a mechanical that only the wrench at the local shop can tackle? No problem. Put away your pride and pull out 35 cents (soon to be 50, thanks to deregulation). Your buddy who sneered at you for riding the city streets will pick you up and take you home in style. Of course, be prepared for a little smack talking on the way. . . .

So, now you have decided to give city riding a shot, by choice or circumstance. You're standing in front of the house, saddlebag jingling, wondering what to do next. Do what comes naturally: ride. Pick a destination; a park that allows bikes, a lake, a nearby trail, and then get creative. This is your city; you know all the back ways to get around. Now use that savvy and turn your city into a playground. Remember that this is supposed to be fun!

Choosing your destination is only the beginning. No longer are you looking for the quickest way to get there but the most entertaining. Think to yourself, "What's between here and there?" Here are some ideas to get those creative juices flowing.

Civilization means structure and structure means lines. In fact, lines are all over the place. Follow them. Follow them so closely that your wheel seems glued to them whether

they're 12 inches wide or nothing but a crack in pavement. You'll be amazed at how your bike wants to stray from the straight and narrow. It'll seem to have a mind of its own. Learn how to curb those crooked tendencies.

Speaking of curbs, ever ride along the top of one? With the added incentive of a sidewalk curb's 6-inch drop (just enough to keep things interesting), you'll be amazed at how your bike is drawn to that imagined abyss. Master this skill and the singletrack at your favorite trail will become child's play.

Maybe you are a log-jumping junky or just junky at jumping logs. Well, there is no better place to practice than those same sidewalk curbs. Big ones, small ones, you decide. Take them straight on, working on fluently lifting that back wheel up and over. Got that down? Start taking them at different angles to simulate how they really are in the woods.

Maybe you're looking to catch a little air. Have you figured any speed bumps into your path? Not those sharp stubby ones that would be better to jump or bunny hop over. Look for those rollers that Mom used to take at 5 mph or else the family minivan started looking like the *General Lee*. Usually found in school parking lots or apartment driveways, these speed bumps are big-air heaven for bikers looking to launch their rigs into the bright blue beyond. Here's a simple formula: pavement equals speed, speed equals air, and therefore pavement equals air. On the more rational side, pavement also gives you greater control at which speed you decide to hit said bumps. A great way to learn.

Got the flight-simulator game beat? Then ride a retaining wall. It might not be the 300-foot cliff Montanans brag about, but that potential 5-foot spill to the pavement below sure will impress the crowd of pedestrians that are certain to gather anticipating that one wrong move. . . .

Cliff hanging not your cup of sport drink? Try some descending. What better way to practice waterbar and washout conditions than a nice set of stairs? You've seen it in the movies, now bring it to your town. Begin with a small series of steps, maybe two or three. Descend by keeping your weight back and hands off the front brake. You want to maintain some speed while doing this. Go too slow and your front tire might not make it to the next step. You fall and look silly. Once you master some short series of steps, gradually increase the length and steepness until the rational part of your brain shouts, "Enough! Stairs are for walking!"

You can also find stairs to ascend. Again start with a short series at a nice grade. Treat them just like a pile of logs. Pull up on the handlebars and power over them. As you gain experience, and confidence, increase the number of steps. A word of caution: after cleaning a few sets of stairs you might experience a slight addiction problem. You're likely to become something of a stair addict and merely walking by one will find you checking for length, width, rise, run, and overall rideability . . . very sad.

What's that you say? Looking for some conditioning training today? Well, pedaling is pedaling, on trail or off. What better way to build up your aerobic base than by hitting the road where the pavement lets you hold a steady cadence and optimal heart rate? Spin until your heart and lungs are content.

Hills? Hills are hills are hills, be they dirt or paved. Looking for elevation in an otherwise flat city? Go where rollerbladers head for hill and cornering clinics: parking structures! A few repeats will do you some good. Just don't forget about those urban trees—they grow 'em thick in there. Careful!

So now you have some ideas not only on how to survive, but conquer the concrete jungle. The key to remember is creativity. You are only limited by your imagination and riding skills, which will improve daily as you explore your city. You can travel a different trail everyday or set up a course using various obstacles to gauge your progress. What starts out as, "Aaaaahhhhh!," will quickly become, "Been there, done that."

Last words of urban playground wisdom. A big hill is still a big hill and a stop sign is still a stop sign. Be sure to obey local ordinances when out to play . . . if unsure what those are, check at your city hall.

GLOSSARY

ALE – Beer made with ale yeast; the most common type of beer found in brewpubs. The short fermentation period and minimum aging requirements of ale make this type of beer more practical for small breweries as it spends less time in the fermentation vessel and more time in the serving tank ready to drink. See also **Lager.**

B&B HOTMILE – Simply put, a B&B Hotmile describes the sweetest section of an already sweet trail. A slice of mountain-bike nirvana. The part of the ride that leaves you grinning like a fool and drooling for more. The true Bike & Brew America goods.

BALLOON-ON-A-STRING – A combination of a loop (the balloon) and an out-and-back (the string). Basically, you travel to a point where the trail diverges onto a loop. Take the loop all the way around. Then return to the trailhead on the out-and-back trail.

BEER – There are two basic types of beer: ales and lagers. The difference is all in the yeast. See **Ale** and **Lager.**

BEER ENGINE – See **Hand-Pumped.**

BREW HOUSE – This is where the magic of brewing actually takes place. Some brew houses are fancy state-of-the-art presentation breweries, and others consist of dairy equipment hidden away in the basement. Regardless of what they look like, all serve the same purpose: to make you fresh, unique beer.

BREWPUB – Accept no imitations. A brewpub is a restaurant or bar that brews its own beer, of which 50% must be for on-premises consumption. Although the various states have different laws further defining a brewpub, this characterization forms the essence.

BRITISH COLUMBIA–STYLE TRAILS or **NORTH SHORE–STYLE TRAILS** – Because the North Shore of British Columbia trail builders and riders pretty much perfected the practice of this insane style of trail that can hardly be called "cross-country," their name has become synonymous with it. This term is about the best way to describe a trail, or section of trail, with a large number of purposefully added obstacles on it. These "obstacles" or "stunts" may include such things as ridiculously narrow bridges, steep ladders, extreme drop offs, ramps, elevated sections of trail (usually raised wooden planks or large logs meant to be ridden along), teeter-totters to be ridden over, stacked log piles and just about anything else that looks exceedingly dangerous or insanely fun (depending on whom you ask).

CARBON DIOXIDE (CO_2) – Most of the beers served on tap use carbon dioxide gas to carbonate the beer and propel it from the serving tank (or keg) through the tap lines to your pint glass. These beers are typically served cold, somewhere around 38 degrees Fahrenheit.

CASK-CONDITIONED (also called **Real Ale**) – A beer is considered cask-conditioned when a secondary fermentation is induced inside the keg (or bottle) from which the beer will eventually be served. This secondary fermentation is the beer's only source of carbonation. A cask-conditioned beer is usually served at cellar temperatures (around 52 degrees Fahrenheit) via a **Hand-Pump.Dirt ROAD** – When all else fails, a nicely maintained dirt road ride is available almost anywhere in the country. Not usually destination rides, dirt roads are still the preferred route for great town-to-town rides and very useful when connecting multiple singletrack trails to create epic rides.

DOUBLETRACK – Also called "two-track," many trails begin as old logging roads, mining roads, fire breaks, railroads, or four-wheel-drive (4x4) roads. These are rediscovered for the use of hikers, bikers, and horseback riders. And, although some may complain that they're not singletrack, sometimes these crazy old roads are little more than glorified goat trails with only one rideable way up, or

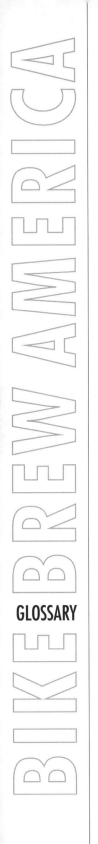

down, and make the best epic rides in the business.

ENDO – An Endo occurs when you unintentionally go over your handlebar headfirst. This stunt happens most frequently when you are riding downhill and your weight is shifted too far forward. Your front wheel comes to a stop either because you applied the front brakes or because your front wheel lodged against an immovable object such as a log or large rock. This situation generally leads to a **Face Plant**, the sudden meeting of your face with the ground. Just the hazards of having too much fun.

FACE PLANT – For whatever reason, the inelegant, rapid pressing of a bicyclist's face into the ground. See also **Endo.**

FERMENTATION – The process of turning wort (the boiled-down, sugary liquid extracted from barley) into beer. Basically (and this is very basic, so take a tour of the brewery the next time you're in a brewpub), the wort is mixed with water, and either lager or ale yeast cells are added to the concoction. A yeast is a tiny (microscopic) single-celled organism that eats the sugar in the solution and whose metabolic byproduct is alcohol and carbon dioxide gas—the building blocks of beer.

GROWLER – The original and traditional method of taking your beer home before there were six-packs. Usually a growler is a half-gallon (64-ounce) reusable glass jug sold at the brewpub for a nominal cost. Once purchased, the growler can be filled with a house-brewed beer, taken off-premises, and consumed at your leisure. Unopened in a chilled, dark place, growler beer can stay fresh up to five days. Once the seal is broken, the beer's best when consumed in one sitting, so make sure you have a couple of friends around.

HAND-PUMPED (or Hand-Pulled) – A traditional serving method designed for cask-conditioned ales, although any beer can be served via this method. A hand-pump (also called a beer engine) uses vacuum pressure to "pull" beer from the keg to the tap. This serving method creates a less carbonated brew, typically served at a warmer temperature (around 52 degrees Fahrenheit) than a typical

American beer. Usually the warmer temperature and reduced carbonation result in a smoother beer with enhanced flavors and exceptional characteristics.

HAPPY HOUR – Usually sometime between 3:00 and 7:00 P.M., during these few magical hours, the beer is discounted, the sun is still shining, and all is right in the world.

HELMET – A light-weight and rather hip-looking device that will help keep your brain properly suspended in your skull. As cool as you think you may be foregoing its use, not wearing a helmet whenever you get on a bike is just plain dumb. Please see **Endo** and **Face Plant**.

HIKE-A-BIKE – A section of terrain impossible or illegal for anyone to ride. Over this section, which is not usually considered a single obstacle where a dismount and remount are required, you must carry or "hike" with your bike. Common hike-a-bikes are large river crossings, unreasonably steep trails (for example, Jacob's Ladder, Moab, Utah), an impassable technical section of trail, or any part of a trail that is illegal for riding your mountain bike.

LAGER – The vast majority of beer produced in the United States consists of American Pilseners, which are made with lager yeast by the likes of Anheuser-Busch, Coors, and Miller Brewing Companies. Occasionally, you'll find a microbrewery or brewpub making a beer or two with lager yeast, although most use ale yeast owing to the longer aging periods required by lager yeast.

LOOP – Just as singletrack is the desired riding medium, a singletrack loop is the desired ride type. On loop rides, you travel in a fashion that brings you back to your original starting position without riding the same terrain twice. Usually some sort of circular situation, the singletrack loop is the Holy Grail of mountain-bike rides worldwide.

MACROBREWERY – Also called a large brewery, companies in this category produce over 2,000,000 barrels of beer per year. Examples in the United States include Anheuser-Busch, Coors, and Miller Brewing Company.

MICROBREWERY – A brewery that produces less than

15,000 barrels of beer per year for off-premises consumption, although many have tap or tasting rooms.

NITROGEN – A growing trend is to use nitrogen to "carbonate" and serve beer. The higher pressure of nitrogen gas means a tight and creamy head and an overall smoother character. A true delight!

NORTH SHORE–STYLE TRAILS – See British Columbia–Style Trails.

OFF-CAMBER – These sections always occur as you traverse the side of a hill and refer to areas of the trail that are slightly tilted, not only in an uphill or downhill direction but in a sideways fashion as well. Often difficult to negotiate even though the grade of the trail can be relatively mild.

OUT-AND-BACK – An out-and-back ride returns you to your original starting position by your riding the same trail back as you rode out. Although not as exciting as a loop ride, the out-and-back is still worthy. Remember, a trail will ride differently in the reverse direction.

PAVEMENT – Not a favorite of most, but still an option. Like dirt roads, paved roads are often used to ride to a trail or to connect different dirt routes together.

PHAT – As in hip, cool, "I wish that were mine," awesome! You may have a phat ride, a phat bike, or a phat time, but you won't have a phat chance for any of that if you don't get out there and ride!

PINT – The almighty pint, a beer drinker's equivalent to singletrack. The most common method for ordering and serving a microbrew in America. Pint glasses range in size from 14 ounces, to the standard 16-ounce glass, all the way to the rare and much desired 20-ounce English or Imperial pint.

POINT-TO-POINT (Shuttle Ride) – Though always fun, a point-to-point ride is the least accessible, because it requires coordination of multiple cars or trucks and drivers. Also called shuttle rides, you leave a vehicle (or arrange pickup) at your destination location (say, the bottom of the mountain) and then travel in another vehicle to your starting destination (say, the top of the mountain) to begin the trail ride back to the arranged destination location. Of all the rides, you can cover the most distance on some of the best terrain (as in "all downhill") on a point-to-point ride. Unfortunately, the need for multiple vehicles, the reliance on others, and arranging the pickup time is often time consuming and prone to error. And retrieving the second vehicle from the trailhead at the top of the mountain delays visiting the brewpub.

REGIONAL BREWERY – One that produces between 15,000 and 2,000,000 barrels of beer per year.

SHUTTLE RIDE – See Point-to-Point.

SINGLETRACK – This is it, what you're all after, the reason you left the road behind and dove headlong into the trees! Simply stated, singletrack is a dirt path too narrow for cars and trucks. But, oh, it's so much more! Singletrack comes in many forms, from smooth and flat to steep and rocky with everything in between. For every variety of singletrack there is someone out there looking for it, and it's all good!

SLICKROCK – Made famous in Moab, Utah, by the classic Slickrock Trail, the term slickrock is now often used to refer to any section of trail that is made of rock. Usually this rock offers unparalleled traction (at least when dry) and a unique riding surface that is much sought out and treasured.

SWITCHBACK – A switchback is a sharp turn up or down an incline. Building switchbacks is a trail-creation method that reduces erosion and helps human-powered machines (including hikers) up a mountain. When properly built, a biker has enough room to complete the switchback without dismounting. This usually requires about 6 to 8 feet of turning radius.

TOWN-TO-TOWN – Often spoken of in only the most hushed of tones, the fabled town-to-town ride is a glorious thing indeed. Typically epic in distance and time, this ride allows the mountain biker to start from town (the brewpub is always nice), travel by bike to the trail, and then return some time later. When planned correctly, the return time usually coincides with **Happy Hour.**

TWO-TRACK – See Doubletrack.

WATERBAR – Waterbars come in all shapes and sizes, but they invariably serve the same purpose: to divert the flow of rainwater from the trail and reduce erosion. Usually, nothing more than a half-buried log, trench, or pile of dirt running almost perpendicular to the trail, these seemingly annoying fixtures are the reason you have pristine single-track instead of a rocked out, eroded, and crumbly mess to ride on. Volunteer to work on a trail maintenance crew to learn more about waterbars and other trail-building techniques.

WIDETRACK – At some point in its life, singletrack can no longer be called thin, or tight, or even narrow. Whether it is from excessive use or by design, there comes a time when a trail is no longer singletrack and not yet a road, even though it is a single dirt path making its way through the woods. Though some of the thrill may be lost, it's still dirt, still mountain biking, and still fun. Enjoy!

INDEX

311

INDEX

313

INDEX

317

INDEX

323

325

TODD MERCER

Todd Mercer is a former collegiate swimmer who realized there was more to sport than the structured confines of the pool. After much time spent scuba diving, rock climbing, and competing in triathlons, he found his true calling in mountain biking. Perhaps a factor in this revelation was how well a pint of fresh beer in the company of good friends tasted after a day on the trails.

Mercer began writing about his outdoor adventures in various club newsletters. Soon his articles were appearing in regional and national magazines. Finally, so there would be no regrets, he abandoned the cubicle world of a nine-to-five computer desk jockey to pursue his dream of traveling and writing. He and his wife, Amanda, a successful prosecuting attorney, sold their nineteenth-century home in Indiana, and along with their dog, Nikki, left behind the secure and predictable for a life on the open road.

They currently live without a fixed address. The red Bike & Brew America truck could be anywhere.